In Living Color

The Cultural History of Television

In Living Color

A Cultural History

BERNADETTE GIACOMAZZO

ROWMAN & LITTLEFIELD
Lanham • Boulder • New York • London

Published by Rowman & Littlefield
An imprint of The Rowman & Littlefield Publishing Group, Inc.
4501 Forbes Boulevard, Suite 200, Lanham, Maryland 20706
www.rowman.com

86-90 Paul Street, London EC2A 4NE, United Kingdom

British Library Cataloguing in Publication Information Available

Library of Congress Cataloging-in-Publication Data Available

ISBN 9781538166574 (cloth : alk. paper) | ISBN 9781538166581 (epub)

This book is dedicated, with love and affection, to
Tony, JuJu, Nijah Bear, King Bing, and Jahni Girl.

Everything I do, I do for you—and the greatest honor of my life
isn't in any of my professional achievements, but in being your Titzie.

I love you little chickens—and don't you forget it for one minute.

Contents

Notes on Nomenclature

Academic wisdom dictates that proper names are first cited in full and then referred to by their last name every time thereafter. Yet because In Living Color: *A Cultural History* mentions more than one member of the Wayans family—to wit: Keenen, Damon, Kim, Shawn, and Marlon—members of the Wayans family are referred to by their first name, or their first and last name, but never merely by their last name, to avoid confusion.

The nomenclature of every other actor—David Alan Grier and Tommy Davidson, for example—follows traditional academic wisdom; proper names are cited in full upon first mention, and surnames only are used every time thereafter.

Acknowledgments

The act of writing a book is a solitary act, to be sure, but I am by no means without a system of support and love that leaves me humbled and grateful. This space, then, is dedicated to these people.

First, and foremost, I need to thank the Universe—for lack of a better way of putting the energy that binds us all—and my two greatest teachers, the Reverend Dr. Lady Auset (and her husband, Lord Ra) and Sorceress Cagliastro of the Iron Ring. It is because of these forces that I am strong—stronger, in fact, than I ever could believe—and for this, I am grateful.

Next, I need to thank the five greatest human beings on Earth: my nephews Tony, JuJu, Nijah Bear, and my baby King Bing Stinkie, and my niece Jahni Girl. *Titzie loves you!*

To the rest of my family: my mom Anna, my sister Marissa, my brother-in-law Cut, my aunt Lydia and my uncle Alfredo, and my cousins Paula (and Dave, Adrianna, and Leo) and Marina (and Jason and Aniyah), Joanne, Anthony Jr. and Philip, Roberta and Dario, Patrizia and Stefano, and all the members of my extended family scattered throughout the United States, Canada, Italy, and Sicily. (There are far too many of us to name you individually—I think I'm personally related to approximately one in every ten Italians walking this Earth, and one in every four Sicilians walking this Earth, without exaggeration.) Quite the motley crew we are . . . and I love you all for it.

To my Rottweiler, Angela—aka Big Ang, aka Fat Fat, aka Fatty McFatterton—for snoring at my feet as I wrote this book late into the night. (As if you can read this thing.) Thanks for saving my life, and my mom's life, literally and figuratively. Sometimes, angels come in human form—and sometimes, they come in the form of fat Rottweilers who eat too much Italian food. I'm grateful you're the latter. Thanks, Big Ang. Special thanks, too, to Hounds Town Doggie

Day Care in Island Park, New York, for keeping her amused five days out of the week while I toiled away at this book.

To my friends in real life: Douglas Friday, Robyn Smith-Kaiser (and Larry Kaiser, and Maverick, and of course, CharStar the Little Rock Star), Marabelle Blue, Jenny "Devil Doll" Gonzalez (and Eric Blitz), Philip Richards (and Jeanne "Panini" Pinnieri-Richards), Ray Monell, Cymande Russell (and Akira), Sesh Foluke-Henderson (and his new, lovely family—I can't believe one of my besties is a papa!), Taalib "Ghetto Philosopher" Wheeler (and Goddess Queen Nefertari), Dr. JonPaul Higgins (and Jonathan Ray), Shaun Lally, Gerard "HipHopGamer" Williams (and RedInfamy), Walter "Lucky Church" Simons (and Vivian Veng), Jasmine O'Day (and Jessica O'Day), Patricia Kuneff, Chrissy Melchiore, and all the people whose names I'm forgetting right now (but who I will gladly remember when the book comes out and do a follow-up post on my website or something). I love you guys, and that's not something I say lightly.

To Christen Karniski and Deni Remsberg of Rowman & Littlefield, for seeing this vision and believing in my ability to deliver above and beyond all expectations. I cannot wait to do this all again in a few months with *The Golden Girls*—and, hopefully, beyond.

To Bettinna, and BettyMedia, for the beautiful cover art. I wept when I first saw it, and I weep anew seeing it in action.

To Antoine DeBrill, for the amazing author photo—and for not making me look like Hillary Clinton in my pics. (Special shout-out to Hillary Clinton, though, and no disrespect intended.)

To Martie Bowser of Role Model Publicity, the greatest publicist a girl could ask for.

To all the people I work and have worked with, who I love and respect and appreciate forever, and whose continued support means the world: Richard Willis Jr., REYN, and Bryan Ransom. The Metropolitan Opera. *Teen Vogue. Vogue Italia.* VH1. *XXL Magazine. The Source Magazine. LatinTRENDS Magazine. Go! NYC Magazine. Interactive One. Vibe. Blasting News. The Inquisitr. Contrast Magazine.* Kool G Rap. G-Unit. Curtis "50 Cent" Jackson (so much love and respect for this man!). Lloyd Banks. Tony Yayo. Kidd Kidd. Mike Styles. The G-Unit Riders. Michael Maddaloni. Chris Lanston. Nassau Community College. Hofstra University. Dr. Kenneth Lampl. WLIR-FM. WBAB-FM. Malibu Sue. Rob Rush. Andre Ferro. Jon Daniels. Keith "Fingers" Steele. Joe Rock. Vinnie "The Chainsaw" Graziano. Amanda Elsheikh. Scott Church. Michael Donati. Sarah Squeaky. Alan Davis. Renee Graziano. Karen Gravano. Big Ang Raiola (God rest your beautiful soul—you truly were one of a kind). *Good Times Magazine. Long Island Entertainment Magazine* (RIP). *Inside Connection* (RIP). Splash News. PR Photos. FlashCity (RIP). WENN. SIPA. Ariel Publicity. John Gilbert Young. Anita Gordy (RIP to the beautiful Ryan). Sam Felipe. The list goes on, and I'm sure I'm forgetting people along the way, but again, you are loved and respected and appreciated. Thanks for believing in the talents of a nerdy Sicilian girl with too many books, too many records, too many smartassed remarks, and too many crazy dreams—and for making all of them come true, and even giving me dreams I never thought I could have and making *them* come true. Y'all are awesome, and I sincerely hope the Universe blesses you and provides for you for all the days of your life.

To the outlets I currently call home: All That's Interesting (John and Jaclyn, thank you for giving me the opportunity to expand my knowledge and write about things above and beyond the music and entertainment industries—and thanks for approving the story about the origins of Anansi, which put me in touch with Stewart Kyasimire, and the rest—as they say—is history). AfroTech, and all the Blavity properties—you are, indeed, my "fam away from my fam."

Micah Davis, *thank you* for being the best deputy editor an old lady could ask for—you deserve the world, and I cannot thank you enough for being who you are and giving me the opportunities you have given me. Shanique Yates, Samantha Dorisca, Ngozi Nwanji, and Michelai Graham—you four ladies inspire me in ways I cannot possibly put into words. I'm looking forward to watching each one of you kick ass and take names, now and in the future, and making all your dreams come true.

Njera Perkins—I love seeing you shine in your new editorial role at POP-SUGAR. You impress me daily, and I hope you keep kicking ass.

Brittni Williams and Katana Dumont—you two ladies are the future. It's an honor to serve as your lead, and I hope you surpass me in ways I cannot imagine right now.

Amaya Woodley, Diorlena Caruthers, Trey Mangum, Sidnee Douyon, Orchid Richardson, Morgan DeBaun, and everyone else who had the faith in me to give me even one assignment—thank you, beyond thanks, for believing in me and my talent, and I hope I make you proud.

And finally, but certainly no less important, *thank you* beyond thanks to Stephanie Ogbogu, for bringing me on board in the first place and introducing me to one of the best places I've ever had the pleasure of working at in my life. This book has a sensitivity, a realness, and a humanity about it because you all are in my life. And a great deal of credit—more than can be put into words—goes to you, Steph, for making that possible.

To the cast, crew, and ancillary folks involved in *In Living Color*—for creating a series that was bigger than any of them could have imagined, and for being a part of a pop culture phenomenon that will stand the test of time. Special shoutout to Keenen Ivory Wayans, whose singular vision launched a thousand proverbial ships—but who, through his leadership, taught us all the most important lesson of family, loyalty, and kindness. Loyalty is rare to find in life, in general—and it's almost nonexistent in the entertainment industry—so the fact that Keenen found it in his professional and personal life is something that's inspirational *and* aspirational. Thank you, all, for being the inspiration behind this *magnum opus* of mine. Above all else, I hope I've done a good job in telling the story of this cultural juggernaut in the context of modern American history, and painted a rich, complex picture that goes above and beyond a topical pop culture book—in other words, I hope I conveyed more than "Homey don't play that" in my words, and that the authenticity of both the show itself—and the critical exegesis therein—shined through above all else.

And finally, I'd like to thank every one of you for reading this book. May you all have the guts to chase your dreams wherever they may lead you, to live your life out loud, to *never* dim your light—and most of all, to speak out against injustice and bad behavior when you see it, no matter what it costs you. I appreciate you all.

Don't talk about it. Don't tweet about it. Don't wish about it.

Be about it, and then *do it*. Period.

Introduction

In 1977, the late, great Richard Pryor launched an eponymous sketch show that NBC, in its infinite wisdom, pitted against ABC stalwarts *Laverne & Shirley* and *Happy Days*, thereby all but guaranteeing it would get clobbered in the ratings. Starring Robin Williams, Paul Mooney, Marsha Warfield, and Edie McClurg—who would all go on to have legendary comedy careers in Hollywood—and, of course, the man himself, *The Richard Pryor Show* was profanity laced, irreverent, and boundary pushing, much like Pryor himself.

In an era that otherwise embraced subversive comedy—*SNL* was already on the air for two years by the time Pryor got his eponymous show, and it was at its peak subversiveness—*The Richard Pryor Show* should have been a critical and commercial darling.

But the critics—almost universally white, almost universally male[1]—were primed at the pump with backhanded compliments.

And lest one think that the "universally white, universally male" commentary is little more than a twenty-first-century attempt to "woke-check" newsrooms, no less of an authority than the Pew Research Center bears that out to be true. According to them, the average newsroom for daily newspapers in the 1970s was 75 percent white and male. Only 25 percent of the newsroom for daily newspapers was female. The twenty-first-century digital newsrooms are no better despite the modern-day window-dressing: Although women make up 47 percent of today's overall workforce, only *33 percent* of the *total media workforce* is female, and that number hasn't changed since 1982. What's more, despite modern-day efforts toward "diversity and inclusion," there's little difference in the nonwhite presence in the newsroom between the 1970s and now. So, then, as now, most opinions shared by newspapers are those of white men.

And that includes the *New York Times*,[2] where John J. O'Connor echoed the belief that Pryor was one of America's most innovative and talented performers. However, in describing the Pryor skits that were unapologetically Black—such as the skit about the "first Black president," nearly forty years before Barack Obama would assume the mantle—O'Connor was, to put it mildly (and perhaps more politely than is merited), befuddled.

He couldn't understand, for example, why the first Black president would consider Black Panther and political firebrand Huey Newton for the position of "director of the FBI." Huey Newton? Surely not *that* Huey Newton, founder of the Black Panther Party (then viewed as an insurrectionist collective and not the social revolutionaries and caretakers that history would, ultimately, prove them to be) and Bobby "Chicago Seven" Seale's longtime compatriot. Presidents were supposed to pick refined gentlemen like J. Edgar Hoover (and all his feather boas) as their trusted advisers, not counterculture revolutionaries who dared to question whether white was right by default. How. Dare. He?

He was perplexed at why Pryor's character referred to his compatriots as "yo, blood!" Blood? Yeesh. How scary. How savage. How . . . Black. Certainly, no white person would deem to refer to their compatriots as "blood." How in the world could that possibly be funny? Clearly, O'Connor would be a stranger in a strange land in the twenty-first century, where white kids from the suburbs use African American Vernacular English—also known as AAVE, and more derogatorily as "Ebonics"—with everyone from their parents to their teachers, and many of its terms (including "blood," interestingly enough) have entered the dictionary as acceptable common parlance. The evolution of English—like every other language—is vital to its survival, though O'Connor and his compatriots surely couldn't have predicted how *Black* the language would become. (Presumably, he thought everyone would still talk like they're in a Shakespearean play or use "groovy" 1960s slang well into the twenty-first century.)

And in the follow-up skit that featured Pryor wearing a poorly constructed wig with locs, O'Connor could only describe Pryor as a "Rastafarian," completely devoid of the cultural context of the hairstyle in the Jamaican community while also seemingly taking a jab at the burgeoning Black Power movement that was gaining increasing prevalence in the United States. "Black Power," in the 1970s, encouraged Black Americans to reclaim their cultural and social heritage while emphasizing the importance of Pan-Africanism, the reclamation of "natural" hairstyles (more than forty years before 2019's CROWN Act codified its acceptance into law),[3] and pride in one's Blackness—concepts that all terrified white Middle America, much like it does in the early part of the twenty-first century.

Interestingly, O'Connor would have found a rich cultural origin story had he just done the most tonsorial of research on "locs." Though historians still debate about the true origin of locs, the first evidence of the hairstyle was found in ancient Egypt, in Vedic India, and among the Minoans of ancient Greece. In

1935—when Emperor Haile Selassie was exiled from Ethiopia after the Italian invasion of the African country—Selassie's Jamaican devotees vowed not to cut their hair until he was reinstated as emperor, and they twisted their hair into locs as a matter of both convenience and reverence. Selassie's devotees followed Rastafarianism—whose name derives from *Ras Tafari Makonnen*, or Haile Selassie's pre-regnant name—and as a result, locs and Rastafarianism became interchangeable, and almost exclusively so, in some people's minds.

But while today's journalists would be all but duty bound to do this sort of cultural research before even attempting to write a commentary on an authentically Black show like *The Richard Pryor Show*—lest they be dragged by their whole hair follicles on Twitter—O'Connor didn't have to do any of that. The white man, after all, was the default setting, and no other context—cultural or otherwise—was required.

And so, after clumsily stumbling, almost fearfully, over his words to describe Pryor's unapologetic Blackness to O'Connor's unapologetically white audience, O'Connor concluded that "it is not, once again, the stuff of family viewing. The fault, however, is not in the star but in the stratagems of schedule planners. If there are any problems about content, the time slot should go but Mr. Pryor should definitely stay."

Sure—let's relegate *The Richard Pryor Show* to the 2 a.m. time slot in a time that Americans typically viewed the so-called "bull's-eye" test pattern, in a time where streaming services were a thing of science fiction and fantasy, and in a time when VCRs were somewhat of a luxury for the average American household. Sounds fantastic, Mr. O'Connor! Let's protect your precious white sensibilities at all costs, sir!

But in an era long before the dawn of social media, O'Connor's word was viewed as bond. After all, he was a *New York Times* pop culture critic, capable of swaying public opinion with just a few words, and with seemingly unfettered restraint or public outcry and pushback. No doubt that in the age of so-called cancel culture, O'Connor would have been skewered mercilessly on Twitter, be made the subject of countless think-pieces across various platforms both mainstream and niche, and ultimately find himself and his career relegated to the dustbin of history—as he would so rightly deserve.

In the same breath, he was also merely saying what everyone else was thinking anyway—Pryor could push the envelope, but only to a certain degree. The minute he started becoming "too Black, too strong" *à la* Public Enemy (vis-à-vis Malcolm X's[4] *Message to the Grass Roots*,[5] of course), he struck fear in the hearts of white sensibilities—the kind who thought "the Negros" (as was acceptable parlance at the time) deserved rights just fine, the kind who would *definitely* vote for Barack Obama for a third term forty years later if only they had the chance to do so,[6] but the kind who believed that equality (no less equity) had its limits.

After all, if you gave Black men (especially) equality, no less equity, what would happen then? They'd buy houses in white neighborhoods? They'd go to college with rich white boys from "good families"? They'd marry your white daughters and have biracial children? They'd vote for a Black president, and that president would actually win? Let's not get carried away with ourselves here.

And that, really, was what had O'Connor—and others, because by no means was his voice the lone one in the din—hemming and hawing about when they referred to "adult" material. Certainly, the subject matter was not something that was so far out in space that it would be impossible to sit on the palate of the average white man in 1970s America. And, no doubt, they've all said worse to better, both publicly and privately. No, "adult" material referred to comedy that dared to be "too Black, too strong" in the face of white normalcy—controversy within controversy, a controversy *Inception* if you prefer.

But it's not like O'Connor and his ilk were unfamiliar with controversy on television. Just five years prior to Pryor's skit about the "first Black president," CBS aired an episode of the hit Norman Lear comedy *Maude* that featured the titular character—portrayed with sardonic brilliance by Beatrice Arthur—pondering over an abortion dilemma, and ultimately receiving one shortly before *Roe v. Wade* was codified into law. It was controversial, sure, but CBS aired the episode regardless, and today, the so-called "abortion episode" of *Maude* is regarded as one of the United States' most groundbreaking comedic episodes in history.

Incidentally, Arthur's Maude Findlay was able to get an abortion on her titular show prior to *Roe v. Wade*'s codification because she lived in the wealthy enclave of Tuckahoe, Westchester County, New York. Contrary to popular misconceptions, abortion was not illegal prior to *Roe v. Wade*—rather, its legality was determined on a state-by-state basis.[7] Prior to *Roe*, thirty of the fifty states banned abortion without exception, sixteen banned abortions except in extreme circumstances (rape, incest, a credible health threat to the mother's life), and three states allowed residents to obtain abortions in a mostly unrestricted way. In pre-*Roe* America, however, New York was credited with having the most "liberal" abortion laws on record—a distinction it maintains to this day—in that it unilaterally allowed women to obtain abortions whenever they so choose, provided the fetus wasn't viable outside of the womb when the woman sought to procure the abortion. But, as plenty of wealthy women from all fifty states are all too happy to tell their children and grandchildren, the right amount of money and a discreet "private clinic" could get the "procedure" (as it was euphemistically termed) done without much fanfare if circumstances truly became dire.

And, certainly, Americans in the 1970s were more in favor of racial equality (58 percent of all Americans supported the passage of the Civil Rights Act in 1964, according to a Gallup poll taken that very same year[8]) than of abortion (only 21 percent of all Americans supported abortion being unilaterally legal in 1972, according to a Gallup poll taken just a few months before *Roe v. Wade* was codified into law[9]).

While *Maude* earned its well-deserved spot in television history, *The Richard Pryor Show* was unceremoniously yanked off the air after just four episodes due to poor ratings, loud clamoring from a highly offended Middle America, and Pryor's insistence on being at loggerheads with network censors.

Pryor, too, was by no means the only comedian to ever thumb his nose at "network censors," but one can't help but wonder if the Powers That Be thought that Pryor, an unapologetically Black man, was too "uppity" for his own good, and that the cancellation of his show was a message reminding him to stay in his proverbial "place," wherever that may be.

It would take until 2010—and a network called TV One, considered an "urban" network catering to the Black American community—for *The Richard Pryor Show* to air again in its original, uncensored format.

Fast forward to 2010, though, and *The Richard Pryor Show* was viewed, rightly, as a show before its time. Sure, it was risqué, but it was far from the shot between the eyes that the 1970s pop culture commentators thought it would be. By 2010, America—both white *and* Black America—had been exposed to such things as Katt Williams's[10] 2006 HBO special *Live: Let a Playa Play*, 2005's *The Boondocks* (and, of course, Aaron McGruder's comic strip of the same name, which enjoyed a life on *Hitlist* and the *Source Magazine* before receiving nationwide newspaper syndication in April 1999), and one other show that we will explore in great detail in this book. As such, Pryor's show was tame—quaint, even—by twenty-first-century standards.

Unfortunately, in 1977, America didn't seem quite ready for a Black sketch show like Richard Pryor's.[11] It was too much for the fragile white minds of 1977, which lived in the shadows of the Civil Rights Movement and the murder of its figureheads in Martin Luther King and Malcolm X, who were painted as violent revolutionaries who dared to upset the status quo, in a tactic that historians would later dub the "Southern Strategy"[12] by the Republican Party and spearheaded, in part, by then-senator Richard Nixon and the equally noxious Barry Goldwater. Battered by the "Summer of Love," the Manson family murders were still fresh in the pop culture zeitgeist, and the seeds of the so-called Satanic Panic were firmly being planted into young minds as conservative Christianity continued its rise into what would, eventually, become the evangelical movement of the twenty-first century.

More's the pity. It would prove, ultimately, to be their loss.

And so it was that in the 1970s, *The Richard Pryor Show* faded from memory, viewed at best as a curiosity for its time—a noble experiment, one that to be sure was paved with good intentions (as the road to hell so often is), but one that deserved to be confined to the dustbin of history.

Or so they thought.

Because in New York City's Fulton Housing Projects, a young Black man raised in a large family of devout Jehovah's Witnesses was taking copious mental notes about this, and other, watershed moments in Black comedy—and the white American response to the same. And he decided that when the time was right, he too would make his mark.

He would eventually leave Tuskegee University just one semester before graduation and team up with Robert Townsend to create the cult classic film *Hollywood Shuffle* before striking out on his own with the cult classic *I'm Gonna Git You Sucka*. The success of those films led executives from the then-fledgling Fox Network to approach him with an idea for his own show. And though he was initially hoping to have a career in films, the young man ultimately decided that he'd like to have a sketch show—one that featured a cast of Black men and women like himself, who could speak to the Black experience and convey it in an authentic way.

Armed with the inspiration provided by Pryor and other groundbreaking Black comedians—and with a *carte blanche* to pretty much do what he pleased from nervous executives from a then-fledgling network called Fox—he created a sketch comedy show that was a direct answer to *Saturday Night Live* yet stood in a class all its own.

The year was 1990.

The man was Keenen Ivory Wayans.

And the show was *In Living Color*.

America may not have been ready for *The Richard Pryor Show*.

It's doubtful if they were ready for *In Living Color*.

But, ready or not, Keenen Ivory Wayans and his motley crew of never-ready-for-primetime players burst onto the scene on April 15, 1990—Income Tax Day!—on a network called Fox.

And after the pilot episode aired, the American pop culture zeitgeist was never the same.

CHAPTER 1

In the Beginning

To tell the story of *In Living Color* in terms of its cultural history, we must address what came before it. *The Richard Pryor Show*, of course, is at the top of that list, but there are countless other cultural—and historical—touchstones to consider when looking at the bigger picture. We must approach the comedy sketches with a critical eye—see what worked then, what still would work now, and what still falls under the category of super-cringe—to get a feel of how experimental, yet effective, this show truly was.

But, most of all, we must listen to the words—the oral history, one of the most essential forms of records keeping throughout time—of the man at the center of this cultural maelstrom himself: Keenen Ivory Wayans. Without his vision, without his commitment, and without his impossible dream, none of this would be possible.

Born on June 8, 1958, in Harlem, New York, Keenen Ivory Desuma Wayans was the second of ten children born to Howell Stouten Wayans and his longtime wife, the former Elvira Green, who was a social worker–turned–homemaker. The family started in Harlem—at 1704 Amsterdam Avenue, to be exact—before moving to "the projects in lower Manhattan" (and, more specifically, the Robert Fulton Housing Projects in the Chelsea district of Manhattan, between 16th and 19th Streets, and bounded by Ninth and Tenth Avenues) when Keenen was six years old.

Like most working-class men in New York, Howell Wayans worked several different jobs to make ends meet for his ever-growing family. "They [the jobs] got progressively funnier as we got older," Keenen said to the Television Academy back in 2013.[1] "He worked for Guinness Harp, as a sales rep. That was the highlight. That was the best job he ever had—company car, expenses—it was a great time. He also worked for Drake's.[2] And that was a great time—because we

And despite its rich ethnic diversity, the backdrop of New York City was far from friendly to Black Americans. Despite Mayor Robert Wagner's assurances[5] that he was "aware" of the needs of the city's Black residents—including housing issues and discrimination—his promises sounded like tone-deaf platitudes. What's more, his assurances of directing "[Police Commissioner] Murphy [to] go full speed ahead with the recruitment and pre-training of minority members for the police services" sounded more like a threat than a salve.

And it was against this backdrop that the Wayans family (and other Black families in New York City) learned to survive—and thrive—together. Despite the looming threat of racism—exacerbated by the tangible fear of extralegal killings of Black boys and men by the (allegedly) corrupt NYPD—and poverty, the children did whatever they could to make a few extra dollars . . . within the bounds of reason, of course.

"That was the other thing—it was always legit," Keenen said.[6] "My parents had very high moral standards. My mom refused to go on welfare, and we never dealt with [crime]. If somebody was selling stolen goods, no matter how cheap it was, that was never entertained. My mother would say 'just because you're *of* the ghetto, doesn't mean you *are* ghetto.' The hustle was always there—so as long as it was legal, it was cool."

But even with Ms. Elvira Wayans's "high moral standards" and Mr. Howell Wayans's incomparable drive to succeed and provide for his family, young Keenen—and, perhaps by extension, the rest of the Wayans siblings—were also keenly aware of their surroundings. It would take Keenen many years to publicly verbalize what was going on—something he ultimately did in 2013, when he spoke to the Television Academy—but the reality remained the same.

The Wayans family, especially the children, were shaped by the experience of the New York City public housing system. The public housing corporation in New York City that provided such housing, known as NYCHA (New York City Housing Authority), was founded in 1935 as the first agency of its kind in the United States, and it continues to remain the largest housing authority of its kind in the United States in the twenty-first century. In theory, the affordable housing developments—which included single-family houses just as often as it included apartment complexes, though the common parlance in pop culture is that they're all "projects"[7]—not only would provide affordable housing and access to social and economic programs to all New Yorkers regardless of their income but also would provide its residents a sense of community that they otherwise wouldn't have.

The reality, however, was quite different.

In the book *Affordable Housing in New York: The People, Places, and Policies That Transformed a City*, editors Nicholas Dagen Bloom and Matthew Gordon Lasner focus on case studies that prove the realities of Mayor Fiorello La

Guardia's public housing brainchildren were very different than their theoretical situations. Rather than providing a sense of community and access to social and economic programs, "the projects"—most of which went up between 1945 and 1965—sterilized the city landscape from an aesthetic standpoint, drove out neighborhood residents who faced a growing concern about plummeting property values, and even destroyed local "mom and pop" shops that previously thrived prior to the construction of these housing projects.

"Massive, centralized, and expensive, America's biggest metropolis condenses and magnifies social inequality," write Bloom and Lasner.[8] "Its poor historically lived in the worst tenements anywhere this side of Dickens's London, while sky-high prices meant nearly everyone, in every era, has endured deficiencies and inconveniences unimaginable elsewhere in the United States."

And, of course, it went without saying that "the projects" were deeply segregated. Both the Harlem River Houses and the Ten Eyck Houses (later, the Williamsburg Houses) were the first two public housing projects to be constructed from the ground up in New York City. The former went up in 1937, and the latter went up in 1938. But the former was "for Blacks only," while the latter was "for whites only." And it went without saying that the disparity in the quality of life was evident between the two housing projects, despite them both being part of the public housing system.[9] "Separate but equal" wasn't a reality either then or now.

It took the Fair Housing Act of 1968 to codify housing desegregation into federal law. But before that, New York City—always more liberal, and arguably more progressive, than the rest of the country—began the process of slow desegregation when it came to their housing projects. And the Wayans family was a part of—as Keenen put it—that "experiment" in the Robert Fulton Housing Projects.

"For us, we were sort of forced to bond more than most families," he said to the Television Academy.[10] "Beyond just being poor, we were part of an experiment. The City of New York started integrating public housing in the 1960s. But the rest of the country was not integrated at that time. So, my housing project was comprised of Puerto Ricans who were brought in from the East Side, Blacks who were brought in from Harlem, and Irish who were in Hell's Kitchen. You had three of the toughest groups put into these eight square block housing developments who had never related to each other—at all—ever—prior to this. And everybody came with their prejudices, and everybody came with their issues, and baggage, and resentments. And it was Hell. Every single day, you fought."

Through this formative experience, the Wayans family learned not only to stick together—thus solidifying their personal and professional relationships as they got older—but also to survive, persevere, and thrive, regardless of the circumstances and regardless of the odds against them.

These traits would come in handy when Keenen decided it was time to try his hand at Hollywood and take his family with him. But Hollywood, at this point in the story, was a far-away dream, one that hadn't quite solidified in young Keenen's mind—and, given the state of television and films in the 1960s, wouldn't involve anything near what he would ultimately become famous for when he became a grown man.

For now, there would be one more lesson to learn.

How were they going to cope with the oftentimes difficult trials and travails of life? What could possibly get them through the worst of the worst—crime, poverty, and racism—and come out on the other side stronger than ever before?

The answer was simple: comedy.

The late, great Steve Allen infamously said, "tragedy plus time equals comedy."[11]

Perhaps that's why the best comedians of all time don't come from privileged backgrounds and gilded cages—but rather, they come from oppressed backgrounds rife with trauma. Whether the oppression is social, economic, psychological, familial, or some combination thereof, the best comedians seem to arise from the ashes of life's worst possible circumstances. They're able to relate to us—and help us relate to each other—in ways that detached wealthy men and women simply cannot do.

To put a finer, more scientific point on it, comedy is a way for both the joke teller and the listeners to get through life easier.[12] We, as a society, take our social cues from comedy—because laughter indicates that the interaction between the comedian and the audience is safe. And by processing trauma live on stage—by naming and shaming the ills that afflict us as people and society as a whole—comedians, and society as a whole, can face the world a little bit easier. The individual audience members, meanwhile, are forced—albeit gently, because comedy is a "social lubricant" that makes tough conversations a lot easier to have—to see things in a different way, resulting in further acceptance of, perhaps, previously foreign concepts.

And as for the comedian? Well, not only does he get to exorcise his demons—or, as psychologists put it, transform trauma through therapeutic humor—but he gets to find like-minded people to share new and interesting ideas, and points of view, with others.

Young Keenen Ivory Wayans wasn't thinking of all this when he was telling jokes with his brothers and sisters in the Fulton Housing Projects. Rather, he just wanted to have a laugh to get through the tough times—and, fortunately for him, the Wayans family was fully supportive of the endeavor, often encouraging each other to have a laugh together.

It certainly made it easier for him, by his own admission, to get through the horror of growing up.

"Every time I would go outside, someone would call me a [n-word]," he said.[13] "And I would be upset. But, one time, my mother saw that I was upset, and she asked me what was wrong. I explained to her what happened—that all these 'big boys' outside called me this name. And she said to me, 'you know what baby? You go back out there, and if they call you a [n-word] again, you tell them to call you 'Mr. [n-word].'"

As darkly humorous as this suggestion was—and for what it was worth, Elvira Wayans's advice worked because her son didn't get his spine rearranged by the presumptive bullies, although Keenen had to subsequently suffer the indignity of being called "every other racial slur" with a "mister" title in front of it—psychologists state that there's an empowerment that takes place when someone chooses to laugh at their trauma, or to attempt to lighten the proverbial load of the trauma through humor. By giving her son the tools to strip the power of the racial epithet away from the bullies in question, Elvira Wayans gave her son—and, subsequently, his brothers and sisters—the tools to empower themselves.

"These social benefits of laughter are likely to enable bereaved individuals to engage in pleasurable social interactions," read one study in the *Journal of Personality and Social Psychology*. "Depressed, hostile, and highly neurotic individuals may engage in more difficult, distressing interactions because they laugh less, thus creating contexts that perpetuate their condition, state, or trait."[14] In other words, had Keenen "matched the energy" that was given to him, the chances are extremely high—from a psychological perspective—that he'd have continued to perpetuate a cycle of violence, with each side one-upping the other each time, until the anger built up to an unsustainable level and resulted in a tragedy for all involved.

And, certainly, there's no shortage of news stories from both the past *and* the present that prove this sort of thing happens far more often than should ever be humanly necessary—sometimes for the most ridiculous of reasons—and doubly so in the wake of the global COVID-19 pandemic.

But indignities from neighborhood bullies aside, Keenen Ivory Wayans would eventually take the comedy routine public, in a manner of speaking. When he was six or seven, he performed an impromptu comedy routine for his mother and her friends, who were paying her a visit at the time. According to Keenen, he put on his father's clothes, took a wine bottle, and adopted the persona of a neighborhood drunk (though Damon would later claim that Keenen was impersonating an uncle). This performance resulted in peals of laughter from Elvira and her friends—and was, arguably, the precursor to the character of Anton Jackson, the drunk homeless man who attempted to entertain beleaguered New York City subway riders on *In Living Color* (though Anton would be played by Keenen's younger brother Damon on the show).

It was his mother's laughter that inspired Keenen to continue to pursue comedy as a hobby and a passion—to the point that it became his singular passion, his raison d'être, and part of the fabric of his very existence.

Like every other aspiring Black comedian of his time, Keenen Ivory Wayans would eventually come upon the works of Richard Pryor—the same Richard Pryor who was too raw for white America, who was too unsafe for Midwestern sensibilities, and who wouldn't last more than four episodes on his own eponymous (and groundbreaking) show—that would serve as the forefather and the quasi-template of Keenen's own.

But while most aspiring Black comedians discovered Richard Pryor through his stand-alone comedy specials and hit records, Keenen Ivory Wayans discovered him through *Dinah!*, a daytime variety show that premiered in syndication on October 21, 1974. (The show would later be renamed *Dinah and Friends* in 1979.)

A precursor to today's variety shows hosted by the likes of Wendy Williams, Shore's eponymous show would feature celebrity guests who would stop by to promote their latest projects. And on the May 23, 1975, episode of the show, Shore had none other than Richard Pryor as a special guest.

And that was the day that Keenen Ivory Wayans happened to tune in.

"I was sitting in the house, afraid to go outside, because a school bully was threatening me," he said.[15] "And I was watching television, and the Dinah Shore show came on. And she had Richard Pryor as a guest. He was doing a whole routine about the school bully, and it was all the things I had just experienced. And I was just laughing and just so amazed that this guy could take this horrible moment and make it funny. And I was just like, who is this man? I want to be like this man."

Keenen's own words demonstrate the psychological symbiosis[16] between the comedian and the audience. Pryor didn't realize it at the time, but by sharing his own experience with a school bully, he was able to connect with a young Keenen Ivory Wayans and give *him* the power to process his *own* experience with a school bully. In so doing, he created a community of like-minded individuals—surely, Keenen wasn't the only young Black boy listening to this routine and processing the trauma of racially charged school bullying—and sparked the careers of more than one of them.

This routine about a school bully would start Keenen on his quest to become "like this man." He wasn't sure how it was going to happen—there were no classes at the local Learning Annex on how to be a successful comedian, after all—but he just knew that this is what he wanted to do for the rest of his life.

Still, it would be another few years before Keenen began to take the idea of being a professional comedian seriously. He wouldn't write his first jokes until he was fourteen years old—and by that time, his audience would be his "smoked out friends," or friends who were high on marijuana (and possibly other psycho-tropic drugs, because this *was* the 1970s, and it wasn't unusual—then as now—for teenagers to experiment with increasingly strong drugs). Keenen, however, chose to avoid the drug scene—whether it was due to a personal preference, his Jehovah's Witness–based upbringing, or some combination of both, the appeal of "getting high" just simply wasn't there for him.

Drugs (or lack thereof) aside, Keenen attended Seward Park High School in the Lower East Side of New York City. The high school, as Keenen knew it, is now closed, having graduated its last class in 2006. Today, it's known as the Seward Park Campus and is home to five smaller schools with specialized ma-triculations. But in Keenen's day, Seward Park High School was known for its notable Hollywood-bound alumni, including comedian Ben Stiller, Hollywood legend Tony Curtis, Zero "Fiddler on the Roof" Mostel, and *The Golden Girls'* very own Estelle Getty. Despite what would eventually become his future, how-ever, Keenen wasn't involved in acting, comedy, or school plays during his time at Seward Park High School.

"People who knew me would say 'I never thought this guy would be a co-median,'" he said.[17] "But people who *really* knew me knew that that was the only thing I ever could have been. So, in big groups, I was always very shy and very quiet. But with my friends, I was the life of the party."

Like most young adults, Keenen really came into his own after high school. After taking a gap year, he enrolled at Tuskegee University in Tuskegee, Alabama—a historically Black college and university (HBCU) that boasted Booker T. Washington as one of its first presidents, and whose distinguished alumni include Super Soaker inventor Lonnie Johnson, rapper Rich Boy (aka Marece Richards), and R&B legend Lionel Richie—on an engineering schol-arship, and that was presumably his chosen career path. Keenen's uncle, who worked with the United Negro College Fund, told him about the Alabama-based university and recommended that his nephew give it a try.

Keenen, though, still had dreams of being a comedian, even though he didn't have a way to get started in the business. Fortunately, his circumstances created the opportunity for him. "I was one of the only students from New York," he said.[18] "And, at lunch time, I would be the entertainment. Everybody wanted to know about New York. And so, I had a captive audience again—I'd be doing my characters, and all my jokes, and I had everybody laughing."

One day, an upperclassman—who was, himself, a fellow New Yorker—caught Keenen's lunchtime act and recommended that he check out "The Improv" when he went home for a visit. Young Keenen was unaware of "The Improv," but as it turned out, it was a legendary breeding ground for all the best comedians in the world, and often the place where aspiring comics would hone their chops.

The Improv was founded in 1963 by Broadway producer Budd Friedman, and its first location was in the Hell's Kitchen district of New York. Originally located on West 44th near the southeast corner of Ninth Avenue, a second location was opened in 1974 in the Fairfax district of Los Angeles, California. Unfortunately, the original Improv in Hell's Kitchen—where Keenen Ivory Wayans and countless other comedians got their start—is closed. The Improv, however, now has more than twenty-five locations throughout the United States, including several locations in Florida, Texas, and Nevada.

But whether an aspiring comedian preferred the East Coast incarnation or the West Coast incarnation of the club, he (or she) was bound to be in good company. Nearly every big name in comedy over the past fifty years—including Richard Pryor, George Carlin, Robin Williams, Freddie Prinze, and Milton Berle—passed through the hallowed halls of the Improv, and Keenen's classmate realized that if his new friend was going to make it in the comedy world, he had to pay his dues at Budd Friedman's pride and joy.

Unfortunately for poor Keenen, his inaugural tryout didn't yield exactly what he'd hoped: "I stood in line with another comedian, Robert Townsend, and I managed to get picked to go on. And it was one of the most surreal moments ever. It was an out-of-body experience. I was standing on the stage, but at the same time, I was able to see myself. And there was only five people in the audience. And there was scattered laughter—but I looked at myself, and I said to myself, 'you're doing it. *You're doing it.*'"[19]

Though Keenen's career didn't take off like a rocket that night, he was standing in line and talking to another comedian who would play an important role in his career going forward, as he'd mentioned. That comedian was Robert Townsend, who would go on to work with Keenen on the groundbreaking film *Hollywood Shuffle*.

But that was still a few years away.

For now, though, Keenen took comfort in knowing that he was able to get onstage and find someplace to call his comedy home. And he was, at last, on the path to making his dreams come true. Yet even he couldn't help but notice the irony of it all: that it took him going all the way to Alabama to find out about a comedy club that was only one mile away from his home in New York City. Later, Keenen would muse that if he *hadn't* gone to Alabama—even if it wasn't for the reasons he'd initially hoped—he never would have made his Hollywood dreams come true.

Philosophical musings aside, his initial audition for the Improv didn't yield a stand-up spot for him. But rather than get down on himself, Keenen chose to attend various comedy shows at the club, where he became a student of sorts. There, he'd watch how various comedians would execute their skits—and he learned what worked, and what didn't, when it came to joke telling, comedic timing, and punchline execution. It took several shows for Keenen to really see the "science" behind his passion, but he was a fast learner, and he got a stand-up slot the next time he tried out at the Improv.

And there was one other skill that he learned at the Improv that, he said, would be the true key to his later breakthrough on *In Living Color*: how to translate his experiences as a Black kid from the projects to "other people." Many people in the Improv's audience were not Black kids from the projects—they were tourists from the Midwest, looking at New York City as an oddity and a Thunderdome of awe. Or they were rich white people from New Jersey and Long Island, what native New Yorkers derisively refer to as "bridge and tunnel" folks (so named because they were not *of* the Manhattan culture, but merely used "the city" as a playground for their own entertainment, only to return to the comfort of their suburban homes in New Jersey and on Long Island when the night was over—a form of being a *colonizer*, if you will), who—much like John O'Connor of the *New York Times*—looked at Black culture as a separate culture unto itself, one that had its own language and mannerisms that were foreign and, dare one say, *savage* in their sheltered, suburban eyes.

The nuances of interpersonal, interracial relationships in the 1980s aside, however, Keenen credits the Improv[20] as his "birthplace," or the place where his comedy career first took off. The manager of the Improv was Chris Albrecht, a native of Queens, New York, who would frequently perform at the club with his partner—and former Andy Kaufmann associate—Bob Zmuda. Albrecht did such a great job performing at the club that Friedman would eventually sell a share of the business to him.

Many years later, when his time at the Improv was all but a distant memory, Albrecht would become a media executive. During his twenty-two years serving as the president of HBO, he ushered in what was eventually called "the new golden age of television," overseeing the signing and development of such shows as *The Sopranos, Sex and the City, Deadwood, Six Feet Under, Entourage, Band of Brothers, Curb Your Enthusiasm,* and *The Wire.*

But before he would turn HBO into a cultural juggernaut, he was credited as a mentor to one Keenen Ivory Wayans, and Keenen frequently said that Albrecht was someone who was instrumental in helping him hone his craft.

And the biggest contribution Albrecht made to Keenen's career was the use of inclusive nuance in his routine. Albrecht told Keenen to use the words "I" and "mine" and not "yours" and "ours." "The more specific you are, the funnier you're going to be," recalled Keenen to the Television Academy.[21] "What I realized was, if I was to come on and say, 'all of our mothers do this,' then people would sit back and say, 'well, I don't know if my mother does this.' But if I were to come on and say, '*my* mother does this,' then people go, 'oh yeah, my mom does that too!' or 'your mom is funny!'"

With that simple, nuanced change in his routine, Albrecht helped Keenen hone his stand-up into one that included the rest of the audience, regardless of the audience member's background. Suddenly, delineations across racial, socioeconomic, and demographic lines were blurred. Keenen wasn't a *Black* comedian[22]—he was a *comedian* speaking about Black culture, and he was *funny*.

Keenen Ivory Wayans was in great company—and competition—in the Improv. In addition to Robert Townsend—who became and remained a lifelong friend and collaborator—Keenen's contemporaries included Larry David, Jerry Seinfeld, Eddie Murphy, Arsenio Hall, and Bill Maher. If iron sharpens iron, Keenen was getting his comedy knife sharpened to a fine, almost deadly, point by these true "iron men" of comedy.

But there was a sense of community, camaraderie, and brotherhood, too. "We looked out for each other," he said to the Television Academy.[23] "No one was allowed to do anything like the other guy. It was the preservation of your point of view that everybody embraced and protected. And anybody who didn't abide by those rules? The club owners wouldn't allow them to perform in the club. And that's what really helped to create my voice."

Alas, New York was proving too big for Keenen Ivory Wayans—and Chris Albrecht. Albrecht had been offered a job as an agent at International Creative Management (ICM), and he lighted out to Los Angeles to take the position. But before he did, he signed five comedians to his roster—and Keenen was one of them. Eventually, Albrecht would also sign Whoopi Goldberg, Billy Crystal, and Keenen's *In Living Color* costar Jim Carrey to his roster.

So, together with Robert Townsend, Keenen drove cross-country to Los Angeles in 1980, hoping to make his dreams come true, and promising to take his family with him if he ever "made it."

While working on his comedy dreams, Keenen began nabbing TV roles to pay the bills and make some important connections. His first role was opposite Irene Cara, best known for cowriting and singing the Oscar-winning song "Flashdance . . . What a Feeling" and the theme song to the television series *Fame*. Keenen, however, began developing a crush on Irene Cara back when she starred in the 1976 musical drama film *Sparkle*.[24] So, he delighted at the opportunity to star opposite Cara in an eponymous television pilot (that, unfortunately, never got ordered to series—a common occurrence in Hollywood, then as now). Undeterred, Keenen went on to book other roles, including *Hill Street Blues* and *Cheers*, where he said "the first line in the first episode" of the series ("Those are our drinks over there!"). But Keenen said that there was something else about his experience on *Cheers* that was memorable, especially as the show became a rousing success: the support system that the actors—especially Ted Danson and Shelley Long, who played Sam and Diane, respectively—had with one another. If he'd ever had the opportunity to have a show, he said, he'd love for his own actors to have the same type of camaraderie.

He also had a regular role as Private Duke Johnson on the 1983 television series *For Love and Honor*, opposite Yaphet Kotto, Rachel Ticotin, and Kelly Preston.

But Keenen would also, unfortunately, get some "stereotypical" roles—roles that catered to stereotypes of Black men as lawless criminals—a theme that would later be lampooned, to great effect, in *Hollywood Shuffle*, which Keenen cowrote with Townsend. One such example of a stereotypical role was the guest appearance he made on the Erik Estrada television vehicle *CHiPS* in 1982. In the premiere episode of season six called "Meet the New Guy"[25]—which initially aired on October 10, 1982—Keenen snagged the minor guest role of a man named "Roberts," who only had one claim to fame on the episode.

"I don't really remember much about that—other than getting arrested," he said.[26] "I was just proud that Erik Estrada was arresting me, and that's what made it special."

On October 5, 1983, he got a chance to perform his well-honed stand-up routine on *The Tonight Show Starring Johnny Carson*. In the 1980s, Carson was notorious for breaking stand-up comedians into the mainstream; performing your routine on the show was tantamount to superstardom, and Keenen's episode—which first aired on October 5, 1983[27]—was no different.

Keenen only had the opportunity to perform a short time, but he made that time count. Donning a silver-grey suit and a striped tie—while pacing nervously and looking nearly unrecognizable to later *In Living Color* fans with his well-coiffed Afro and a clean-shaven baby face—he kicked off his routine with a remark about bringing his older brother, Dwayne, to Los Angeles, to "cool out" from the tensions he'd been under in New York. Dwayne had just gotten fired from his job at McDonald's, and the eldest Wayans child blamed "the man" for his firing. Keenen's routine—which got thunderous applause from the audience—consisted of making his brother's conspiratorial musings the butt of the jokes, with proclamations about the need for "the white man" getting "Dwayne" after they'd already taken down Malcolm X and Martin Luther King. Black people were making too much progress, said Keenen, and white people believed they all—including poor Dwayne Wayans, aspiring McDonald's manager—needed to be stopped before things got out of hand.

"That was the greatest moment of my career," Keenen reflected to the Television Academy.[28] "When you're first starting out, you think of 'the biggest thing.' And, for me, the biggest thing was to be on *The Tonight Show Starring Johnny Carson*. And for me to be there—I can't think of a way to describe it, other than, like I said, when you step into your dream."

But Keenen also acknowledged that, like many young comedians getting their "big break," he was nervous to be on such a big stage and in front of such a rapt national audience. So, he said, he quoted a line from the film *Risky Business*—"sometimes, you just gotta say, 'what the fuck!'"—and ran out onstage. And, after his performance, even Carson himself was impressed—so much so that he asked Keenen to come sit next to him after the routine. Keenen called it "the dream on top of the dream."[29]

Though his profile was raised by his appearance on *The Tonight Show Starring Johnny Carson*—thus making the auditioning process easier and putting him in a "different class" of comics—his career trajectory didn't change until he teamed up with his old friend, and fellow Improv alumnus, Robert Townsend to make movies of their own accord. And, by his own admission, both he and Townsend had an ignorance about the process of filmmaking—all they had was gumption and a desire to get it done, which is how it got done.

Or, to put it more explicitly, "the fact that we were too stupid to know that it was not possible made it possible."[30]

For their first film, he and Townsend laid out different articles of clothing to represent the different characters they wanted to portray. They would then take turns improvising the characters in front of a video camera and making note of what did and didn't work. This piecemeal method ultimately worked, and the pair had come up with a script.

Now came the next problem: they didn't have any money to make the film. They had no connections to financiers, they weren't independently wealthy, and they were clueless about things like budgeting, camera crew, and lighting. Initially, the plan was for the pair to book their acting jobs all over town—and pool their resources together to make the film as gigs came through. But that process would be long and arduous, especially if their sole source of income was random acting gigs at SAG (Screen Actors Guild) scale rates.

But then, Robert Townsend had what Keenen called a "stroke of luck."

"Robert got a credit card in the mail," he said.[31] "And he applied, not only for that, but for ten other credit cards, and got 'em all. And we used the credit cards to make the movie. The locations were the outside of my house, and the inside of Robert's apartment. We didn't have the money to rent out a restaurant, so we rented out the parking lot to the restaurant and hung a sign on the wall outside the restaurant . . . but that's where all that ghetto poverty came into play, because 'problem-solution, problem-solution.'"

Shades of Keenen's father, Howell, and his ever-persistent hustle to make ends meet doing everything from working in Drake's cake factory to selling wholesale items at retail prices certainly can be seen in the pair's drive to make this film by any means necessary.

A promotional shot from *Hollywood Shuffle*. From left to right: Lou B. Washington, Robert Townsend, Keenen Ivory Wayans. *Samuel Goldwyn Company/Photofest © Samuel Goldwyn Company*

The movie in question was *Hollywood Shuffle*, which was released in 1987 and is considered a cult classic today. A semiautobiographical film based on Townsend's experience of being told he wasn't "Black enough" for certain stereotypical roles in Hollywood, *Hollywood Shuffle* starred Townsend and Wayans alongside a bevy of Black actors and actresses including *What's Happening Now!!* star Ann-Marie Johnson as Townsend's long-suffering wife, *Good Times* and *227* star Helen Martin, and legendary comedian John Witherspoon.[32] Keenen's brother, Damon—who finally was old enough to join his brother out west—also had a bit part as a bodyguard.

Hollywood Shuffle would use a lot of the authentically Black double entendres that *In Living Color* would become legendary for. And, unlike its television descendent, *Hollywood Shuffle* didn't have to engage in exposition, because it knew its audience wouldn't need it. The main "superstar" in *Hollywood Shuffle*, for example, was a man by the name of "Batty Boy" (played by Brad Sanders). The surface pretense was that Sanders's character played a bat on television— and naturally, many white people thought Sanders's character was an Adam West–as–Batman send-up. The Black audience, however, knew better: in Jamaican *patois*, "batty boy" is slang for an effeminate gay man.

The film was equal parts social commentary and dark comedy, and it established Townsend as a legitimate power broker in Black Hollywood.

But while the film also gave Keenen a great opportunity, he didn't view *Hollywood Shuffle* as *the* step he needed to make as his entrée into Hollywood. (It was, however, "a" step, in his mind's eye, and no less important to the overall body of work he would eventually amass.) But, more important to him, the success of *Hollywood Shuffle* gave Keenen the money he needed to make his own movie, *I'm Gonna Git You Sucka*. The film, which received a limited release on December 14, 1988—and a wide release on January 11, 1989—was a parody of so-called "Blaxploitation" films that Keenen—and others in his age group—grew up watching. With a meager budget of $3 million, *I'm Gonna Git You Sucka* went on to gross $13 million during its release, making it a bona fide indie hit and establishing Keenen as a power player on par with his good friend.

And yet, it was a film that—in a different pair of hands—would never have become the success it ultimately became.

"What I didn't know was that the movie was never supposed to see the light of day," Keenen said to the Television Academy.[33] "The studio I made the movie with had a video deal, and they had to make a certain number of movies to fulfill the terms of that video deal. *I'm Gonna Git You Sucka* was one of those movies [under the video deal]. And I didn't know this, but I made the film, and I was so upset by the materials that I saw because I felt like they were trying to sabotage the film. But I said to the head of distribution—I don't know where I got the balls—'you can't kill this movie. Here's what you don't understand: there hasn't been a Black film in 20 years. Imagine that there are no white movies—and someone puts one out. You're going to go. You know why? Because you haven't seen yourself in 20 years.' Then they released the movie in five markets—not New York or LA—going up against *Twins* with Arnold Schwarzenegger and Danny DeVito. They spent $200,000 in publicity and sent me to these markets to do some press. Well, the box office numbers come out—and *Twins* was number one, but *I'm Gonna Git You Sucka* was right there, at number two."

That's when United Artists—the studio in question—realized that they had a potential hit on their hands. So, they ramped the film's release up to the next level: they broadened the theatrical release of the film to New York, pinning it against the Kevin Kline vehicle *The January Man*, which was open in fifteen hundred theaters in contrast to *I'm Gonna Git You Sucka*'s two hundred theaters.

The end result?

The January Man made $1.9 million and was universally panned by critics.[34] *I'm Gonna Git You Sucka* made $1.6 million and received universal acclaim, especially from Black critics, who were thrilled at Keenen's aplomb at parodying—and, at the same time, paying tribute to—the Blaxploitation genre.[35] Sure, there were plenty of people who didn't "get it"—Roger Ebert,[36] for one—but to be honest, Keenen wasn't really talking to them anyway.

But the success of *I'm Gonna Git You Sucka* opened another door for Keenen, one that would ultimately place him forever into the annals of pop culture history.

Shortly after *I'm Gonna Git You Sucka* was released, Keenen hosted a screening for the film for all the executives of the film studios. After the screening, the calls started coming in—and one of the first was from a then-fledgling television network called Fox. This surprised Keenen, because Fox didn't send its film executives to the screening—so initially, he thought he was pitching a film to the network.

"I go to the meeting, and it's not the film department—it's the TV department," he told the Television Academy.[37] "And I was disappointed at first. But then, they explained to me that they had a new network—they said, we really want to push the edge, and we loved the movie."

Garth Ancier, who was the president of Fox Entertainment, told the *Hollywood Reporter* that he was hoping someone would bring a particular idea he'd had in the back of his head to life. "I kept index cards of promising ideas on a corkboard behind my head. One card just said 'Black *Laugh-In*.' We needed someone to bring it to life," he told the outlet.[38]

Ancier was clearly in a mode of "throwing things to the wall and seeing what sticks" when he suggested a "Black *Laugh-In*." Best known for launching the careers of Goldie Hawn, Lily Tomlin, and former *Family Feud* host Richard Dawson, *Laugh-In*—officially, *Rowan & Martin's Laugh-In*—was a sketch comedy show that ran for 140 episodes on NBC, and it frequently took aim at the 1960s counterculture with sexually charged innuendo and pro-conservative "comedy." *Laugh-In* also took aim at the burgeoning civil rights and antiwar movements, so despite its later reputation of being a symbol of the 1960s counterculture, it was actually quite "square" in its subject matter. Clearly, Ancier had no idea what Keenen had up his sleeve, and it didn't have a thing to do with phrases like "you bet your sweet bippy!" and "sock it to me!"

And then, Keenen recounted that the executives said the words that would forever change his life—and the course of pop culture history.

"They said, 'you can do what you want to do,'" he recalled to the Television Academy.[39] "I said, 'Really?' So, I left, and I thought about it, and I said, 'okay. I got somethin'.'"

CHAPTER 2

You Can Do
What You Want to Do

With the green light in hand, Keenen went to work creating his television comedy opus. He already had three skits in hand—"Men on Film," which featured two effeminate gay men giving Siskel-and-Ebert-style commentary on films (which would eventually be encompassed under the "Men on . . ." series that included commentary on art, books, and television); "The Homeboy Shopping Network," which featured two street hustlers selling boosted items on a QVC-like network; and "Homey D. Clown," a disenchanted children's party clown with questionable ethics and a memorable catchphrase[1]—but not much else.

Still, everyone who was coming on board knew that Keenen had *something*, even if they didn't know exactly what it was quite yet. Naturally, the first people to come on board were members of the Wayans family—Damon (who'd already had some minor success in Hollywood[2] and was a *Saturday Night Live* alumnus[3]), Kim, Shawn, and later Marlon—who believed in their older brother, on instinct. The eldest Wayans brother, Dwayne—the beleaguered McDonald's manager who was the butt of the jokes on Keenen's inaugural *The Tonight Show Starring Johnny Carson* routine—would also periodically appear in various *In Living Color* sketches as an extra.

"I was a teenager," Shawn told the *Hollywood Reporter* in 2019.[4] "Keenen was telling me that he was working on something and might have something for me. He was always Superman to me. I've been watching my brother do some incredible [stuff] since I was 5."

Damon, however, saw his brother's nascent television vehicle as an opportunity for something else. "I never got in the business to be a star," he said to the *South Florida Sun-Sentinel* in 2013.[5] "I got in it to be funny and as therapy, as a way for me to talk about my life and what I was going through."

With the Wayans family locked and loaded, their younger members brought their friends along to audition for their big brother. Damon recruited his *Earth Girls Are Easy* costar Jim Carrey, while Kim recruited her friend David Alan Grier, who was a veteran of Broadway and radio.[6] Though Grier auditioned for the show with Susie Essman, Chris Rock, and Martin Lawrence—none of whom got a part on the show, though Rock would later reprise his "Cheap Pete" character from *I'm Gonna Git You Sucka* on later episodes of *In Living Color*—it took Kim's convincing to make him sign on to the show. "I wasn't a standup comedian—these guys all had characters and stuff, and I thought this wasn't really my forte, but it was the best decision of my life," he said at the Tribeca Film Festival in 2019.[7]

Incidentally, despite Damon's invitation, Carrey almost didn't take the show. Carrey kept asking for more and more money, and when Keenen wouldn't meet his demands, he would turn it down. Published reports suggested it was because Carrey felt he already "had a career" and didn't need *In Living Color* to "make it." At one point, Thomas Haden Church was being considered in place of Carrey, but ultimately, Fox cut a separate deal with Carrey to get him the money he felt he deserved, and he ultimately signed on to the show.

DC native Tommy Davidson, who was an in-demand stand-up comedian[8] at the time he auditioned, also felt there was something special about Keenen's nascent show. "We knew what it was gonna do. There was so much energy built up and anticipation because America needed something new," he said at the Tribeca Film Festival in 2019.[9]

Rounding out the cast was comedian Kim Coles,[10] actress and singer T'Keyah Crystal Keymáh, and actress Kelly Coffield. Of the inaugural cast, only Carrey and Coffield were white; this alone made the show an anomaly on television at the time.

With the core cast in place, the show needed a name. Tamara Rawitt, a co-producer on *I'm Gonna Git You Sucka*—who was also commissioned by Keenen as a writer and a producer for the new show—recalled an old NBC tagline,[11] and as such, *In Living Color* was born. The name was just as much of a hat-tip to the Peacock network as it was a play on the cast's predominant phenotypes—and it was also a swipe at *Saturday Night Live*, whose cast was exclusively white at the time.

In fact, *Saturday Night Live*'s demographics are well worth noting in this context. The 1989 cast was composed of Dana Carvey, Nora Dunn, Phil Hartman, Jan Hooks, Victoria Jackson, Jon Lovitz, Dennis Miller, and Kevin Nealon. Its featured players were A. (Alan) Whitney Brown, Ben Stiller, Al Franken, and Mike Myers. Every single cast member—and every single featured player—was white. In fact, of the 153 players to ever appear on *SNL* in its forty-five-year history, only 20 of them—including Damon Wayans—were Black.

With all the important elements in place, the cast and crew went to work shooting the pilot. Keenen chose to replace the "Homey D. Clown" skit with

"The Wrath of Farrakhan," a *Star Trek* send-up that featured Carrey parodying fellow Canadian William Shatner's best-known character of Captain James Tiberius Kirk in all his campy glory, and Damon adopting the role of the controversial Nation of Islam leader.

Grier, who played Spock, hilariously described Damon's Farrakhan as "a former calypso singer" in the skit, making a mostly obscure reference to Farrakhan's early career where he was known as "The Charmer" and sometimes known as "Calypso Gene." In fact, a year before Harry Belafonte released his classic album *Calypso*, Farrakhan—under his birth name, Louis Gene Walcott—released about a dozen calypso-style songs, including a particularly offensive track called "Is She Is, or Is She Ain't?" which was laden with transphobic references to Christine Jorgensen's gender reassignment surgery—one of the first of its kind that gained mainstream recognition in the American zeitgeist.

With references to Uhuru's (Kim Wayans) "nappy wig" and Spock's snapping at Kirk's "Caucasoid" behavior, Farrakhan inspires the beleaguered Starship *Enterprise* crew to revolt against the oppressive white regime on the ship.

As one might imagine, the white network executives were more than a little nervous.

"By the time the pilot was finished in 1989, I had left," Ancier explained to the *Hollywood Reporter*.[12] "Peter Chernin[13] took over. But I saw it and I know a lot of people at Fox were offended by it. I made my thoughts known to Fox chief Barry Diller that it was a valuable show and to go forward with it."

Despite Ancier's campaigning for *In Living Color*, the pilot sat in what Rawitt called "long-term parking"[14] for six months. Fox executives may have told Keenen that "he can do what he wants to do," but they didn't think he'd take it *that* literally, it seems. Maybe, they pondered, a few potential directives would have been in order?

For what it was worth, the Fox executives—including Chernin and Diller—weren't so much concerned about "putting Keenen in his place" as NBC had done to Pryor all those years ago. Rather, they were concerned about how Keenen's comedy would be received by the Black community at the time.[15] How much pushback would Fox get? Would their fledgling network be over before it even started? The social and economic impact of *In Living Color* on the network couldn't be overstated—the success of the network almost entirely hinged on it, in fact—and Chernin and Diller knew that *In Living Color*'s audience would be predominantly Black, especially in the beginning. If Fox lost them, it would be a proverbial wrap.

But this, perhaps, is one of those cases where well-meaning white liberal concern falls short of the mark, not out of any malice, but out of ignorance—or, perhaps more correctly, a "blind spot"—of the nuances of Black culture. Much like the *New York Times*'s John O'Connor had no clue about why Pryor's audience would find Huey Newton's appointment to the "first Black president's cabinet" hilarious, Chernin and Diller had no clue how "Men on Film" or "The Wrath of Farrakhan" would be funny to *In Living Color*'s prospective audience. Insulting gay Black men *and* a Black supremacist? Was no cow too sacred to slaughter?

Keenen, perhaps, also picked up on this blind spot and decided to demonstrate how he knew what his audience wanted.

"The intent of the show was to include *everybody*," Keenen said to the Tribeca Film Festival in 2019.[16] "We're gonna include *everybody*. Everybody's gonna laugh. [The pilot] sat on the shelf for a year. They wouldn't air it. And then, I met with Peter Chernin and Barry Diller. And in walks a group of guys— all white guys, suits—like, they came in, very quietly, with their clipboards. And the guy starts to tell me that they'd screened the TV show. And he starts telling me the audience's reactions—but he's not telling me what they laughed at. He's telling me what they *felt*. I was like, 'whoa.' Then, they started interviewing me. And the guy says, 'tell me your vision of the show.' And I start talking about the show, and I go, 'I think it'd be revolutionary!'"

Keenen then went a step further and invited Chernin down to the first rehearsal of "Men on Film" after Diller made clear that the skit would never get airtime. Chernin reluctantly agreed to Keenen's request and watched the skit— to coin a phrase—"in living color."

"It was like a bomb went off in the studio audience," Keenen recounted to the *Hollywood Reporter*.[17] "People were stomping their feet and clapping and laughing. Barry stood there watching. His face didn't move. But then he turned to me and said, 'OK,' and he left. So, we were able to do it."

While Keenen tried—and ultimately succeeded—at winning over the Powers That Be at Fox, Rawitt was talking up the press about *In Living Color*, serving as the show's de facto publicist. She managed to get a copy of the pilot over to a journalist at *Details* magazine,[18] who absolutely fell in love with it and wrote about it in the December 1989 / January 1990 issue of the magazine. In the article, the journalist questioned why the show hadn't been aired yet on Fox. Rawitt promptly faxed the article over to the executives, and the article— combined with the rousing live response to the "Men on Film" sketch— prompted Fox executives to finally give a green light to air the *In Living Color* pilot, which aired for the first time on April 15, 1990.

Of course, if you ask the executives *today* what they thought of the show, they completely deny any potential hesitancy about airing the pilot episode of *In Living Color*. Chernin, in fact, told the *Hollywood Reporter* that everyone who saw the pilot—from the executives to the advertisers—"went crazy for it" and that the network knew it had a hit on its hands. This, of course, begs the question: if that's the case, why did it sit on the shelf for at least six months, if not a year, before it finally aired?

In any event, the intro alone let the audience know they were in for a treat unlike anything they'd seen before—or since.

But the show had hit a minor snag: the first logo for *In Living Color* got some pushback from the rock band Living Colour, who sued Fox and Ivory Way Productions—Keenen's production company—claiming trademark violations over the show's logo and name of the show, which they claimed was "too similar" to their own. According to their lawsuit, Ivory Way Productions approached Living Colour to use their song "What's Your Favorite Color" as the theme song, and the band denied their request—and the band felt this trademark violation was retaliation by Fox and Ivory Way Productions for the denial. Fox subsequently changed *In Living Color*'s logo to something more monochromatic, but other details of the lawsuit—including any settlement terms—remain undisclosed to this day.

The intro song was Heavy D and the Boyz's "In Living Color,"[19] and the refrain was a nod and a wink to the directive to Keenen from Fox executives: "You can do what you want to do/In Living Color!"

In the first two seasons, the intro featured the cast members playing with brightly colored paint against a white painter's tarp, followed by a segue into a set that was meant to be on a New York City rooftop. On this rooftop, DJ SW-1—the alter ego of a teenaged Shawn Wayans,[20] who was too young to be featured in any of the skits that had decidedly adult humor—was on the ones and twos as a group of five gorgeous women known as the "Fly Girls" danced a tightly choreographed routine of all the hottest hip-hop dance moves seen in the clubs of the time. They would then open the rooftop door and let Keenen Ivory Wayans out to do a brief intro to the show before the sketches were launched.

America had never seen anything like it.

And they loved it.

The Fly Girls, too, deserve more than a passing mention here—because they were just as integral to the show's success as the talented cast of characters.

While Jennifer Lopez is, unquestionably, the most famous Fly Girl of all, she didn't join the lineup until the third season of the show. *In Living Color*'s inaugural season featured Cari French, Carrie Ann Inaba,[21] Deidre Lang, Lisa Marie Todd, and Michelle Whitney-Morrison. Each of these dancers came with successful dance and entertainment careers of their own, and their routines were choreographed by the inimitable Rosa "Rosie" Perez.

Dancers and variety shows go hand in hand—but these women weren't Barbara Boylan dancing with the Mouseketeer Bobby Burgess on *The Lawrence Welk Show*. Like the cast of *In Living Color*, almost all the Fly Girls were Black, Latina, or another "minority"—in fact, white girls were in such short supply as

The Fly Girls. *Fox/Photofest © Fox*

Fly Girls that the most common Google search term that brings up Lisa Joann Thompson's name is "blond Fly Girl."

"Five multicultural girls were going for their dreams and not afraid," Inaba told *People* in 2006 about her Fly Girl experience.[22] "I felt so at home."

And it went without saying that square dancing and fox trotting weren't on the dance card, and Welk's big brass band wasn't playing in the background, either. Rather, SW-1/Shawn Wayans—and later, DJ Twist/Leroy Casey—would spin the hottest hip-hop, rap, and house music that was making its way from the underground as these women—dressed in the hottest, most colorful B-girl gear for maximum impact—smurfed, ramboed, and cabbage patched for the audience at home and in the studio as the sets were shifted and the next sketch was prepped.

Mainstream hip-hop, in fact, owes just as much of a debt to *In Living Color* as it does to *Yo! MTV Raps*—more so, in fact, when you consider how many more people watched as *In Living Color*'s premiere episode[23] pumped hip-hop music into American homes during the prime-time hours and paired the music with the dance moves of the Fly Girls. To the average straight and virile American male, the sight of the Fly Girls dancing to Queen Latifah was far preferable to the sight of Ed Lover and Doctor Dre[24] wiggling along to "The 900 Number" by the 45 King. Besides, *In Living Color* aired in prime time, while *Yo! MTV Raps* aired at a random time in the afternoon when most people were still at work.[25]

But the Fly Girls weren't just the feminine analogues of the predominantly male *In Living Color* cast. Rather, they represented a specific type of woman: the women of New York City's outer boroughs of Bronx, Queens, Kings (aka Brooklyn), and Richmond (aka Staten Island). First immortalized in song in the 1985 hip-hop classic "Fly Girl" by the Boogie Boys,[26] the Fly Girl was bold, opinionated, and unapologetic. She had her own ideas, and she wasn't afraid to let the world know she had them. Her style—the ability to pair one or two high-fashion pieces with common, less expensive staples; "bamboo earrings, at least two pair/a Fendi bag and a bad attitude"—was often imitated, but never duplicated.

In short, she was an urban goddess—Mary Magdalene of Queens Boulevard, Lady Godiva of Flatbush Avenue, Venus on the Half Shell riding the Staten Island ferry—and she oscillated between being worshipped and objectified, an urbanized form of the Madonna-whore dichotomy, and a feminist quandary that persists in twenty-first-century hip-hop to this very day.

The Madonna-whore dichotomy is one that sees female sexuality as a black-and-white zero-sum game: women are either "good girls" who lack sexuality of any kind and thus merit respect (Madonna, so named for the mother of Jesus Christ, not the pop star), or they're "bad girls" who are hypersexual and thus merit no respect (whore). Sexuality, of course, is a sliding scale, and a woman's respectability has nothing to do with whether she's asexual, hypersexual, or anything in between—which is why modern feminist theory postulates that the Madonna-whore dichotomy is nothing more than another way to reinforce the patriarchy—and, more specifically, the white patriarchy.

But the Fly Girl cared about none of these things. She was, unapologetically, New York—as much a part of the fabric of the Big Apple as the Empire State Building, Times Square, and Central Park. When people think of the stereotypical New York woman, the Fly Girl is the default setting.

"A Fly Girl on *In Living Color* is beautiful, has a gorgeous body, and her own personal style," said Perez, who choreographed the troupe.[27]

"She's somebody who has her stuff together," said Deidre Lang, who was a Fly Girl for all five seasons of the show.[28] "Somebody who has all the moves."

"[She's] the kind of girl that every man dreams of having, and every girl dreams of being," said Jossie Thacker (nee Harris),[29] who was a Fly Girl in the last two seasons of *In Living Color*.

More important than having a body, a face, and her own sense of style—not to mention a milkshake that brought all the boys to the yard years before Kelis mellifluously sang about it—a Fly Girl had to wrap all these things in the bow of self-confidence—as Carrie Ann Inaba found out when she first auditioned to be a Fly Girl and got the job at almost the exact same second she flung off her jacket to perform her trial routine. "Keenen always said that I got the job the moment I walked in because my outfit was so bad and I had so much confidence," she told the *Hollywood Reporter* in 2019.[30]

No one had ever seen dancers like Fly Girls on mainstream television prior to *In Living Color*. Writing for the *Baltimore Sun* in 1991,[31] Michael Quintanilla sniffed that the girls were nothing like the June Taylor Dancers, seemed befuddled that their personal style was a mix of "street chic, haute couture and K-mart blue-light special," and could barely hide his bemusement as *In Living Color*'s costume designer, Michelle Cole, described the androgyny—which, today, would be called gender fluidity—that the Girls adopted in their personal style. It was a mix of "a little bit of boy, and a little bit of girl," a style that the average outer boroughs New York woman wore—and continues to wear to this day—as equal parts form and function, a matter of both budget and convenience (it's either the rent or the Louis Vuitton, and no true Fly Girl would be caught dead with a designer purse and an eviction notice).

It's interesting that Quintanilla's sole frame of reference was the dance troupe called the June Taylor Dancers, who couldn't have been more of the antithesis of the Fly Girls if they'd tried. Choreographed by the Midwestern, and decidedly white, Marjorie June Taylor, her namesake dancers were the backup for *The Jackie Gleason Show*, which aired in various incarnations from

1952 until 1970. Their signature style was a high-kicking chorus line reminiscent of the New York City Rockettes, and it went without saying that the June Taylor Dancers were all uniformly anemic, pale, lithe, and white. Throughout the entire history of the June Taylor Dancers, there was only one Black dancer: Mercedes Ellington, granddaughter of the legendary Duke Ellington, who joined the lineup in 1963 at the pinnacle of the civil rights era and shortly before the Civil Rights Act was codified into law. "The Fly Girls are like little runway models coming out at the start of the show. But their look is not about dresses and heels," Cole said to the newspaper.[32] "It's about contradiction, things you wouldn't think go together, but do."

Cole had the unenviable task of explaining the New York City je ne sais quoi to a random journalist in Baltimore, without the benefit of smartphones, the internet, YouTube, or social media. Given the cards that were stacked against her, she did a pretty good job.

But the Fly Girls on *In Living Color* had to work overtime to get that je ne sais quoi that came naturally to outer borough girls. Perez said that when she first started working on *In Living Color*, her schedule was "hectic" and sometimes took ten or twelve hours out of a day to complete. That's because she'd be doing everything from picking the music to editing the music—and even had to clear the licensing rights for the music (which is something that's normally done by someone *other* than the choreographer—but hey, "you can do what you want to do!").

"Everyone was so new to the business," said Perez.[33] "It was just kinetic, the energy—it was electric. And hip-hop was huge in New York, and it was huge in the music. But it wasn't huge in the mainstream."

Perez knew more than a little about the dance style she was trying to teach these wide-eyed young women with dreams of superstardom. After striking out to Los Angeles from Brooklyn—with aspirations to study biochemistry while helping a struggling young cousin who already had two children—Perez got plucked from the City of Angels' dance clubs to become a dancer on *Soul Train*. But her hip-hop dance style was a curiosity to Don Cornelius, who had never seen anything like it—or like Perez herself—before.

"Don Cornelius did not want to see how I really danced—I was doing hip-hop, and it was foreign to people out in California," she told *Esquire* back in 2014.[34] "They only knew about popping and locking, so they were not keen on hip-hop dancing. Don was like, 'No, no, no. You're a girl.' I was like, 'What? This is really weird.'"

Nevertheless, she made quite a splash on *Soul Train*, so much so that when Spike Lee caught her act in a nightclub, he hired her for her first major acting role in *Do the Right Thing*. From there, she began choreographing music videos for the likes of Janet Jackson, Bobby Brown, and LL COOL J.

But Perez's allegedly hard-scrabble New York background also hid a secret: her dance routines for the Fly Girls were rooted in a much more sophisticated locale. "I knew how to choreograph because I was part of the cheerleading squad in upstate New York," she explained to *Elle* back in 2014.[35] "And I knew how to give them [the Fly Girls] a personality and style because I am a geek and I loved to stay at home and watch television and watch one of my favorite movies again—*Viva Las Vegas*—[I] saw Ann-Margret and thought 'That's who they are.'"

Regardless of whether Perez got her inspiration for the dances from Brooklyn or Bryn Mawr, she had to get them out to the rest of the world. But Perez was concerned because the dancers who were ultimately chosen for the show didn't know how to do the B-girl dance moves that came so naturally to her—to which Keenen was quick to remind her that teaching them was part and parcel of her job description (presumably after she cleared the mechanical licenses for the music).

"I was a technical dancer," said Lang.[36] "I didn't know what hip-hop was, but I think if you start out, like, doing ballet—which is kind of like the core of dancing—I think you can do anything. [But] nobody had ever seen this before—and Keenen said that you're going to set a standard for dancers out there."

Keenen—as he usually was—was right. Women who tuned in to *In Living Color* were keenly aware of the Fly Girls—and they wanted to look like them, dress like them, dance like them, get the attention from men that they got . . . and yes, even *be* like them.

And as for the men? *C'mere shorty, lemme holla at you for a minute.*

Even in the twenty-first century, the Fly Girls' impact continues to be felt. Writing for Nerdist, Tai Gooden minced no words about the impact of the *In Living Color* dance troupe on the popular culture as we know it today—and how YouTube now serves as a time capsule of sorts to forever preserve the legacy these women left behind, to influence every generation hereinafter.

"Were the Fly Girls the originators of women's hip-hop fashion or dance? Absolutely not," said Gooden.[37] "But their visibility on TV provided an affirming platform to lots of women and girls, especially Black ones. It further confirmed to them that their culture, hair, and style were amazing. They still set a standard of what it means to be talented, cool, and straight up fly."

No doubt, then, that the Fly Girls would be a TikTok sensation today—or even back then, if social media was a thing. But because this was 1990, and "personal computers" felt light-years away in affordability to the average American household,[38] people had to content themselves with catching the Fly Girls once a week on *In Living Color*.

And they all acknowledged that this was a group effort—that, like Keenen did when he first joined forces with Townsend on *Hollywood Shuffle*, their ignorance was their gift. They were all crazy enough to believe that they could do it—and that's how it got done.

"There was magic in the skits, and the Fly Girls had this cult following," Inaba told the *Hollywood Reporter* in 2019.[39] "Rosie Perez pushed us hard. She didn't know how to pronounce words like 'pirouette,' but it didn't matter. She had a vision."

Indeed, everyone on *In Living Color* had a vision—even if they didn't have a clear path, or a road map, on how to get there. All they knew is that they could do what they wanted to do—and they did it all for the culture.

CHAPTER 3

For the Culture

The main key to *In Living Color*'s success was that it would create—and flaw-lessly execute—sketches that dealt almost exclusively with Black subject matter. Keenen, Damon, Jim Carrey, and the rest of the writer's room—Les Firestein,[1] Pam Veasey,[2] Greg Fields,[3] Marc Wilmore,[4] (and, later, his brother Larry[5]), Buddy Sheffield, Steve Tompkins, Fax Bahr,[6] Adam Small,[7] Paul Mooney,[8] and countless others—were unafraid to try new things with their skits. But the com-mon thread that ran through every skit was that it was unapologetically Black before it was fashionable to be so.

Naturally, not every skit was revolutionary in its writing or its delivery. Many skits dealt with the topical issues of the day—one infamous skit from the first season featured Keenen and Damon poking fun at Milli Vanilli,[9] and Jim Carrey quickly became known as the go-to impersonator for Snow and Vanilla Ice, white rappers who had booming careers in the 1990s but were, rightly, seen as donning musical blackface for performing music that was, at the time, exclu-sively the domain of Black people (and, to put a finer point on it, almost exclu-sively Black men)[10]—and, as such, reached a broader audience with their appeal.

But there were some skits that were strictly "for the culture"—for the Black American culture of the 1990s—and they've stood the test of time today. And it was just as much a function of the quality of the writer's room as it was to the ragtag group of talent that he cobbled together from his siblings' suggestions and group of friends.

"Everyone that Hollywood didn't know what to do with, I knew what to do with," he said on HBO's *The Black List* in 2009.[11]

This incomparable combination led to the creation of some of the most incredible skits specifically designed for the culture—for the Black culture—and that continue to stand the test of time today.

✳   ✳   ✳

Note: By no means is this a comprehensive list of all In Living Color *sketches. This is solely a list of the best of the best that still stand the test of time in the twenty-first century, and why they continue to resonate with modern audiences. Topical sketches are often the product of their time, and* In Living Color's *topical sketches are no exception.*

The Homeboy Shopping Network

SEASON 1, EPISODE 1

A send-up of the Home Shopping Network (today merely known as HSN), "The Homeboy Shopping Network" featured Keenen and Damon as The Iceman and Whiz, respectively, and first debuted on the pilot episode of the show. Dressed in jeans, T-shirts, backwards caps, and oversized clock chains (a nod and a wink to Public Enemy—and specifically, the group's hype man William "Flavor Flav" Drayton)—in other words, the typical hip-hop fashion of the day—The Iceman and Whiz would run in the back of a truck dazzled with graffiti and "The Homeboy Shopping Network" in colorful letters, while proclaiming "show 'em what we got!"

The basis of the joke was, of course, that the items "fell off the back of a truck"—as "stealing items" was euphemistically dubbed back then—and The Iceman and Whiz would offer everything from televisions to VCRs at steeply discounted prices.

The Iceman and Whiz are also in on the joke, as The Iceman offers car phones,[12] car stereos, and car alarms to the viewer—completed by Whiz's deadpan remark, "and if you act now, we can probably get the car." Jewelry was also available to the viewer, though "some of it was broken in transit."

And if you were interested in purchasing any of their wares? Call the nearby pay phone at 555-4396. (Cell phones were, apparently, too cost prohibitive, even for enterprising young men like The Iceman and Whiz.)

Naturally, the first call The Iceman and Whiz get is from an irate gentleman (voiced by Carrey), who recognizes his wife's ring in the collection of pilfered wares, and this is (also naturally) followed by a string of expletives and threats to Whiz's life. (The pair brush it off by saying "another satisfied customer!")

Next item up for proffer is a television like the one you get at some of the better hotels (with the gag, of course, being that the TV *was* from one of the better hotels—and it came with the special fancy stand to prove it), along with some free Gideon Bibles "if you act now!"

Now, what good would a television be without the next item up for proffer? Yes, that's right, a satellite dish (a luxury item at the time[13]) is the next item! Except this one was an even more luxurious item because it was plucked, somehow, from NASA, with The Iceman and Whiz promising you could talk *directly to the astronauts* courtesy of this oversized satellite dish (though what one would talk about with the astronauts once the transmission was dispatched is anybody's guess).

And lest you think that things couldn't get any more outrageous, The Iceman and Whiz have an ATM as the final item up for sale. Of all the items up for proffer, the ATM was the rarest of all: Though they first came out in the late 1950s and early 1960s, it would take until the late 1990s and early 2000s for the ATM (Automated Teller Machine) to enjoy ubiquity. So, at the time Iceman and The Whiz were offering it up for sale, it was a very rare item indeed.

But our newly beloved enterprising entrepreneurs couldn't enjoy the proceeds of their sales because the party is broken up by the "blue light special"—specifically, the blue and red lights of the NYPD, who managed to find the enterprising thieves. (Can't imagine how, or why, because they flew *so* far under the radar.) The Iceman and Whiz do, however, promise to be back next week—but "on a different corner."

It's worth noting that thanks to this iconic sketch, the phrase "Mo'money! Mo'money[14]!" entered the common vernacular, though Damon actually first said the phrase during a "Weekend Update" segment during the brief period he was a featured player on *Saturday Night Live*. Nevertheless, this was the first of many legendary sketches to come, and the audience was hooked on both the sketch, and the show, from this point forward.

Follow-up "Homeboy Shopping Network" sketches: "Homeboy Shopping Network: Used Car Sale" (season 1, episode 5), "Mo'Money with Wiz & Ice" (season 1, episode 9), "Homeboy Shopping Network: Hollywood Homeboys" (season 2, episode 7), "Homeboyz Shopping Network" (season 3, episode 16).

Great Moments in Black History: First Black Man on the Moon

SEASON 1, EPISODE 1

Believe it or not, this sketch shows up on "Black Twitter" in the twenty-first century, often as a joke involving a minor accomplishment (i.e., "first Black woman to straighten her hair") that gets uproarious laughter when it's referred to as a "great moment in Black history." Whether the tweeter realizes it or not, each one of those "great moments" is a nod and a wink to *In Living Color* and this sketch series.

In the inaugural sketch, Davidson[15] serves as a Levar Burton–esque host who goes on to introduce the "great moments in Black history" and the ordinary men and women who contribute to them. In the premiere sketch, Grier pays tribute to a Black man named Slick Johnson, who allegedly orbited the moon with Neil Armstrong, Michael Collins, and Buzz Aldrin. But Armstrong got word that he only had enough fuel to take two out of the three astronauts safely back to Earth with him—and it went without saying that poor Slick Johnson was left behind. An embarrassed NASA subsequently deleted all references to Johnson from its records (it was too soon for websites, after all).

Depending on how you read this sketch, this is either a swipe at NASA and its nearly uniformly white employee base,[16] or it's poking fun at conspiracy theorists who believe there's a global agreement between the world's most powerful leaders to denigrate Black men and their accomplishments. Maybe it's both. Either way, the skit is hilarious in both its delivery and its simplicity.

Follow-up "Great Moments in Black History" sketches: "Great Moments in Black History: The First Self-Service Gas Station" (season 1, episode 4), "Great Moments in Black History: The Jheri Curl" (season 3, episode 13), "Great Moments in Black History: The First Record Scratcher" (season 4, episode 22), "Great Moments in Black History: The First Def Comedy Jam" (season 5, episode 20).

Equity Express

SEASON 1, EPISODE 1

In the late 1980s, American Express released a series of commercials that had a film noir quality to them and featured a businessman talking into the camera and discussing a problem he had with his recent transaction—a case of fraud, a travel issue, a problem with a purchase, all the typical trappings of credit card usage. This was followed by an American Express customer service agent talking into the camera on how he (or she) helped the customer. The premise, of course, was that American Express's first commitment was to customer satisfaction, no matter what it took.

But it went without saying that the businessman—and the AmEx customer service representative—in the commercials were white. And the situations they presented—far-flung vacations in Bangkok, for example—were also out of reach to the average working-class Black American.

It's worth noting that, in the 1990s, credit card transactions were nowhere near as ubiquitous as they are today. Back then, credit card transactions were often reserved for "big-ticket" items—everything else was either paid via cash or check. In fact, a 1989 *Orlando Sentinel* article suggested that paying for "small-ticket" items—in their example, "a Big Mac and fries"—was more of a hassle than it was worth because of the paperwork involved (registers weren't on computerized systems at the time). But as registers shifted to a more computerized system, credit card use would become more ubiquitous. "During the 1990s there will be a proliferation of self-service credit transactions, using devices like the card-readers attached to some gasoline pumps in a few parts of the country. He sees more video rental machines and ticket dispensers that allow consumers to slip in their cards, get what they want and slip away," the outlet predicted, and correctly so.[17]

In Living Color did a send-up of the AmEx commercials with their own "Equity Express" commercial/sketch, featuring Coffield as the customer service representative and Grier as the beleaguered customer. And their issues didn't involve far-flung vacations or a Coach purse purchase.

Grier's character wants to purchase a shirt at a bespoke clothing store, but he doesn't have cash, so he presents the sales representative his "Equity Express" card. This prompts a call from the store manager, who is (as Coffield put it) "suspicious of a customer who was trying to use his Equity Express card" because he "wasn't the right *sort* to carry a gold card, if you know what I mean." (In today's parlance, the customer service rep would be "saying the quiet part out loud.")

When the customer service representative runs the card, Grier scoffs and says he knew his credit was good because he'd just paid the bill. He then produces all the forms of identity that the manager asked for—driver's license, birth certificate, mother's maiden name—and tries to play it off, because "this had happened before." That Grier was used to these sorts of issues tells a larger story, one that the Black audience was all too familiar with: statistically, then as now, Black Americans are more likely to have lower credit scores, get higher interest rates on their mortgages (if they even get mortgages at all), and are more likely to get lower lines of credit—if they even *get* credit at all—than their white, Asian, and even Hispanic/Latino counterparts.

That wasn't enough for Coffield, who smiles a Karen-esque smile and informs the audience that she "wasn't giving up so easy." She then gets the customer on the phone and asks him an obscure question: "Who was the winner of the Bob Hope Invitational Tournament in 1978[18]?" This angers Grier, who tells her to "kiss my butt, bitch!"

"I had him," says Coffield. "Use of obscenity over interstate phone lines is a federal offense.[19] So, I asked the store manager to stall him while I called the police."

The store manager's idea of "stalling" Grier involves giving him the red-carpet treatment—wrapping his T-shirt in a gift box, serving him hors d'oeuvres, performing magic tricks—until the police show up. After being wrongfully arrested, Grier sues Equity Express and won, "but it was still fun to do, and the store manager was grateful."

Equity Express—don't leave your crib without it!

The groans and *ooohs* from the audience notwithstanding, the skit works because the premise is quite *real*—and it's still very real today.

One can't help but see this skit in a darker light in the wake of the George Floyd murder on May 25, 2020, which happened simply because a shopkeeper believed Floyd was trying to pay for his wares with counterfeit money (an eerily parallel situation to the one presented in "Equity Express"). It would be interesting to see how (or even *if*) *In Living Color* would approach the Floyd murder—and the subsequent extralegal massacre of countless Black men since that time—if it were on the air today.

Whether we want to admit it or not—and frankly, nobody wants to admit it, or at least not as much as they should be admitting it—Black men are never given the same deference, the same respect, and the same benefit of the doubt in the business world as their white counterparts.

This was true in 1990—and as much as we'd like to think things are completely different today, we still have a long way to go.

The fact that this skit could still be performed in the twenty-first century and still land a powerful punch is proof positive that things aren't where they should be in the United States. And that needs to change. It's long overdue.

Follow-up "Equity Express" sketch: "Equity Express Blue Dot/Kennedy Carte Blanche" (season 3, episode 13).

Arsenio and Marion Barry

SEASON 1, EPISODE 2

Arsenio Hall, who had a very popular nighttime television show at the time, was frequently the butt of the jokes on *In Living Color*, and Keenen often parodied Hall with wicked glee. Snarky comments were made about Hall's close, quasi-fraternal relationship with Eddie Murphy ("and don't you forget it!"), Golden Retriever dogs were in the audience barking (a snarky reference to Hall's signature "Dog Pound Cheer," which featured audience members pumping their fists and barking like dogs), and Hall's body movements—and booty!—were presented in an overexaggerated fashion.

It's worth noting that despite being the butt of many of Keenen's jokes, the truth is, Keenen and Hall were (and are) very good friends. In fact, Keenen was the one who introduced Hall to his longtime collaborator and lifelong friend, Eddie Murphy.

But the true humor in this episode was in Hall's guest: controversial DC mayor Marion Barry.[20] Throughout the skit, Barry was rubbing his nose with a handkerchief (a nod and a wink to his crack-cocaine addiction, whose most common symptom includes a persistent runny nose) and claiming he was being "wrongly accused of a crime."

Keenen, for his part, played Hall as an ignorant buffoon, questioning Barry on how it felt to be a sex symbol, and confusing Barry's "book" with "being booked" (that is, being arrested).

Critics would often take Hall to task for inviting "political firebrands" on the show, and they claimed that Hall's interest in politics "killed the ratings."[21] So, at times, Keenen's parody of Hall felt less like good-natured ribbing between two friends and more like dogpiling onto a bad situation. Still, the Hall parodies also showed how impressions can be at the heart of good comedy.

Follow-up "Arsenio Hall" sketches: "The Arsenio Hall of Justice"[22] (season 2, episode 22), "Arsenio Hall: Dare to Say Hmmmm"[23] (season 3, episode 7), "Arsenio Hall Harasses Eddie Murphy" (season 3, episode 17), "Arsenio Hall, Whoopi Goldberg, and Jay Leno: Undigable Hosts" (season 4, episode 27).

Ridin' Miss Daisy

SEASON 1, EPISODE 2

As the name implies, "Ridin' Miss Daisy" was a send-up of the Oscar-winning film *Driving Miss Daisy*, which starred Morgan Freeman as Hoke Colburn, the driver to the late Jessica Tandy's cantankerous titular Miss Daisy Werthan. In less than ninety seconds, Keenen took the joke *exactly* where you think he would—to Coffield's Miss Daisy's back seat—to thunderous laughter and applause from the audience.

As ridiculous and, arguably, juvenile as the punchline to the skit was, it was just as much of a critique of the film itself. Consider that *Driving Miss Daisy* and *Do the Right Thing* were both released in the same year—1989—and both were purportedly films meant to be watershed moments in race relations in the United States.[24] But while the former was nominated, and ultimately won, the Best Picture Oscar, the latter was completely shut out of the awards ceremony.

Spike Lee's recent commentary[25] about the ultimate impact of the two movies sums it up quite nicely, however. In 2014, *Selma*—about Martin Luther King Jr.'s groundbreaking Civil Rights March in the Alabama town—was nominated for Best Picture (it lost to *12 Years a Slave*, and the commentary writes itself) and Best Original Song (for "Glory" by John Legend and Common, and it won). However, director Ava DuVernay was not nominated for best director. Speaking to the *Daily Beast* in 2017, Spike Lee snarked "join the club!" before reflecting on how *Driving Miss Daisy* shut out his own film—and how, ultimately, it didn't matter in the long run, because "nobody's talking about motherfuckin' *Driving Miss Daisy*. That film is not being taught in film schools all across the world like *Do the Right Thing* is. Nobody's discussing *Driving Miss Motherfuckin' Daisy*."

With this in mind, perhaps, then, it's best if the film is remembered by Keenen and Coffield's parody, and not the film itself.

Oswald Bates for the United Negro Scholarship Fund

SEASON 1, EPISODE 3

Thanks to social media, we all know at least one person like Oswald Bates—someone who thinks he's so intelligent but couldn't be a bigger idiot if he was paid to do so. He's the type of guy who uses big words, yet has no clue what they mean, and the result is nothing short of a word salad (think any politician's speech, on either side of the aisle, after 2016).

Speaking on Oswald, Keenen said that he represented "every brother who thinks he's educated."

In the inaugural sketch, Oswald (played by Damon Wayans) is speaking directly into the camera for the "United Negro Scholarship Fund" (a send-up of the United Negro College Fund, whose slogan was "A Mind Is a Terrible Thing to Waste," and whose irony will be well apparent very shortly).

"First of all, we must internalize the *flagellation* of the matter by transmitting the *effervescence* of the *Indonesian proximity* in order to further segregate the *crux* of my *venereal infection*,"[26] he begins, sounding extraordinarily like a Trump presidential speech before his presidential run was even a glimmer in the Republican Party's eye.

And it just gets worse (and progressively more hilarious) from there.

As he continues to talk in his nonsensical way, the camera pans away to reveal that Oswald is, in fact, delivering this speech from behind bars—after which a voice-over comes on and encourages the viewer to give to the United Negro Scholarship Fund, because "a mind is a terrible thing to develop without help." The upshot, of course, is to "stay your butt in school," which seems like a fine message to send to young people of all stripes these days.

Critics of the sketch saw it as an indictment of Black men—and, as Keenen's own words suggest, perhaps it was. He was, however, taking aim at a certain type of Black man—one who means well but is misguided, perhaps, or one who arrogantly believes he's much more intelligent than he is.

But the point, in fact, is that this is one of those sketches where "if he was talking to you, you'd understand him." In other words, Damon's character wasn't meant to be understood by white men and women—especially privileged white men and women—but by *In Living Color*'s predominantly Black audience. And, certainly, by no means was it meant to be used as evidence of "white superiority" by a particularly noxious subset of society.

But the layers of societal rot addressed by the Oswald character are self-evident: the mass incarceration of Black men, the prison industrial complex, functional illiteracy[27] among Black men,[28] and Black men adopting a "white" persona to feel empowered in a society that makes them feel disempowered by its very existence.

Writing for the *Journal of Black Studies*, Wayne Blake and Carol Darling note that the misplaced adoration of white men led to the conundrum that many Black men in 1990s society faced. "The white male has been identified as protective, condescending, and generally patriarchal with respect to women," they write. "Displaying dominant, aggressive, and often violent behaviors towards women are also characteristics of the white male's sex role. This belief has kept African American males from adopting a part of the culture's definition of masculinity because they have failed to realize that because Black men's experiences are different, then their roles must also be different from white males."[29]

Whether this sort of larger social commentary was intentional or not is, of course, up in the air—but it does open the door for a larger conversation to be had about such things, and how we can ameliorate them in the future.

Follow-up "Oswald Bates" sketches: "Oswald Meets the Parole Board" (season 2, episode 15), "Visiting Day for Oswald" (season 2, episode 25), "Oswald Bates: The Silence of the Lambs II" (season 3, episode 2), "Oswald: 48 Hours Again" (season 3, episode 9), "The Law Offices of Oswald Bates" (season 3, episode 30),[30] "Oswald: Booked on Phonics" (season 4, episode 17).[31]

Anton

SEASON 1, EPISODE 4

The first appearance of Anton Jackson—a homeless man and entertainment aficionado who often tries, in vain, to entertain beleaguered New York City subway riders—was in season 1, episode 4 of *In Living Color*.

To this day, there isn't a New York City subway rider who doesn't groan whenever they hear "ladies and gentlemen, may I have your attention please!" And, of course, those are the first words Anton says when he arrives on the subway car.

Though Anton had the first shades of Keenen's impersonation that he performed all those years ago for his mother and her friends, the actual character himself was performed by Keenen's younger brother, Damon, and Anton would eventually become one of Damon's most memorable characters.

But though Keenen may have seeded the Anton Jackson ground with his initial impersonation of a drunk person for his beloved mother and her friends, Damon told *UPROXX* that he drew his inspiration for Anton Jackson from two far darker sources: first, from his uncle Gene—brother of his mother, Elvira—who was a heroin addict; and second, from a potential suitor of his sister Deidre, who tried to impress the unsuspecting Wayans family matriarch by complimenting her on her big butt ("now I see where Deidre got [it] from") and did speedballs (a mix of heroin and cocaine, speedballs are infamous for being the cause of comedian John Belushi's death). It's interesting to note that two brothers can have the same mother and father, grow up in the same home and under the same circumstances, yet draw inspiration from two completely different places.

In any event, Anton has all the qualities of a standard subway busker—gross habits (such as picking his nose and wiping it on the passengers), questionable talent, and a complete lack of ability to read the room and just keep quiet, even after Grier (as the passenger) begged him to do so.

But he also had an ineffable charm, which made him a hit with the audience (even if the subway riders couldn't wait to get away from him). Anton would subsequently make appearances in other skits and other circumstances, most infamously in "Po'People's Court," a send-up of the legendary *The People's Court*.

Follow-up "Anton" sketches: "This Old Box with Anton Jackson" (a send-up of "This Old House"—season 1, episode 8), "Anton on Po'People's Court" (a send-up of *The People's Court*—season 1, episode 10), "Anton: Army Recruitment Office" (season 2, episode 2), "Anton's Thanksgiving" (season 2, episode 10), "Anton in the Burbs" (season 2, episode 16), "Anton: Shakespeare in the Park" (season 3, episode 3), "Anton and the Undercover Journalist" (season 3, episode 11), "Anton: Suburban Marriage" (season 3, episode 21), "Anton Gets Rich" (season 3, episode 24), "Anton at Comic Relief" (season 4, episode 6).[32]

Black World

SEASON 1, EPISODE 5

One of the most underrated—but most powerful—*In Living Color* sketches is one that doesn't get as addressed in mainstream culture as much as, say, "Men on Film" (which will be discussed in greater detail later—and, in fact, it gets its own chapter) or "The Homeboy Shopping Network." It's "Black World," a one-off sketch performed by T'Keyah "Crystal" Keymáh.

In the sketch, the diminutive Keymáh plays Chrissy, a little girl who is waiting in a theater for her mother to finish her cleaning job. While she waits, Chrissy addresses the audience to talk about a place she likes to go in her imagination called "Black World."

For the next three minutes, Keymáh delivers equal parts social commentary (with references to political prisoners in South Africa, suffering under apartheid—including Nelson Mandela) and satire, pointing out how little Black girls are aware of their Blackness—and how the world around them responds to it—in a way that little white girls are not.

It's hard to convey to twenty-first-century young people just how pivotal the release of Nelson Mandela was to the movement to end apartheid—or why little Black girls in the late 1980s and early 1990s were so in tune to the racially charged environment of South Africa. But perhaps it's worth noting what was going on at the time this pivotal sketch was recorded: Nelson Mandela was ultimately freed from prison on February 11, 1990. Subsequent negotiations to end apartheid began on May 4, 1990, and continued until April 27, 1994, when it was finally abolished. To give a better frame of reference in terms of the show: three months before *In Living Color*'s first episode aired, Nelson Mandela was freed. And less than three *weeks* before *In Living Color*'s final episode, apartheid was finally abolished. That means throughout nearly the entire 127-episode run of the show, apartheid was still legal—and practiced—in South Africa.

So, while Keenen et al. were free to do what they wanted to do, in living color, in the "good old U. S. of A.," men and women who looked like the cast of *In Living Color* were being subjected to brutal conditions in their native land—to the point that a similar cast lineup featuring white cast members associating with Black cast members would have been a crime. And in apartheid-era South Africa, it was illegal for Black people to set up businesses in white areas, meaning that the mere incorporation of Ivory Way Productions would have been a crime in South Africa.

Is it any wonder that Chrissy dreamed of a "Black World," where all the Black people were free, including Nelson Mandela?

"And the white people don't follow you around and ask you if you have some money, like they know you didn't have any money, because your mother didn't give you any money, because she didn't have any money," she says, sadly, in a childish voice. "Because they, because they not there anyway because the Black people own the store, and they are nice to you—and the white people—I dunno where they are. They must be back in white world."

She also points out that, in Black World, Black Barbies are the norm, and not the exception.

And then, at the end of the sketch, Chrissy's mother calls her off-camera, and she sadly waves to the camera, ready to face the harsh realities of an unkind world outside of the preconstructed "Black World" of her imagination.

Even looking at the sketch through twenty-first-century eyes—in the wake of the summer of Black Lives Matter and the extreme polarity of the country in the wake of the Trump presidency—"Black World" remains a poignant testament to how far we need to go, as a country, for full *equity* and equality.

Jheri's Kids

SEASON 1, EPISODE 6

Because no cow was too sacred to slaughter on *In Living Color*, the "Jheri's Kids" sketch was a send-up of the annual Jerry Lewis MDA Labor Day Telethon, which ran until 2010, when Lewis parted ways with the Muscular Dystrophy Association. From 1956 until 2009, the telethon raised more than $2 billion for the Muscular Dystrophy Association. In 2020, the Muscular Dystrophy Association launched a new version of the telethon. But this one was social media based, and it was hosted by Kevin Hart.

Lewis's humor was very family friendly, but by the 1980s, it was seen as the typical "Borscht belt" humor that it really was, and it fell out of favor with the younger generation.

In this sketch, Carrey adopted the Jerry Lewis persona, and it was the perfect opportunity for the Canadian comedian to showcase the slapstick physical comedy that would, eventually, make him famous worldwide. Carrey's Lewis impersonation was replete with exaggerated facial expressions, a funny walk, and a nasal intonation that was all too familiar to fans of Lewis.

But rather than raise money for the MDA, "Jheri's Kids" raised money for Black men from Compton, California,[33] who became addicted to the Jheri Curl product.[34] Davidson played one of the "addicts" in question,[35] and he claimed that his woman left him "because she was tired of washing the pillowcases, man!"[36] He then claimed he was a "walking fire hazard."[37]

The good news, though, was that Davidson had finally gotten past his Jheri Curl addiction and was going to get a flat-top shortly after the fundraising event was over.

At one point in the sketch, Carrey was so amused by the song he had to sing—a parody of "You'll Never Walk Alone"—that he broke character and laughed at the finale. True to form, Davidson picked up the slack and sang the final lyric ("put that greaseball under a *caaaaaaaaaap*!").

What's perhaps most important to note is that Carrey was doing an un-apologetically Black sketch, but he never once stepped into territory where he didn't belong. In other words, he didn't don the Jheri Curl himself, and neither did he denigrate or otherwise insult Davidson's character for being "addicted" to the hairstyle. This skit is a perfect example of the difference between *appreciation* and *appropriation*, and none of the white cast members on *In Living Color* ever crossed into the latter territory during the "Keenen era." Whether it was because Keenen and the writers simply wouldn't allow it, or the white cast members simply knew better, or both, the fact is, they did it—nobody complained—and neither Carrey nor Coffield ever felt like they were being "canceled" or otherwise silenced for not donning comedic blackface.

And this was in the 1990s, that mythical time that certain political parties claim there was no "political correctness," and how things were so much better back then, because everyone could say what they wanted without fear of retribution, and couldn't we ever go back to those times for the sake of the children?

Do with that information what you will.

Ted Turner's Very Colorized Classics: Casablanca

SEASON 1, EPISODE 7

Ted Turner—the media mogul who founded networks like CNN and TBS—was a very vocal proponent of colorizing old movies in the 1980s. He made headlines in late 1988, when he and his team secretly began colorizing *Citizen Kane*. Naturally, the outcry from the Hollywood establishment was that Turner was committing nothing short of "sacrilege" for doing this.[38]

But there were plenty of people—*In Living Color*'s writers included, apparently—who felt the outrage was a bunch of much ado about nothing, and they decided to make a comment about it. The outrage certainly sounds like a bunch of much ado about nothing when viewed through twenty-first-century eyes, with today's content creators being unapologetically heavy handed with filters and Photoshop like it's second nature.

The sketch featured Carrey as Turner,[39] sitting in a lounge chair and serving as the host of the "very colorized classic." But if the critics thought that Turner adding a little bit of blue to Orson Welles's magnum opus was the equivalent of lèse-majesté, the *In Living Color* treatment of the film would have been straight-up regicide.

Humphrey Bogart was replaced by Billy Dee Williams (played, of course, by Keenen in one of the most pitch-perfect impersonations of the *Mahogany* actor in history, although this isn't Keenen's best-known impersonation of Williams—more on that later), and the first thing he says is "of all the jive joints in the world, she had to bring her big butt into mine."[40] And who's playing the piano in this jive joint? Why, none other than Stevie Wonder (Tommy Davidson), of course!

Yes, Ted Turner certainly brought plenty of color into the classic films. You might even say he did it "in living color." And *Casablanca* never looked better.

The "Ted Turner's Very Colorized Classics" sketches also take on a special importance when you think about how many old movies featuring an exclusively white cast have been rebooted to feature Black casts since *In Living Color* went off the air. From *Cinderella* starring Brandy and the late Whitney Houston (1997) to *Steel Magnolias* starring former *In Living Color* musical guest Queen Latifah, Phylicia Rashad, Alfre Woodard, and Jill Scott (2010), and even to 2014's re-imagining of *Annie* starring *In Living Color* alum Jamie Foxx and Quvenzhané Wallis, Black actors have now come to realize that they don't have to be depicted as "the help" or—worse yet—"the slaves" in films. No, now Black actors can see themselves—whether young or old—as the *stars* of a mainstream film.

"Very Colorized Classics," indeed.

Follow-up "Ted Turner's Very Colorized Classics" sketch: "Ted Turner's Very Colorized Films—Redd Foxx's The Kid" (season 1, episode 10).[41]

President Jackson's Farewell Address

SEASON 1, EPISODE 8

In 1990, it was almost impossible to fathom the day that America would have a Black president. Barack Obama's presidency was still eighteen years away, and the Black men and women who were young adults during the time *In Living Color* was on the air were still smarting from the after-effects of the civil rights era—not so much for the forward motion, but for the resultant violence from the usual law enforcement suspects (encouraged by the likes of the allegedly feather boa–buying J. Edgar Hoover, of course).

But in 1984, the Reverend Jesse Jackson ran an unsuccessful campaign for president as a Democrat, becoming the second Black person—after Shirley Chisholm in 1972—to do so on a national level.[42] Jackson would run again in 1988, and he more than doubled his results from the first time around. Nevertheless, he was still seen by many in the traditional DC political establishment as a "fringe" candidate, one whose progressive views were an outlier and not the norm, and he was far from seen as a serious political contender.[43]

In the *In Living Color* sketch, "President Jackson's Farewell Speech" was delivered on December 22, 2000. Keenen, who played Jackson, tells the audience that he is delivering the last press conference of his presidency. It's interesting to note that Keenen plays Jackson with many of the same mannerisms that would later be ascribed to Obama—slow, deliberate speech; pointed hand gestures when drawing emphasis to a particular statement—but, unlike Obama, Keenen's Jackson was played with an exaggerated Southern drawl, which was a sharp reference to Jackson's upbringing in Greenville, South Carolina.

Jackson lists his accomplishments in a sort of rhyme scheme—one might even say he was rapping or delivering a spoken word performance—as he talks about going from "the outhouse to the White House," as is typical of Baptist ministers to turn tragedy into testimony.

He then turns the questions over to the pool of DC journalists (a very obvious hat-tip to the sketch on *The Richard Pryor Show* about the first Black president—and unsurprising, considering Mooney was a writer for both shows), and the first question comes from Keymáh, who asks if Jackson ever feared an assassination attempt "as the first Black president."

"My administration did fear assassination, either by strangulation, decapitation, or driving through the South without identification," he says, clearly keeping with the rhyme scheme. "So, I took several precautions to ensure my safety . . . I also, as all my predecessors have, kept Dan Quayle as a vice president."

Despite being considered one of the "most active vice presidents in history," James Danforth "Dan" Quayle was seen by many in DC as an incompetent lightweight, incapable of handling complex matters that involved great intellectual heft. That's because most of his statements were contradictory and nonsensical (such as the time he made reference to the slogan "A Mind Is a Terrible Thing to Waste" of the UNCF [formerly the United Negro College Fund] as "What a waste it is to lose one's mind"), and matters weren't helped when he infamously misspelled "potato" as "potatoe" in front of a classroom full of elementary school students in New Jersey, to the ridicule of both the students and the press around him. Quayle, for his part, refused to take responsibility for the gaffe, blaming the elementary school's index cards for containing the spelling error. The running joke in DC, at the time, was that Quayle was kept as President George H. W. Bush's vice president for Bush's safety, because no American in their right mind would attempt to assassinate Bush knowing that Quayle was next in line for the presidency.

As for his greatest achievement as president, Jackson claims that he passed a law forbidding performances from LaToya Jackson and Tito Jackson, Michael Jackson's arguably less musically talented siblings. And, for what it's worth, Jackson—who is referred to as "Brother President" by the journalist played by Coles[44]—felt he kept the most important promise he made to the American people, which was to "keep hope alive."[45] But it wasn't about keeping hope in the promise of a new day alive—no, it was about keeping the cryogenically frozen Bob Hope alive "for another hundred years."

A straight line can be drawn (and has been consistently drawn) between this *In Living Color* sketch and *The Richard Pryor Show*'s sketch "The First Black President." In Pryor's skit, "The First Black President" was the fortieth president of the United States,[46] and he was articulate, intelligent, and charming—much like Obama himself would be nearly forty years into the future. But Pryor's First Black President wasn't afraid to drag the white establishment by its short and curlies, which probably did him no favors when it came time to save the show from the chopping block. With Pryor's First Black President clearly happy to engage in friendly banter with the "journalists from *Ebony* and *Jet*" and engaging in a call-and-response with *As-salamu alaykum* and *Wa'alaykumu s-salām*,[47] it's perhaps no wonder that O'Connor could barely contain his contempt for Pryor in his *New York Times* review of the show. "The nerve of this Black man" is silent, but only barely, in O'Connor's review.[48]

Arguably, Keenen's depiction of Jackson as a slow, subliterate Southerner with an exaggerated drawl—as opposed to taking Pryor's more straight-ahead excoriation approach—made the depiction easier to digest by the white audience. Furthermore, it stands to reason that Keenen was almost hyper-aware of this— he *was* a comedy disciple of Pryor's, after all, and any Black comedian worth their weight in salt would know about the pushback Pryor faced from the white establishment, if they hadn't already experienced it themselves—and played it as safe as possible while still packing a hard comedic punch. It certainly helped that Keenen chose to only make passing references to political figures, toned down Jackson's more progressive platforms (which were seen as downright radical in those times),[49] played up his Southern-ness[50] to comedic effect, and chose to excoriate political figures that were already tied to the whipping post—Quayle was low-hanging fruit thanks to that "potato/potatoe" mess.[51]

Still, this sketch is yet another example of the show's willingness to directly tackle Black subject matter and integrate it into mainstream America, even if they had to do so in the most delicate way imaginable.

Follow-up "Jesse Jackson" sketch: "Jesse Jackson's Children's Books" (aka "Green Eggs and Gubment Cheese") (season 3, episode 4).

Cephus and Reesie Mayweather

SEASON 1, EPISODE 8

Cephus and Reesie Mayweather were a part-Gospel, part-R&B duet that were also a married couple, who had a residency at the Mirage on the Vegas strip.[52]

Like typical Vegas acts, Cephus and Reesie were clad in over-the-top green rayon suits and matching gold boots that shimmered with every move.

Portrayed by Grier and Kim Wayans, the pair would sing "funkified" versions of nursery rhymes ("Pop Goes the Weasel"), which the viewer could get on their compilation greatest hits album. And it was important for the viewer to "act now," because let's be real, Cephus and Reesie were going to give a "special touch" to any song you could possibly imagine. And who could possibly resist? (For $11 "in cash," you could mail away for a greatest hits album that came with a special ten-carat gold-plated tooth just like the ones Cephus and Reesie wear!)

But nothing could compare to the pair's original tracks, which included "We Tight" and "Get Off the Lord's Bus If You Ain't Got Correct Change."

Unlike many of the other sketches on *In Living Color*, the Cephus and Reesie sketches were funny simply because they *were*. There was no deeper meaning behind the songs, there was no social commentary, and there was no comment about all of life's trials and tribulations. This was the typical humor that the younger members of the Wayans family would eventually become known for in both films *and* television: funny skits for the sake of being funny, Black humor that appealed to the mainstream in equal measure.

Follow-up "Cephus and Reesie Mayweather" sketches: "Cephus and Reesie's Broadway Tour" (season 2, episode 3), "Cephus and Reesie: The Christmas Album" (season 2, episode 12), "Cephus and Reesie: Last Request" (season 2, episode 19), "Cephus and Reesie: Bar Mitzvah" (season 3, episode 5), "Cephus and Reesie: Toons for Tots" (season 4, episode 13[53]).

Hey Mon: Hedley Airlines

SEASON 1, EPISODE 9

This sketch was one of many that featured the Hedleys, a West Indian (and, to put a finer point on it, Jamaican) family that dealt in the trope of having multiple jobs (the Hedleys each had fifteen jobs) to make ends meet. Damon Wayans played the patriarch of the family, and they were running their own airline in this sketch. Damon was the pilot, the in-flight chiropractor, the ticketing agent, the baggage handler, the head steward, the navigator, "and me own co-pilot to boot." His daughter, Margaret (Coles), was the stewardess, cook, restroom attendant, rent-a-car agent, air traffic controller, and engine mechanic. His wife, Hilda (Keymáh), was doing laundry on the wing of the plane—and she appreciated the cold because "it dried her laundry in one-*toured* (one-third) the time."

"And the rude boy[54] serving a drink is my lazy son Byron [Davidson]," continues Mr. Hedley, who apparently is embarrassed that Byron only had one job and wore a uniform that made him look like Isaac from *The Love Boat* (though Byron felt that the uniform gave him "authority")—and "we all know he hasn't had a job in a long time."

For the jokes throughout "The Hedleys" to work, the viewer had to subscribe to a form of an *immigrant advocacy trope* (IAT), which depicts immigrants from poorer countries—in other words, the West Indies, Mexico—as "job stealers." The crux of the trope is the belief that poor immigrants from far-flung countries—especially Black and brown immigrants—come to the United States with the sole intention of stealing jobs from hardworking Americans, who are unemployed and poor because of this influx. (And, certainly, there's a certain political party that campaigns, in part, on this fictional trope.)

But, as the children of immigrant families from all over the world—and especially from poorer countries—will tell you, their parents do the jobs that American-born laborers simply won't do. What's more, because the jobs are low paying—sometimes, even below minimum wage—their parents must take several jobs to make ends meet. Jamaican families, like the Hedleys, are one such family—and their reasons for resonating with the *In Living Color* audience, many of whom were of West Indian descent themselves, are obvious. Those viewers could see their own family in the Hedleys and felt "seen"—sometimes for the first time in their lives.

And then there was the subversiveness of the "Hey Mon" sketches: the cast was able to sneak in Jamaican *patois* obscenities—with the first salvo being delivered by Damon as the Hedley patriarch, who referred to his lazy son Byron/Davidson as a "*bloodclaat*"[55]—without much pushback from the Fox censors (but there was a collective "Oh! *Whoa!*" from the audience, who caught on all too quickly), because, quite simply put, the white censors[56] had no idea what they were saying.[57]

But the Black audience—especially those of West Indian and, more specifically, Jamaican descent—knew exactly what they were saying, and they loved it. And that was all that really mattered.

Follow-up "Hey Mon" sketches: "Hey Mon: Hedley Hospital" (season 2, episode 1), "Hey Mon: Hedley Court" (season 2, episode 19), "Hey Mon: The Hedleys vs. the Wans" (season 3, episode 4).

Homey D. Clown

SEASON 1, EPISODE 9

Season 1, episode 9 introduced a character that can also be considered one of *the* definitive characters on *In Living Color*: Herman Simpson, better known as

Homey D. Clown. The character was one of the first to be licensed from the show,[58] and his likeness spawned such merchandise as T-shirts, stuffed socks (which were used to beat unfortunate victims), and even a video game.

The "Homey D. Clown" video game was released in 1993, so the graphics, sound effects, and gameplay were primitive, to say the least. In the game, a very pixelated Homey—in all his 8-bit, MS-DOS glory—would go through a maze, collecting random items and interacting with random villains who either just wanted change for the subway, or who made fun of Homey's clown suit. In 2020, at the height of the COVID-19 pandemic lockdown, gamers for the outlet Ars Technica did a review of the speed run game for a piece called "Summer Games Done Quick," and the quality of the game can be summed up in one phrase that they uttered at the beginning of the review: "This game aggressively farts at you."[59] It would be interesting to see what a Homey D. Clown app would do in the year 2021, however.

In any event, in the inaugural episode that featured the character immortalized by Damon, the cast members (including Grier, Coffield, Davidson, and Keymáh) are dressed as children at a birthday party, and their excited mother (Coles) informs them that she has hired a clown to entertain them for the occasion.

But she didn't hire just any clown—she hired Homey D. Clown.

And the kids got an experience they wouldn't soon forget.

When Davidson excitedly asks for Homey while dancing around, the misanthropic clown responds with a smack upside his head and a dirty look. This got thunderous laughter and applause from the audience, who presumably had their fair share of dealing with badass kids hyped up on sugar at birthday parties—and probably wished for a "Homey" in their own lives as preternaturally *exhausted* parents.

"Aight, kids, I'm Homey D. Clown," begins Damon, who is dressed in clown makeup, a hilariously bad red wig that made him look bald on top, flouncy oversized shoes, and a multicolored jumpsuit. "You ready to have some fun? Aight. What'chall want me to do for you first?"

Keymáh's character raises her hand and asks for a "clown dance."

Homey looks to the camera, breaking the fourth wall, and nods sarcastically. "Yeah. Degrade myself, huh?" he asks the little girl, sternly, before whacking her over the head with a sock filled with a tennis ball for her insolence. "I don't think so. Homey don't play that."

Incidentally, "Homey don't play that" became the definitive catchphrase for the character and spawned many bad impersonations by rich suburban white boys who thought they were "down with the brothers," in what can only best be described as one long *Malibu's Most Wanted* cosplay years before the Jamie Kennedy–led film would be released. And—no surprise—one of the *Malibu's*

One of Damon Wayans's most beloved characters, Herman Simpson, aka
Homey D. Clown. *Fox/Photofest © Fox*

Most Wanted writers was also in the *In Living Color* writer's room, so it all ties neatly together.

So, with the option of a clown dance squared away, Coffield is next to volunteer. "You can slip on a banana peel and fall on your butt!" As Homey slings the "sling-sock" over his shoulder, Coffield removes her party hat, apparently ready to take the blow. But he avoids smacking her—perhaps in a rare moment of self-contemplation, or perhaps knowing that the optics of a white child getting hit by a Black clown would have raised all sorts of hell for him by their prototypical Karen mothers—and paints a scenario that involved his brains and blood splattering on the floor, all for the kids' cheap thrills, before informing them again that he didn't think so, Homey don't play that either.

And the skit proceeded from there, with Homey D. Clown getting progressively more abusive—such as kicking a cream pie in Davidson's face (which made him feel "totally dissed") and stealing a dollar from Grier ("Homey may be a clown but he don't make a fool of hisself!")—until he finally reveals why he was playing a clown in the first place.

"I guess it's because I've got so much love to give," he says sarcastically, looking straight at the camera and breaking the fourth wall. "And it's part of my prison work-release program. So, I've got five more years of this clown crap."

He then starts telling a story that "has an important message," and in true *In Living Color* fashion, it once again deals with race relations in the United States. Homey went to a restaurant, presumably to patronize the establishment called "Chez Whitey,"[60] only to be hassled by the maître d'[61] who informs him that a tie is required to eat at the establishment. Homey then informs the unsuspecting restaurant employee to "get them ties out of my face before I kick your ass," and the hilarious accompanying drawing features Homey choking the life out of the maître d'.

"But unfortunately, Monsieur Snowflake[62] didn't hear Homey correctly, so he had no choice but to keep his word," he concludes.

The moral of the story, of course, is that "Homey don't play that!" And this garnered cheers and applause from the kids, who couldn't get enough of Homey's take-no-prisoners attitude.

In 2015, Damon told *UPROXX* that his inspiration for the character came from two sources: an old *Saturday Night Live* sketch he used to perform,[63] and Paul Mooney himself.

"Paul Mooney, he was the angriest Black man in the world, and he prided himself on that," he said to the outlet.[64] "Like, he wouldn't even pitch ideas for sketches in front of white people. 'Not in front of the white people, Homey. One on one, me and you, Keenen, and I'll tell you everything. Not in front of the white people.' And he would say 'Homey,' you know, 'Homey this, Homey that. Oh Homey, Homey. Not in front of the white people, Homey.' So, this guy, Sandy Frank—these are writers—and Matt Wickline said, you know, this is funny. The clown who won't perform. So, they wrote Homey D. Clown and I put the angry Black man voice on Homey D. Clown because I just thought it was appropriate, and the rest is history."

If nothing else, Homey D. Clown taught kids the importance of setting boundaries, of never degrading yourself and your self-worth for a paycheck, and of calling out racism when it happens no matter the consequences. "Homey don't play that," indeed.

Follow-up "Homey D. Clown" sketches: "Homey D. Clown's One-Stop Carnival" (season 1, episode 13), "Homey D. Clown: When Homey Met Sally" (season 2, episode 2), "Homey D. Clown: Homey Claus" (season 2, episode 12), "Homey D. Clown: Home E. Cheese" (season 2, episode 14), "Homey D. Clown: Homey Sells Out" (season 2, episode 24), "Homey D. Clown: Homey Meets the Man" (season 3, episode 1), "Homey D. Clown: Homey at the Circus" (season 3, episode 13), "Homey D. Clown: Kindergarten Substitute Teacher" (season 3, episode 22), "Homey D. Clown: Homey's Son" (season 4, episode 7).[65]

The Brothers Brothers

SEASON 1, EPISODE 11

A send-up of the equally nonthreatening Smothers Brothers,[66] the "Brothers Brothers" are a pair of brothers, with the last name Brothers, who are both named "Tom, after their uncle."[67] In a word, they are as far away from the *In Living Color* audience as you can get: they play 1950s-style variety show music, they sing along in harmony without any rhythm whatsoever, and they feel that *other* Black people are the problem, which is why it's their duty to remediate the issues with a song.

Keenen and Damon once again teamed up, this time to portray "The Brothers Brothers," and the premiere sketch was "sponsored by White-Out."[68] They opened the sketch with a theme song that was equal parts satire and commentary on the parlous state of affairs on network television, with one such memorable line as "the network wants Blacks/but they don't want them real/so Oreos like us get a hell of a deal." ("Oreo," an insult that first gained traction in the 1960s, refers to a Black person who "acts white"—and it comes from the Oreo cookie, which is black on the outside and white on the inside.)

Then Keenen's "Tom" makes a knock-knock joke, with "Spike" being the person at the door.

Spike who?

"I hope it's not Spike Lee, that troublemaker," he says. "What's *his* problem?" *Nyuk nyuk nyuk.*

And then came a nod and a wink to *Hollywood Shuffle*, the film Keenen and Townsend made way back when, which took aim at the Hollywood establishment that felt Townsend wasn't acting "Black enough" for certain roles.

"So, it's hidey-ho, as I dig out my 'fro, we all play the same parts whatever the show," they sing. "The guys are all pimps, and each chick is a ho—if we just sell out, we'll be rollin' in dough."

A more self-aware television executive would have the good sense to start making changes—or, at the very least, have the pride to crawl under the nearest desk in shame. *Yikes.*

Then came an ode to Bill Cosby's character on *The Cosby Show*, Heathcliff Huxtable, whose wife Claire was a lawyer. "As Black folks all know, it's the average life," they sing in praise, "with a six-bedroom house, and a cute little pup, and some well-behaved kids that don't get knocked up."[69]

The Cosby Show is an interesting study in complexity—and it's one that isn't often discussed without extreme polarization from both sides of the debate, proving that we, as a society, have lost the art of nuance in our interpersonal and intellectual discourses.

On one hand, the show depicted a "wholesome" Black family that flew in the face of racial stereotypes, and the character of Dr. Heathcliff Huxtable became a beloved "father figure" for many young Black Americans who grew up watching the show, especially if their homes lacked a similar kind father figure in the house. On the other hand, *The Cosby Show* was also one that allowed a different sort of "color-blind" racism to flourish—one that's more insidious because it's wrapped in a veneer of gentility.

Writing for *Salon*, Chauncey DeVega notes that while Cosby was thumbing his nose at Norman Lear's depictions of Black poverty as a trope (à la *Good Times* and *Sanford and Son*), his show also did the viewing public a disservice by avoiding the realities of the racism of the time (and which still exist today). What's more, Cosby released a book in 1992 called *Childhood*, and one of the "funny anecdotes" that Cosby told in the book was about "drugging his dream woman with Spanish fly," and his stand-up routine had a similar sketch.

So, while Cosby had one "face" he showed the public, the truth was certainly a lot more insidious.

In addition, Larry Wilmore (who was one of *In Living Color*'s writers) frequently, and to this day, speaks out about how terrible Cosby was as a human being, and how he went out of his way to mistreat Wilmore's mother—and many *In Living Color* sketches weren't exactly complimentary to "The Cos."

On the other hand, in 2015, Damon told the hosts of *The Breakfast Club* that he didn't believe all the women who were coming out against Cosby and felt that there might be a larger force at play (and, as a Black man who most likely has been on the receiving end of some of the same types of microaggressions, he'd know better than anyone else). And perhaps as can be expected, this opinion drew fire from the blog-osphere, with many twenty-first-century commentators "woke-checking" Damon's past sketches on *In Living Color* and using them in a flawed argument to "prove" that Damon was, somehow, a "rape apologist" (when there's no concrete evidence to substantiate such claims).

But both Wilmore's experience with Cosby, and Damon's experience as a Black man, are valid experiences—even if they didn't have the best way of putting it into words in either case.

In short, there's no "correct" answer to the Cosby question—because whether you take one side or the other, a marginalized group (women, Black men) feels slighted. Maybe the *only* answer is, two things can be true at the same time: Dr. Heathcliff Huxtable had a positive impact on the Black community, but Bill Cosby was a man—a human being—and therefore deeply flawed. These truths aren't mutually exclusive—and neither should they be.

Though the "Brothers Brothers" sketch seemed innocuous and almost quaint on the surface, it's one of the more brutal, thumb-your-nose sketches in *In Living Color*'s repertoire. It takes direct aim at the depictions of Black men and women on television, outright states that networks don't care about true Black voices, and implies that Black men who refuse to play "the game" with these ridiculous depictions will find their careers unceremoniously sidelined by network executives—but those who play the game, those who sell their souls for rock 'n' roll (or, in this case, Hollywood fame and fortune at the expense of their authentic Blackness) will be rewarded with fame and money, even if it's at the price of their soul. And who would know better than Robert Johnson?[70]

And the sketch does it all with a Colgate smile. It's a Trojan horse of a sketch—one that you don't see coming until after the punch has landed. But throughout the sketch, Keenen and Damon never lost their exaggerated, pearly white smiles, and the result was the equivalent of a comedic atomic bomb. Keenen and Damon didn't need to engage in rage—screaming, crowing about conspiracy theories, or other toxic behavior to get their point across—because, as Keenen's mother so aptly taught him way back in the Robert Fulton Housing Projects, forcing your bullies to address you as "Mr. [N-word]" is far more effective.

Follow-up "Brothers Brothers" sketches: "The Brothers Brothers: Two Sistas for Two Brothers" (season 2, episode 10), "The Brothers Brothers: Tom and Tom for the Arizona Tourism Commission" (season 2, episode 13), "The Brothers Brothers: Tom and Tom at the Country Club" (season 2, episode 18), "The Brothers Brothers: Black Like You" (season 3, episode 3), "The Brothers Brothers on *The $100,000 Pyramid*" (season 3, episode 23).

Calhoun Tubbs

SEASON 1, EPISODE 11

If Damon's definitive *In Living Color* character was Homey D. Clown, Grier's definitive *In Living Color* sketch was Calhoun Tubbs, a congenial (but talentless and annoying) blues singer who would break out into offensive blues songs at the drop of a hat, which were often prefaced with "I wrote a song about it. Would you like to hear it? Here it go."

Inevitably, of course, nobody ever wanted to hear it, and the song would often cause the listener to either cry harder, fight more, or otherwise get offended.

But for his inaugural Calhoun Tubbs sketch, Grier explained his origins—such as where he got the nickname "Hard Fingers" from (he played the guitar for thirty-six hours straight back in 1947, "for no reason at all"). He'd been in the business of "the blues" for seventy-five years "and still tryna make it." (He, of course, wrote a song about it. Would you like to hear it? Here it go.)

And though he never quite made it in show business, he did manage to wave to a few famous folks through the years, including Stepin Fetchit,[71] who "talked exactly like a white boy, when he wasn't workin'."[72]

So, the skit progressed, on and on, with Calhoun bragging at one point that he wrote "twelve thousand *new songs*" as part of his new gimmick, which was preferable to his previous gimmicks that resulted in his car parts being stolen and a life of obscurity.

"But I got to look on the bright side," says Calhoun. "I've been a success at being a failure for seventy-five years."

In subsequent skits, the songs would get progressively more annoying and offensive. At one point, he delivered the songs at a funeral, and that went as well as you'd think.

In 2018, Grier told the *A.V. Club* that his idea for Calhoun Tubbs came after one of his castmates paid a visit to his dressing room and told him he needed a "signature character." So, Grier recalled someone from his past.

"Damon Wayans came to my dressing room, he said, 'Look, you have to have your own signature character,' and we just started talking," he said to the outlet.[73] "He helped me come up with Calhoun Tubbs, which was based on old blues singers, [specifically] on a guy named Shakey Jake that used to perform around Ann Arbor where I went to school at University of Michigan. He's like a campus mascot. But Shakey Jake was a terrible guitar player. He couldn't sing, but for some reason, all the kids loved him. So that was what the whole impetus of the character was: a really horrible blues singer."

Follow-up "Calhoun Tubbs" sketches: "Calhoun Tubbs on the Campaign Trail" (season 2, episode 10), "Calhoun Tubbs Mentors a British Rock Star" (season 3, episode 11), "Calhoun Tubbs: Prison Performance" (season 4, episode 18), "Calhoun Tubbs: Chuck E. Cheddar" (season 4, episode 29).

I Love Laquita

SEASON 1, EPISODE 12

In terms of "sacred cows" in American pop culture, none are quite as sacred as Lucille Ball and *I Love Lucy*. Considered the *grande dame* of modern television, Ball was a beloved comedic legend whose titular show is also considered one of the greatest of all time. To this day, people are still fascinated with Lucille Ball and her husband/costar, Desi Arnaz—and are still making movies about her and making her a Twitter trending topic.[74]

So, you already know what that means: it was prime fodder for *In Living Color*.

But their reimagining of the television classic wasn't so much a send-up as it was a reimagining. (Think of it as a pop culture "What If . . ." more than a parody sketch, as in "What If Lucille Ball Was Black?"[75]) In the "I Love Laquita" sketches, Carrey played the Ricky Ricardo character (though he was "Ricky Marcado"), and Kim Wayans played "Laquita," the Black Lucy analogue. Unlike Ball—who was impeccably dressed in a proper 1950s hoop dress, housewife-approved pearls, and proper heels in every scene—Laquita was dressed in a skin-tight, leopard-print bodysuit with a matching bandana, glimmering gold chains, and garish makeup. "Hi, honey!" was replaced with "Hey, baby! Gimme some sugar!" And when "Ricky" asks about dinner—a bit of an inconvenience, considering Laquita is in the middle of polishing her nails—he is informed that he would be treated to an evening of steamed pig's feet.[76] This meal displeases Ricky, who informs Laquita that he's expecting an important producer over for dinner, and he needs to impress him.

Unlike Lucy Ricardo, though—who spent her days hoping that Ricky would put her in his show, to no avail—Laquita "Marcado" had a career of her own, and she asks Ricky if his producer friend would be interested in a female rapper as a potential act.[77] Unfortunately for Laquita, Ricky didn't want his long-suffering wife to interfere with his quest of getting into show business and calls her burgeoning hip-hop career a "harebrained scam." He then plans to depart for the Chinese restaurant to pick up a meal "fit for human consumption" (if men have nothing else, they'll always have the audacity . . .); on his way out, he informs her that the cable man is on the way.

But before Laquita can catch him to confirm what he'd said—since, apparently, she didn't hear him from in the kitchen—Ethel (Coffield) pops in.

Laquita fills her friend in on the impending VIP house guest and tells her to prepare the "Salt-N-Pepa" routine that they'd been practicing. After Coffield agrees, a man (Grier) appears at the door and identifies himself as a representative from Continental Television.

Laquita thinks it's the producer that her husband was waiting for, so she immediately invites him in and gives him the VIP treatment—puts his feet up, gives him a comfortable chair to relax in—as she demands her friend to get him a glass of something nice to drink—and, more specifically, "ripple!"[78]

Ethel and Laquita then perform their routine for the Continental Television rep, who is clearly impressed and gives them a round of applause. He then informs the ladies that he has a "service contract" that needs to be signed, which Laquita interprets as a television deal (in actuality, it turns out to be a contract for the cable television service).

But before Laquita can sign on the dotted line, the representative informs her that "nothing can be signed until I take care of the physical connection." But no need to worry, because this was his twelfth appointment of the day, and it "shouldn't take longer than five minutes." (Of course, there are a few notable exceptions, such as the one lady that took "almost two hours" to get the physical connection going, and "her box" was "rusted shut" by the time they found it.)

Laquita, of course, thinks he's suggesting she hop on the casting couch,[79] and she's highly offended by the insinuation not only that she would cheat on her beloved Ricky but also that she would compromise her integrity for the sake of fame. Nevertheless, a girl's gotta do what a girl's gotta do—she'd clearly been wanting fame for the longest time[80]—and she confers with Ethel to decide.

"Just think about it, Ethel!" Laquita says to her friend. "We could be on *Showtime at the Apollo*[81] and *The Byron Allen Show!*"[82] After Ethel acquiesces, the Continental Television rep asks where "they want to do it."

This earns even more consternation from Laquita, who informs the representative that they're "not freaks! We're going to do it in the *bedroom*, of course!"

When the ladies hear that the Continental Television representative has more than "100 feet of cable," and that he's going to feed it to her through the window, Ethel panics again, and begins to have second thoughts about this little "arrangement."

"Oh, come on, Ethel," pleads Laquita. "You know Fred ain't throwing down in the bedroom anyway."

Ethel finally acquiesces, then informs the rep that he can "do her first, then her friend." But the still-clueless rep continues with the double entendres and informs her that he can "get a splitter and turn the both of you on."

At long last, Ethel and the rep make it into the bedroom, where Ethel presumably removes her clothes. Laquita listens in from behind the door, and the man shouts, demanding to know what Ethel thinks she's doing.

Just then, Ricky and his producer friend (Davidson) walk in, obviously in the middle of sharing a joke, and oblivious to the mess going on around them . . . until Ethel emerges, dress asunder and makeup smeared all over her face, informing Ricky that she got free cable for the *whole* building.

And with this, Ricky folds his arms in anger, and says "Laquita!" in a similar way that Ricky Ricardo called for Lucy. And, like Lucy, Laquita looks at the camera and cries.

It's a brilliant sketch in its simplicity, and it pays tribute to *I Love Lucy* while putting a unique spin on a comedy classic. And while, certainly, it dabbled in the risqué, it never crossed the line into disrespectful or the pornographic. In so doing, it became a classic all its own.

Follow-up "I Love Laquita" sketch: "Laquita Sings the Blues" (season 2, episode 8)—a send-up of "Lady Sings the Blues," which featured Billy Dee Williams reprising his role of Louis McKay, so clearly he wasn't too bothered about Keenen's various depictions of him.

Benita Buttrell

SEASON 1, EPISODE 13

It wasn't just the men on *In Living Color* who got a chance to shine. Kim Wayans, the sole sister of the Wayans family who had a regular gig on the show, also created a signature character of her own in Benita Buttrell.[83] And, like her friend Grier, Kim said she drew inspiration from her own life experiences when creating the character.

"She was basically inspired by some of the women in my neighborhood that we grew up with, that would just sit around on the bench all day talking about people's kids," she said at the Tribeca Film Festival in 2019. "I won't name anyone in particular, but she knows who she is. She's famous now. You can't tell her she's not a star, because she knows who she is. She knows I immortalized her as Benita."[84]

The sketch would open outside of a New York City brownstone, and Benita Buttrell would open the window with her laundry in hand, ready to hang them out on the clothesline[85] to dry. This setup gave Kim the opportunity to break the fourth wall, where she'd talk directly to the viewer about the latest neighborhood gossip.

But before she could get into the nitty-gritty, she introduced herself, informing the viewer that she'd been here "all her life," and she knew the ins and outs of the neighborhood better than anyone else.

Kim Wayans as Benita Buttrell, who isn't one to gossip, so you ain't heard it from her. *Fox/Photofest © Fox*

The fun in the Benita Buttrell skits would be in the setup: a neighborhood friend would pass Ms. Benita by, Ms. Benita would say something overly nice and fawning, and then break the fourth wall and deliver a searing insult about the same person she was just kissing up to.

Even her own godson, Charles—"Chucky-Wucky, Chuckster, you gonna give your godmama a kiss?"—wasn't safe ("that's a crackhead in the making right there").

And after each searing insult, Benita Buttrell would deliver her catchphrase that, much like her brother's "Homey don't play that," became ubiquitous among white kids in the suburbs: "I ain't one to gossip, so you ain't heard that from me."

The frequent target of Benita Buttrell's gossip was the invisible Ms. Jenkins—good old Ms. Jenkins—"I *dare* somebody say something bad about Ms. Jenkins, honey!"

But don't worry, because Benita Buttrell delivered. "She is something else, honey. Just don't let her take her shoes off in your apartment," she snarked.

*Follow-up "Benita Buttrell" sketches: "*Benita Buttrell: Uninvited Guest" (season 2, episode 4), "Benita Buttrell: Block Captain" (season 2, episode 15), "Benita Buttrell: Carnival Booth" (season 3, episode 3), "Benita Buttrell: Witness for the Prosecution" (season 3, episode 11), "Benita Buttrell: Class Reunion" (season 3, episode 20), "Benita Buttrell: Delegate" (season 3, episode 29), "Benita Buttrell at the L.A. Riots" (season 4, episode 1), "Benita Buttrell: Holiday Volunteer" (season 4, episode 11), "Benita Buttrell: Physician's Office" (season 4, episode 13).

Frenchie

SEASON 2, EPISODE 6

If the character of Frenchie reminds *In Living Color* viewers of someone familiar, it's because Keenen Ivory Wayans made it so.

"One night, I was hanging out with Eddie [Murphy]," he told the Television Academy in 2013.[86] "And he was getting dressed, getting ready. And in his closet, he has a rack of clothing that his fans have sent to him. So, it was all these bad versions of the *Delirious*[87] outfit. So, we were laughing about that, and I held one of the outfits up and say, 'I should wear this out tonight.' He goes, 'that would be hilarious.' So, I put it on. And then, he had this Rick James wig, so I put the wig on. And then he had this guy that worked for him named Federov, who had this cheap gold chain with an "F" on it, so I was like, 'yo, Fed! Let me borrow that!' So, I put the chain on. And then, he had these glasses—they were called gazelles—with all these studs on them, so I put that on, and I was like, 'that's the look.' So then, I said, 'who am I?' And then I said, 'I'm going to be your cousin Frenchie from Augusta, Georgia.' That's when I started doing this country bumpkin, and we were laughing about it, and he was like, 'man, you ain't going out like this.'"

And Murphy was right—Keenen had one more piece to add to the puzzle. He went into Murphy's refrigerator, pulled out a sausage, and stuffed it down the side of his leg "so I looked like I had the biggest *schlong* in the world." They went out that night, and Keenen was dancing in the most exaggerated way, making the sausage bop up and down between his legs, which earned him plenty of looks—and not all of them bad—from the women in the club that evening.

"And so, I take all the classic disco chants—like 'the roof, the roof is on fire'—and I'm just messing them up," he said.[88] "Like, 'the roof! The roof! Somebody done shit on the roof!' And I'm just, like, having so much fun. And Eddie—*tears* are pouring down his face because he's like, 'this dude's insane!'"

But that wasn't even the apex of the evening. That honor went to the moment that Keenen met Rick James.

"So, we're at the club, and Rick James is there," Keenen continued, "and he comes over and says 'hi' to Eddie. And I'm standing there, and Eddie doesn't want to introduce me, but I keep trying to make my way over. So finally, Rick says, 'who is this guy?' And Eddie says, 'this is my cousin Frenchie from Augusta, Georgia.' And Rick has a drink in his hand, and I snatched his drink, and I go, 'what's up, man!' and I just chug his drink down."

Ultimately, James and the Mary Jane Girls[89] squired Keenen away from the club in their limo, because they'd grown quite fond of Keenen—or, more accurately, "Frenchie." But the point of the story, Keenen said, was to show the importance of a comedian remaining committed to the character. Throughout the evening, Keenen never once broke character, and neither did he reveal his identity.

But ultimately, he didn't have a choice in the matter—because Murphy had purposely left Keenen's change of clothes back at the house. So, even if he wanted to break character—or reveal his true self—he couldn't.

That fateful evening birthed a character that would forever be immortalized on *In Living Color*. With this season 2, episode 6 sketch, Keenen took the character from that hilarious night and immortalized him forever in the annals of pop culture history.

The premiere "Frenchie" sketch opens in a "Save the Dolphins" fundraiser. The host of the party is a man named Benny (Davidson) who is also an acquaintance of dear Frenchie's—and who would become the target of most of Frenchie's misadventures in subsequent sketches. Frenchie informs the security at the door that he's a friend of the host after he is not-so-politely informed that the event is by invitation only.

Frenchie, as one might imagine in his bad *Delirious* outfit (complete with yellow fringe!), wasn't used to such a "classy affair" that served mini hot dogs in a blanket, "but luckily, I brought these hot wings!" He then summarily dumps the hot wings on the waiter's service tray.[90]

Benny then questions how Frenchie got his information to get into the party. Frenchie informs Benny that he'd taken his license plate number and contacted the DMV[91]—who put Frenchie in touch with Benny's ex-wife. And, after talking to her for five minutes, she gave up all the information he needed—with a "you clearly deserve one another" as a send-off.

Frenchie took that as a compliment. Benny begged to differ.

The rest of the evening involves Frenchie being a well-meaning, but clearly ignorant, goof—such as when he explains to a prospective date that he was nicknamed "Frenchie" because he took French in eleventh grade and liked to kiss that way too . . . only to slobber all over the woman's hand when she offered it to him to kiss. Or when it was explained to him that the event was a fundraiser for the dolphins . . . and he was confused, because "it was the Rams that need the help!" And when Benny tries to compliment a woman's "gorgeous gown," Frenchie informs her that it looked like the same one his mother got "from the Home Shopping Club!"

Not exactly high praise.

But Frenchie ended up redeeming himself, even with the Asian guest he referred to as "Bruce Lee" earlier in the evening[92]—namely, by offering the guests some cold duck he'd brought with him for the event, since clearly, the champagne wasn't hitting right.[93] He was dismissive—rightly—of a party guest who tried to display his intellectual superiority by dropping Ivy League university names, and he ultimately slaughters the *bougie* man's ego by demonstrating (albeit unintentionally) how unimpressed he was with his credentials.

And the best part of the night comes when Frenchie throws it back to that fateful night in the club with Eddie Murphy and asks the piano man to play some Rick James. (He was a white man, and he clearly didn't know any Rick James songs—not even "Super Freak." *Shameful!*) But Frenchie still gets the people dancing and, eventually, wins all the guests over.

In subsequent sketches, Frenchie always ended up winning the crowd over, no matter how awkward or ill placed the circumstances. Whether he found an old hook-up buddy in Alcoholics Anonymous, or he visited another old hook-up buddy in her Lamaze classes, Frenchie was the unlikely hero who ended up saving the day and turning every frown upside down. And his catchphrase—"I'm hip, I'm slick, and all the women love my GI Joe with the kung-fu grip!"—demonstrated that even with his comical looks, he had no problem pulling the ladies. Frenchie may have looked like a pimp out of a Blaxploitation film, but he wasn't malicious or ill meaning. To the contrary: his ridiculous getups betrayed his kind demeanor and affable charm.

It's easy to see from this inaugural sketch how the Frenchie character was so easily endeared to the likes of Eddie Murphy, Rick James, and the Mary Jane Girls: however ignorant he may be—and, certainly, he said and did more than a few cringe-worthy things—he was a genuinely well meaning, and kind, a man who just wanted to see people have a good time.

Follow-up "Frenchie" sketches: "Frenchie at a Bachelor Party" (season 2, episode 16), "Frenchie at the Opera" (season 2, episode 25), "Frenchie Goes to Alcoholics Anonymous" (season 3, episode 10), "Frenchie at Lamaze Class" (season 3, episode 15).

Handi-Man: The Justice Legion of America

SEASON 2, EPISODE 11

Years before Marvel and DC Extended Universe (DCEU) movies became the cultural and film juggernauts that they are today, *In Living Color* was bringing their own version of the superhero to the small screen. But their caped crusader was a man by the name of "Handi-Man" (Damon Wayans) whose superpowers weren't exactly on par with the likes of Superman or Batman.

The inaugural sketch opens with an intro by a Superman-like figure[94] (Carrey) announcing to a rapt audience—in between puffs on a cigar—that the "Justice Legion of America" just settled an affirmative action lawsuit brought against it by the United States.

"Apparently, the Legion has shown a discriminatory preference for white men and incredibly beautiful white women," "Superman" says.[95] "As part of our settlement, without denying or admitting our guilt, I'd now like to present our newest members."

The first superhero introduced was the first Jewish superhero,[96] "Beard Man!" And, as one might expect, "Beard Man" was a Hasidic Jewish man who came complete with a *kittel*, a dark three-piece suit, and a black hat. He also wore a menorah on his chest to indicate that his superpower was . . . keeping candles burning for eight days, presumably.

Next up was Chi-Go, the human computer, who was "our first Oriental."[97] He wore the flag of Japan in a bandana wrapped around his head.[98]

And then there was "Angry Woman," the first Black feminist lesbian superhero[99] (portrayed by Kim Wayans in full Angela Davis mode, albeit with a lot more color in her getup). She wore the lesbian Venus symbol—that is, a Venus symbol crossed with a raised fist—on her chest.

"And last, but certainly not least, let's give a warm Justice League[100] welcome for the newest handicapped superhero, Handi-Man!" finishes Carrey's "Superman."

At that point, Handi-Man (Damon Wayans) stands up, dressed in a blue getup with a white cape and the International Symbol of Access (ISA)[101] on his chest. As he stands up, it becomes clear that he was suffering from some sort of palsy, which generated peals of laughter from the audience.

Handi-Man wanted people to know that if they doubted "the power of the handicapped," that there was a "new sheriff in town, and this is his badge."

As he talks, a "Bat signal" of sorts is generated outside featuring (what else?) the ISA instead of Batman's logo. (Licensing issues with the Batman logo, apparently.) That prompts Handi-Man to inform the audience that there was someone who needed his help. He then flies out the window into a men's bathroom, where he is met with a man in a wheelchair (Davidson) who can't get into the disabled stall.

"This guy has been in the stall for *over an hour*—and he's not even handicapped!" Davidson shouts.

"Say no more—wheel back," Handi-Man says, pushing Davidson back. He then rips open the door to find a gentleman sitting on the toilet reading the newspaper. When he refuses to leave the stall even after being demanded to do so, Handi-Man quips, "Uh-oh! Looks like somebody's about to join the ranks of the disabled!"

The pair then fight, and it ends with Handi-Man dunking the offender's head in the toilet and flushing it for good measure.

"Never underestimate the powers of the handicapped!" Handi-Man says, winking at the camera.

Now, clearly, this can be seen as a problematic sketch by the well-meaning—but still misguided—white liberal types. But, as Damon explained to *The Breakfast Club* hosts in 2015,[102] "the only people that were offended by the sketch were those that *weren't* handicapped."[103] To put it much more frankly: there's no need for anyone who isn't handicapped to feel offended on behalf of someone else, especially if *they* aren't offended. It's best to assume that the presumptive offended party is an adult who can make decisions for himself/herself, and if they're not offended, neither should you be, however well-meaning your intentions are. To do otherwise is, frankly, infantilizing and insulting.

It's also worth mentioning that Damon knew more than a little about the subject matter at hand: he was born with a club foot, thus qualifying him as "handicapped" or "disabled," whichever term is preferable these days. In fact, he told the *Baltimore Sun* in 1995[104] that he had only one dream growing up, and it didn't have anything to do with stand-up comedy.

"My dream was to wear Nikes," he said. "I wanted to get out of orthopedic shoes and dunk a basketball."

When he was younger, he underwent several surgeries to correct the club foot, which improved his gait and his appearance. Despite this improvement in his appearance, he told the *Sun* that he didn't get his first pair of "nice" (that is, non-orthopedic) shoes until he was in junior high.

If Damon can't poke fun at himself and his disability—thus taking the power back for himself and others like him—then who can? And if we accept that trans comedians can effectively write trans comedy—if we can accept that Black comedians can effectively write Black comedy—then we can *also* accept that Black *and* disabled comedians can effectively write (and, in Damon's case, execute) Black and disabled characters for laughs.

So, if a well-meaning, but misguided, group of people is offended by "Handi-Man," it's more *their* issue than it is Damon's—or *In Living Color*'s. And, frankly put, the sketches are nothing short of brilliant both in their subject matter and their execution—and for a Black and disabled man to portray a Black and disabled superhero (even for laughs) at a time before the DCEU spent millions of dollars to bring Cyborg to life, and at a time when concerns about "tolerance" were nowhere near trending topics, is nothing short of a remarkable feat.

Follow-up "Handi-Man" sketches: "Handi-Man's Evil Twin" (season 2, episode 22), "Handi-Man: The Adventures of Handi-Boy" (season 3, episode 5), "Handi-Man and the Tiny Avenger" (season 3, episode 14), "Handi-Man: The Sequel" (season 3, episode 21), "Handi-Man Loses His Powers" (season 4, episode 8).[105]

Fire Marshall Bill: Home Safety

SEASON 2, EPISODE 14

"Let me show ya something!"

That slogan is instantly recognizable for fans of *In Living Color* because it meant that Fire Marshall Bill was coming to the stage.

The inaugural Fire Marshall Bill sketch—titled "Home Safety"—opens with a scene of a normal Black family in the 1990s. Father (Grier), Son (Davidson), and Daughter (Keymáh) are gathered around the television, sitting on a putrid yellow velveteen[106] couch, as Mother (Kim Wayans) cooks a roast in the kitchen.

"Honey!" shouts Father, "How's that roast coming along?"

Mother informs the family that the roast is coming along just fine—in fact, it's almost ready!

Just as Mother makes the announcement, the sound of a fire truck's siren can be heard in the background. Son runs to the window upon hearing the sounds, and he sees that the fire truck is "really close, Dad."

There's a knock at the door.

Dad tells his concerned family to relax, there's nothing to worry about— "I'll handle this."

He opens the door, and in walks Fire Marshall Bill—charred skin, charred lips with an exaggerated smile, talking a bit like Gomer Pyle, and dressed in remnants of a fireman's outfit.

"Nice to meet ya, folks! Fire Marshall Bill here," he begins.

Father, being polite, invites him in.

It would prove to be hilarious for the audience but devastating for the family.

As it turns out, it's National Fire Safety Week, and Fire Marshall Bill is going door to door checking on fire hazards. He offers his inspection services to the family—"it's free!"—which the unsuspecting family politely accepts.

The first target of Fire Marshall Bill's fire safety was Father's pipe—"pipes, cigarettes—the number one cause of domestic fires."[107] He takes the pipe from the father, puts it in his mouth, and utters his infamous catchphrase: *Let me show ya something!*

Jim Carrey as Fire Marshall Bill on *In Living Color*. Fox/Photofest © Fox

Fire Marshall Bill then starts out with a plausible scenario that could cause a fire—"now, say one night you're drifting off to sleep on the couch, and the pipe falls out of your hand"—and turns it into something so ridiculous that the screams of laughter naturally follow: "Now you start dreaming that you're having a little barbecue, you pull out a can of lighter fluid"—at this point, he sprays the lighter fluid everywhere—"*boom!*"

Cue the camera panning to the fire and the worried family desperately trying to put it out.

And it just got increasingly more ridiculous from there. From Fire Marshall Bill's proclamation of "I caught fire so many times, I can't even feel it anymore," to Fire Marshall Bill suggesting that an acceptable after-dinner trick would involve sticking a fork in an exposed electrical socket,[108] to him ultimately burning down the family's whole house after lighting a match with his teeth, Fire Marshall Bill thrived on being outrageous.[109]

In terms of iconic Jim Carrey characters, Fire Marshall Bill ranks up there with Ace Ventura, The Mask, and even his version of The Riddler in 1995's *Batman Forever*. As with all of Carrey's comedic fare—save for his most recent efforts in the 2019 Showtime series *Kidding*, which had a darker, more sardonic tenor—Carrey's brand of humor fell decidedly in the "slapstick" category and got its laughs from physical stunts usually meant to bring harm to the teller of the joke. As one of the few white performers on the show, it would be impossible for Carrey to use comedy to speak on the societal ills plaguing the Black community in the 1990s, unless he planned to adopt the persona of a KKK member or Jimmy the Greek (and that wasn't too high on anyone's list). So, Carrey's style of comedy on the show is not only in the "slapstick" category but also the "absurdist" one.

But if we define comedy by Steve Allen's definition—if we believe it to be tragedy plus time—then we already know that one of Carrey's most infamous characters would spring forth from tragedy.

And, as he told *WTF with Marc Maron* in 2020,[110] that's exactly what happened even in the case of Fire Marshall Bill.

"[He] was born out of a sketch . . . called the Death Wish Foundation. It was a sketch about kids who were passing away, and their posthumous wish is what we were concentrating on. My posthumous wish as this sick kid was to go to an amusement park after I died. So, it would be me, on the rides, flopping around in the seats on the roller coaster like *Weekend at Bernie's*. That didn't get on, but the character stuck. The character became Fire Marshall Bill," he explained.

So, if you bear in mind that Carrey is supposed to be portraying a *deceased* character, it makes the dark humor behind the character even darker. Whether you find it funnier or not is up to you, of course, but that added layer to the character is certainly a good thing. Even in comedy, multidimensional characters stand the test of time.

Follow-up "Fire Marshall Bill" sketches: "Fire Marshall Bill: Classroom Safety" (season 2, episode 18), "Fire Marshall Bill at the Sports Bar" (season 3, episode 16), "Fire Marshall Bill: Teppanayaki Restaurant Safety" (season 4, episode 17), "Fire Marshall Bill: Magic Show Safety" (season 5, episode 7),[111] "Fire Marshall Bill: Honeymoon Hotel" (season 5, episode 18).

Les and Wes: Twin Stars

SEASON 2, EPISODE 16

Les and Wes Rawls were conjoined twins portrayed by Damon and Keenen, respectively—who else, really, could pull this one off?—who also happened to be in the comedy business.

In the inaugural sketch, it's evident that Keenen and Damon were struggling to keep a straight face when they were delivering the first lines—and being that this was the second season of the show, *In Living Color* fans already knew that this meant the Wayans brothers were up to no good.

The idea behind the sketch was that, on the surface, Les and Wes loved one another—they didn't have much of a choice in the matter, really, because they were literally stuck together—but it would only take a few seconds into the comedy routine for the barely hidden tensions to surface. From grabbing the mic away from one another while sucking their teeth, to throwing shade about their respective circumstances, the comedy routine was *hilarious* because it was *so* terrible.

After a tomato lands straight on Les's face, the pair head backstage. Les is under the impression that they "killed" it, but Wes is of a different opinion, and the sketch takes a quasi-dramatic turn when Wes informs Les that he is "splitting up the act."[112]

Les informs Wes that they need one another like Abbott needs Costello—to which Wes replies that they need one another "like Michael [Jackson] needs Tito."

The sketch then cuts to John Tesh and Leeza Gibbons[113] hosting a special segment of *Entertainment Tonight*, where they'd interviewed Wes from the set of his new film with Steven Spielberg. As Tesh and Gibbons are talking to Wes, the camera pans out to Les, who is sound asleep next to Wes. Apparently, separating them only went so far.

"Now Wes, in a moment here, we're going to show our folks at home a clip from your new movie," deadpans Tesh. "But first, I want to ask you about that other guy that you used to work with. Whatever happened to him?"

"That guy was actually my brother," Wes stutters as Les snores. "And, uh, we don't really keep in touch anymore. But I'm sure wherever he is, his heart is with me. I know mine's with him."[114]

At this point, Les wakes up. "Where am I? The doctor says I should be in bed. Where am I?"

Tesh and Gibbons continue to ignore Les, and Gibbons quips, "I'm sure you can keep us cracking up all night, but why don't we take this time to roll that clip from your new movie?"[115]

The sketch then cuts to the "action scene" from the movie *Lone Wolf*, and needless to say, *all* of the blows from the "bad guys" landed on Les. Even the shots fired from the guns of the bad guys landed on Les.

The sketch then cuts to Les reading a book called *Severe Depression* in bed as Wes entertains two beautiful groupies. One of the groupies asks Wes what happened to his brother, which prompts an eye roll from Wes.

"But brothers shouldn't fight," says the other groupie.

Wes then promises the groupies that he'll call his brother in the morning— "I promise!"—but, for now, it was time to return to the business of lovemaking. (And did it go without saying that one of the groupies was literally lying right on top of Les and ignoring his entire existence? Of course, it did.)

The sketch then cuts to Les working at a burger joint and getting all sorts of abuse from his manager (Davidson) before the phone rings. The scene then cuts to Wes—who is standing next to Les in a three-piece suit, wearing a pair of sunglasses, and talking on a cell phone[116]—asking his brother to put the past behind them.

"In fact," says Wes, "I found a way we can work together again."

The final scene of the sketch cuts to Wes—a movie star in his own right— signing autographs as Les serves as his majordomo.

This is one of the more complex sketches on *In Living Color*, and because there's a *gravitas* to the story line—even though, at its core, it's very funny— there's a sympathy that's conveyed to the characters as well.

Follow-up "Les and Wes" sketches: "Les and Wes: On the Run" (season 3, episode 8), "Les and Wes: Go West, Les and Wes" (season 3, episode 28).

Prison Cable Network's Win, Lose, or Draw

SEASON 2, EPISODE 17

From 1987 until 1990, one of the hottest game shows on NBC was *Win, Lose, or Draw*. The premise of the show was simple—and silly: two teams, one male team and one female team, would compete against one another. The team was composed of one celebrity and one contestant, and the teams would take turns drawing pictures on white sketch paper. The teammate would then have to guess what the "artist" was drawing; the contestant with the most points would win a cash prize.

And so came this send-up of this silly show in this recurring sketch series. Now, to be clear: the "Prison Cable Network" sketches weren't a set of sketches that tried to focus on a "cable network" per se, but on the prisoners in the sketches themselves. The standout character was Angel (Davidson), who is the first one we see in this sketch and is the presumptive "host" of this version of *Win, Lose, or Draw*. Angel is a Mexican American—which is nothing if not an interesting choice for a Black man to play—who had a jovial demeanor and seemed to be the natural choice to host this show.

And that was especially true when compared to the other options, such as "Charlie Magic" (Carrey), a psychotic murderer who was based on Charles Manson; Tiny (Grier), a rapist who has an unhealthy obsession with women's body parts (especially "breasteses"), and—in later sketches—the Death Row Comic (Keenen), a Hannibal Lecter type who was frequently shown behind a steel door and who could only be seen through a slot.[117]

There were plenty of references to prison culture throughout the sketches— for example, Hector's "girlfriend" Chico would hold onto his vest each time he'd go up to the white paper, implying that he was Hector's "prison bitch"—and, certainly, the audience caught each one. Long before *Orange Is the New Black*, Coffield, Keymáh, and Kim portrayed women prisoners who stuck together behind bars, no matter how different they were (Coffield, for example, was nicknamed "Lobotomy" and was portrayed in a medically induced coma for everyone's sake, including her own). Long before *Oz*, Davidson, Grier et al. gave a clue to "Middle America" about what went on behind prison bars.

The "Prison Cable Network" sketches—as they would eventually become known—showed the prisoners having a humanity, and wanting human things (friendship, gameplay), despite the severe nature of their crimes. Even if it was inadvertently accomplished—and, no doubt, it most likely was—these *In Living Color* sketches showed a different side to prison life . . . but it also gave a clue about the true brutal nature that also awaited prospective prisoners long before countless documentaries and HBO specials gave us all more information about that than, perhaps, we all ever wanted to know.

Follow-up "Prison Cable Network" sketches: "Prison Cable Network's Fall Promos" (season 3, episode 5), "Prison Cable Network: Mr. Cell Block Beauty Pageant" (season 5, episode 4), "Prison Cable Network: Lights Out with the Angel" (season 5, episode 26).[118]

Clarence Thomas: Sweet Clarence's Badass Song

SEASON 3, EPISODE 3

In 1991, President George H. W. Bush nominated Clarence Thomas to the Supreme Court to replace Thurgood Marshall, who had just announced his retirement. Bush, clearly, thought he could merely replace one Black man with another—but while Marshall had nothing but the respect of his colleagues (albeit hard earned), Thomas had nothing but their consternation.[119] Thomas also met with opposition from many women's groups and civil rights groups thanks to his objectionable stances on equality and abortion, and this was all *before* Anita Hill[120] brought allegations of sexual harassment against the presumptive Supreme Court judge.[121]

And the opinion of Thomas among the *In Living Color* writers—and, indeed, the Black community as a whole[122]—was that Thomas was excessively servile, especially to the white people he'd hoped to impress in the Supreme Court. And that was made evident from the opening scene of the inaugural Clarence Thomas sketch—whose name itself was a send-up of the 1971 Melvin Van Peebles–directed Blaxploitation film *Sweet Sweetback's Baadasssss Song*—where Thomas is seen serving coffee to his fellow Supreme Court justices.

"Just call me Clarence!" Grier, who portrayed Thomas, says in a nasally voice as he sits down on command. "I just wanted to make sure that everyone started their day with a nice hot cup of coffee. Just wanted to make sure everyone's happy. You know me: nothing wrong with kissin' a little *butt*!"

It was pretty evident that *In Living Color* chose *not* to be subtle with their depiction of Thomas as an "Uncle Tom"–like character.

The first case the Supreme Court hears is a case about discrimination, brought by a man by the name of Kareem Johnson (implying with the name, of course, that the petitioner is Black). As the justices unanimously vote against the claim, Thomas stands up and says, "*Double* nay!"

When Coffield's Ruth Bader Ginsburg admonishes Thomas and asks him to discuss the case, Thomas scoffs and says that Johnson is nothing but a whiner. "You let *one* Black guy complain about discrimination, and the next thing you know, it's *The State of Washington v. Kool and the Gang*," he says, sarcastically. "Let him get a job the old-fashioned way. *Let him earn it*."

Anyone who has spent more than five minutes talking to an "anti–affirmative action" type—assuming one can last that long listening to such nonsense—might recognize the more noxious aspects of Thomas's statements.

Thomas then gets up, *again*, to serve his fellow Supreme Court justices, pouring coffee and offering bran muffins to his colleagues.

Next up is the case of the *Springfield Police Department v. Hector Rodriguez Gonzalez.*

But when prompted for his opinion, Thomas replies, "Uh, *me*? How were the rest of you guys gonna vote?"

When Ginsburg claims she's going to vote in favor of the police department, Thomas opines, "I mean, come on, they fired *four* warning shots. Unfortunately, three of them hit the guy. But *hey!* If you're gonna jaywalk in front of Winchell's, don't come crying to us."

He then concludes this forceful statement with, "I say . . . whatever the rest of you guys say."

The lead justice (Carrey) then informs him that he needs to calm down, since he's going to be in the job for the rest of his life. "You're just like Daryl Gates[123]—they can't get rid of you," he quips, to screaming and thunderous applause from the audience.

"So let me get this straight," asks Thomas, "no matter what I do—no matter who I piss off—I'm here to stay?"

When greeted with the affirmative, the servile act drops. He refuses to get the justices any coffee, his "white" accent drops, and he calls Ginsburg "baby." Ginsburg is shocked, and she asks why he suddenly changed his mind when, just five minutes ago, he was ready to vote in favor of the police department.

"Five minutes ago, I was a Black judge appointed by Bobo the White President," he remarks sarcastically. "And now? I'm your darkest nightmare."[124] He then breaks out into song—and he sings (what else?) a parody of "Shaft."

Aside from creating a fantasy world where Thomas has even just the slightest bit of a backbone, this sketch explores a variety of uniquely Black issues from "code-switching"[125] to excessive servility to white supremacy and does so in a brilliant way—all while taking some well-deserved aim at Justice Clarence Thomas.

Follow-up "Clarence Thomas" sketch: "Clarence Thomas: I'm Going to Girlie World" (season 3, episode 3).

Bill Cosby for the Cosby Condom

SEASON 3, EPISODE 12

This sketch was aired on *In Living Color*'s Valentine's Day special, so it goes without saying that they were raring to go with the most irreverent of sketches to celebrate the holiday of love.

The "Bill Cosby for the Cosby Condom" sketch was announced as the "first-ever condom commercial on national television,"[126] and it featured Jamie Foxx as "The Cos," who adopted a pitch-perfect tone of America's favorite television dad.

"Did you ever notice how I would do all these routines?" he begins, already letting the audience know where this was going, and once again saying the quiet part out loud. He goes on to say that he does routines about children, because he likes children, but then "they grow up and become teenagers, and I don't like them anymore, because *they're stupid!*"

He then explains that his son[127] feels like his "pudding pop" is on fire[128] every time he goes to the bathroom, qualifying him as "stupid" under "The Cos's" definition. And it's all because he refused to use protection—which is why he was endorsing the "Cosby Condoms."

The commercial was very much presented like Cosby's extremely popular (at the time) Jell-O commercials, with the "different flavors, and the different colors." But then came an intimation from Foxx-as-Cosby that he was using it on women who weren't his wife, Camille (which is why Camille was rolling her eyes, per Cosby's description, in the commercial).

"So, before you dip your spoon into the pudding," he says, to screams of laughter from the audience, "make sure you're wearing the Cosby Condom."

It's very easy to react to this sketch using today's lens (especially about Cosby) and think it's problematic. That, however, is an unfair assessment—and even by 1990s standards, the sketch was anything *but* problematic.

First, nowhere in the sketch is Cosby showcased as "America's dad." It's clear from the way he's written, even here, that he's a creep and a maladaptive curmudgeon[129] at best—even though he is wearing one of the "ugly sweaters" that Heathcliff Huxtable would wear on *The Cosby Show*. Second, though it isn't outright stated, it's heavily implied that Cosby isn't exactly appropriate when it comes to dealing with women who aren't his wife.[130]

But what *is* worth exploring, however, is the obvious elephant in the room: If so many people knew about Cosby and his predilections—and, at the very least, he was inappropriate by his own admission under oath—why didn't anyone say anything?

There's no easy answer to this question, except to say that things were merely different back then. Back then, it was okay to use fear to subjugate women—to make sure they had *some* power as was allowed by law, but not *too much* of it, lest they out-earn or out-perform their male counterparts—and the only way to really do that, effectively, was to pit women against each other . . . and to threaten the ones who were left standing with being blacklisted and otherwise left to rot on the unemployment line.

And even if someone spoke up—even if someone *did* say something before Cosby finally admitted to it under oath—who would believe them? Who would listen? In 1990, more than six hundred thousand women were raped—which was *five times* the amount that was reported to the Justice Department. One study published by the *New York Times*[131] reported that 92 percent of all rape victims said that a huge contributing factor to whether they reported their rape was the guarantee of confidentiality—something that wasn't guaranteed in every state of the union.

And so, with this tenor of fear, retaliation, and retribution—plus the omnipresence of a beloved, and powerful, man in the entertainment industry—silence was the golden rule when it came to reporting such things.

If anything, this sketch—and many others like it—only prove that many people were already saying the quiet parts out loud. Many people were telling the truth of the matter long before the proverbial dam finally broke with that fateful Hannibal Buress stand-up routine in 2014[132]—but "the truth" was hidden behind the veneer of comedy, as good comedy so often is.

So, the next time a comedian tries to tell you a joke, *pay attention* to what's being said. There just might be more than a little bit of truth behind all that laughter.

CHAPTER 4

Shades of Richard Pryor

WHEN *IN LIVING COLOR* WAS TOO RAW FOR TV

Despite Keenen et al.'s best efforts, there were times when *In Living Color* was too raw for TV. Even though the brass at Fox gave Keenen the initial directive to "do what you want to do," it seems they should have told him that even that directive had its limits.

It would have only been fair, really—and it would have saved them *and* him a lot of aggravation.

"We had several approaches with the censors," he told the Television Academy in 2013.[1] "Most of my week was spent on that. Ultimately, we found common ground. But prior to that, we used to make his life[2] miserable. The advantage that we had was the slang [vis-à-vis the Jamaican *patois* in the "Hedleys" sketches], so we knew that there were things that we could say that he had no idea what they meant. And so, we would get away with murder."

Keenen then recalled a particular sketch in which the censors informed him that the cast couldn't say a particular term. He didn't remember what the term was at the time—and after all these years, what does it really matter anyway?—but he proposed what he thought was a fair alternative.

"Okay," Keenen said.[3] "So can I say, 'Toss my salad'"?[4]

The censor agreed.[5]

It took absolutely no time at all for the phrase in question to get defined to the censor—but that was, of course, *after* the sketch aired. Naturally, the censor was enraged at Keenen afterward—and Keenen's hand gestures suggested that the censor would have strangled him, Homer Simpson style, if he thought he could get away with doing so. But Keenen was the Bart Simpson to this poor censor's Homer, and while it probably sent the censor to an early grave with a widow maker heart attack, Keenen delighted in the role, and still gets a wicked glimmer in his eye every time he tells the story to this day.

That said, there were times that not even Keenen's mischievous charm—or outright protestations—could save a sketch from the chopping block, especially after its initial airing.

It must be made clear that exploring the issues within these sketches is not an attempt to "woke-check" *In Living Color*. It's completely unfair to look at a twentieth-century sketch show—and a twentieth-century Black sketch show, at that—through a twenty-first century lens. Comedy is always a product of its time, and what was acceptable at the time it was written isn't always acceptable in the modern era—which is why when comedy translates throughout the generations, it's seen as a classic or a timeless sketch (such as the ones discussed in the prior chapter). And even beyond the boundaries of "acceptability," there are some things that just fall flat over time (consider, for example, all the classic "Greek comedies" that make no sense to modern schoolchildren that were side-splittingly hilarious in the age of antiquity).

It's also unfair to suggest that Hollywood—or New York—or even comedy itself is being "reactionary" simply because society's standards (which were always a sliding scale to begin with) slid in favor of treating a more marginalized group with more dignity and respect than to make them little more than a badly drawn caricature. Because, with a little empathy, it's easy to see how it would be very easy to put yourself in the shoes of "the other." Just as one wouldn't want to be a target of a particularly nasty joke, neither would anyone else—especially if that "anyone else" has, like many others, been historically marginalized by the white patriarchy.

On the other hand, one must also be wary of "overregulating" comedy. If marginalized people cannot talk about what plagues their own communities, who, then, can—or should? White people? Yeah, we see how well *that* turned out. And if said marginalized community's concern is that comedy is "reactionary" because they're forbidden from talking about their own issues, perhaps it's worth exploring why that is. Who are we, who are *not* of the culture, to say what can and can't be said among those who *are* of the culture?

These sketches were either cut from syndication, cut from the DVD version of *In Living Color*, or both—at least at one point or more in their existence[6]—and but for the existence of YouTube, they would have become an urban legend a long time ago. It's worth exploring why they're problematic, while also understanding why they were funny in their time. And it's also worth positioning these sketches in the grand scheme of the sliding scale of societal morality *without* overstepping where we should, and shouldn't, speak on the issues they present.

*   *   *

Note: This is not a comprehensive list of all In Living Color *sketches. This is solely a list of sketches that were either too raw for their time, too raw for today, or both—and why that is so. Again, what society finds acceptable—and unacceptable—is a sliding scale, and it always has been. What worked back then may not work today—and again, it cannot be overstated that this analysis is, by no means, meant to "woke-check"* In Living Color. *But if something was too offensive for its time, but no longer offensive today, it's also worth exploring why this is so.*

Bolt 45—The Lost Sketch

SEASON 1, EPISODE 4

From 1986 until 1991, Billy Dee Williams was a spokesperson for the Colt 45 malt liquor brand.[7] Williams helped the brand skyrocket to unsurpassed heights during his time as the spokesperson, with some estimates putting the total barrel sales at more than 2 million at the height of Williams's spokesperson career.[8]

But, as these things are often wont to happen, the "young lions" (in this case, Keenen) often want to depose the "old lions" (in this case, Billy Dee Williams). Williams's brand of debonair—made famous in films like *Brian's Song, Mahogany, Lady Sings the Blues,* and of course, *Star Wars Episode V: The Empire Strikes Back*[9]—was seen as out of fashion by a young man like Keenen in the 1990s, especially as hip-hop and a gruffer, more "alpha male" (for lack of a better turn of phrase) paragon was taking hold in the pop culture consciousness.

And so, in what would be the first—but not the last—time that Keenen would impersonate the suave actor with pitch-perfect precision, *In Living Color* parodied the infamous commercials that sold cheap malt liquor to the unsuspecting populace.

The beginning of the sketch started out much like Williams's Colt 45 commercial: Keenen, dressed in a dapper tuxedo and adopting a voice that sounds like it could melt butter, explains that when he invites his lady over, he likes to prepare the finest food and wear the finest clothes before cracking open a can of "Bolt 45" for her enjoyment.

The doorbell rings, and "his lovely" (Coles) walks through the door in a skin-tight leopard-print dress, squealing in delight as she kisses him.

As she takes off her shoes and squawks about how the bus made her feet tired,[10] the butler (Grier) offers her a Bolt 45. She swills the malt liquor straight from the can, then demands a paper bag[11] and a straw since "she's a lady."

As "Billy Dee" continues to talk into the camera about the "rich flavor" of the harsh malt liquor, Coles's lady of the evening swipes the cans off the silver serving platter and stuffs them in her bag. The camera continues to pan between the smooth, dapper Billy Dee with his caramel voice and the brash, messy lady of the evening with her accent reminiscent of Fran Drescher from *The Nanny*.

That's when Billy Dee informs the audience that Bolt 45 has five times the alcohol content of the average stout beer, "so it gets any lady in the mood for what I'm after."

One can almost immediately see where this is going.

Billy Dee throws the tablecloth and all the accoutrements off the table and commands the lady of the night with the words "let's get busy, baby!" He proceeds to scoop her up—as she's burping and slurring—toss her onto the table, and thrust her leg over his waist; the camera then pans out to "Bolt 45," with the implication being that Billy Dee is about to "score," as he calls it in the sketch.

Whether you interpret the "lady of the evening" as drunk or passed out, *legally speaking* (in other words, *not* in the context of this sketch, but in the context of "if this were a real-life scenario, these would be the laws in play"), she's in no position to consent to sex. There is *arguably* a gray area for "drunk sex"—many an adult has knocked back a few too many with a lover in preparation for an amorous evening, and everyone wakes up fine and happy about it all, if a little hungover the next day—but there's *never* a gray area for "passed-out sex." So, depending on whether you see the "lady of the evening" as drunk or passed out is whether you see this sketch as "playing too hard and fast with boundaries" or "encouraging date rape."

The sketch stayed in the gray area until 2013, when Keenen confirmed that it meant to depict date rape.[12]

"The joke was, they [the Colt 45 advertisements] tried to make Colt 45 like a 'date drink,'" Keenen told the Television Academy in 2013.[13] "[But] this is like lightning in a bottle. Two hits of Colt 45, and you're under the table. So, we did the 'date-rape'[14] approach, but with Billy Dee, so it makes it seem fly. And the censor made us cut out, after a certain point [referring to the end of the sketch, where the camera pans away from Billy Dee getting ready to have sex with his date]. We fought, but I was ultimately fine with it."

According to Keenen, though, on the actual date of airing—which was May 5, 1990—the broadcaster got the wrong cut, which created the uproar, and the person responsible for it nearly lost his job. Whether you believe that story or not—and it does sound murky, at best[15]—the result was still the same: outside of the initial airing, the "Bolt 45" sketch never again made it to the air. It doesn't air in syndication, it doesn't appear on any DVDs, and it never would have seen the light of day again were it not for the enterprising efforts of a few renegade YouTubers who have preserved it for all of posterity.

The question we must ask ourselves is that of one: is the sketch funny?

If we look through the lens of the twenty-first century, no, it isn't. The twenty-first century is the century of the #MeToo movement, episodes of *Law &*

Order: SVU and the saint-like Lieutenant Olivia Benson, the #TimesUp movement, social media, and the great Hollywood reckoning that took down the likes of Harvey Weinstein and Bill Cosby.[16] And to be clear: date rape is wrong—*all types* of rape are wrong—and if we're going to give deference to minor victims of sexual assault, that same deference should be given to adult victims of sexual assault. In this case, it's an all-or-nothing deal: either *all* rape jokes are funny, or *none* are funny, and it's best to err on the side of caution and say that *no* rape jokes are funny in the twenty-first century and beyond.[17]

But that was not the climate in the twentieth century. Things were far different back then, even though it was only about thirty years ago (as of this writing). Was it funny for its time? Arguably so, even with the intimations being what they were. Poor taste, bad judgment, wrong cut—but it is what it is.

Was the sketch, on its face, depicting rape? It was not. It was a problematic sketch, sure, but it wasn't an explicit depiction of Keenen raping a woman on screen. *That* would have sparked a completely different discussion, and there would be no question that the sketch wasn't funny by *any* standard or in any era.[18]

Again, it cannot be overstated that the sketch is problematic—one that would *never* be made today—but, once again, it needs to be viewed through the lens of the times, not through the modern lens. There's no shortage of films and television shows that would never be made today yet are still considered "classics"—with *Breakfast at Tiffany's* and its racist depictions of Asian people being right at the top of that list. But it's important to discuss *why* things evolve over time—*how* it helps shape our understanding of the world around us—because merely "canceling" things without having a nuanced conversation about how one can do better, and provide room for growth, doesn't cultivate an environment conducive to that growth.

"If you look at it now, you'll see that it wasn't anything bad," Keenen told the Television Academy in 2013. "It was just, for that time, and the context of the sketch being date rape, it was just . . . another one of those *In Living Color* moments."[19] That isn't the best of answers—and certainly not the worst of answers—but, again, this statement was still made four years before the virality of the #MeToo movement—and four years away from seeing the ugly side of rape and how it impacts its victims for the rest of their lives.[20]

Did Keenen et al. intend to cause malice with the sketch, or with subsequent statements? Definitely not. As he made clear at the Tribeca Film Festival in 2019, the intent was *always* to "include everybody"[21] in his sketches. *Nobody* was safe from Keenen's critical eye.

But could it be done differently today, with perhaps a more sensitive eye, and still be funny? It would be tricky but still doable. By Keenen's (and Grier's) own admission at the Tribeca Film Festival in 2019, you can only work with what you know at the time—basically, when you know better, you do better.

So, with that in mind, it's perhaps best to view the infamous "Bolt 45" sketch as a product of its time—but one that's worth viewing if solely to spark a larger, healthier conversation about what does, and doesn't, work in comedy, and how it evolves over time.

Then again, when the "Bolt 45" sketch was pulled from the show, it was replaced with a sketch about the Exxon oil spill, which was dry, dull, and boring—and hasn't become funnier with time—so make of that what you will.

Vera DeMilo

SEASON 1, EPISODE 10

The first episode of *In Living Color* that featured Vera DeMilo (played by Carrey) is one that does not air in syndication, which should already be a harbinger of things to come.

In the Vera DeMilo sketches, Carrey plays a female bodybuilder who has conspicuously large muscles, and a conspicuous bulge in her shorts, as she competes against the toughest and buffest of men. In the inaugural sketch, Grier plays an announcer for the Sweethearts Bodybuilding Competition, "here in beautiful Las Vegas, Nevada, it's the greased-up pose part of the competition!"

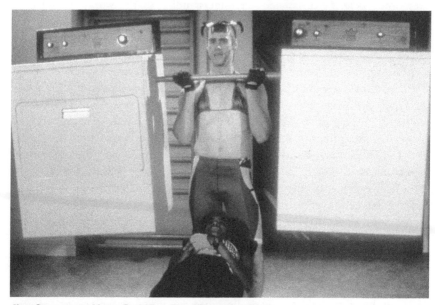

Jim Carrey as Vera DeMilo. *Fox/Photofest © Fox*

The first competitor was "Sarah Sunkiss" from Salamander, California. "Sarah" was a beautiful, curvy Black woman who had a few muscles, but "there's not a lot of muscle mass, and still quite feminine. And quite frankly, I don't like it, and neither do the judges."

Next up was "Carla Meals" from Beaverton, Wisconsin. Like "Sarah," Carla was a beautiful, curvy Black woman who had a few muscles. And, like "Sarah," there wasn't a lot of muscle mass.[22] That was no good, either.

And finally came the competitor that everyone was coming to see: Vera DeMilo.

It went without saying that Vera was far more "ripped" than her competition—she *was* a man, after all—and there were several references made to the question of her gender ("she's the only competitor who goes to the bathroom standing up!"). At the time, the audiences couldn't get enough of Vera—she garnered loud cheers each time she appeared in a sketch—but, again, this is not a sketch that would be made today when viewed through twenty-first-century eyes.

It's pretty easy to draw a straight line from Vera DeMilo—a trans woman being played by a straight man—to the more nasty, transphobic forms of "comedy" that aren't accepted today.

Consider the blowback from Dave Chappelle's recent Netflix comedy special, *The Closer*, where he referred to trans women's "moose knuckles" (in other words, male genitalia in its totality) and "Adam's apples," among other things—and got scorched by both the public and Netflix in response. Whether you found his comedy special funny or not,[23] there was a whole group of people[24] who felt slighted, singled out, and marginalized.[25]

Recall, once again, that the golden rule of comedy is "don't punch down."

"I absolutely believe that a straight comic can tell a joke about trans people that is funny for everyone," trans comedian Jaye McBride said to CNN,[26] when discussing Chappelle's controversial special. But, McBride clarified, there are some parameters—and those parameters include leaving jokes about genitalia on the cutting room floor. That would mean that the Vera DeMilo sketches—with the constant references to her breasts (or her lack thereof), her muscle tone (and her excessive amounts thereof), and the thrusting of her midsection to emphasize the bulge in her pants—would qualify as "not funny" by McBride's definition.

Now, in fairness to *In Living Color*, you can't view a twentieth-century sketch through a twenty-first-century lens, as has been previously stated. And in a rare moment of hope for humanity, today's Vera DeMilo GIFs are used on social media, not to attack trans men and women, but to poke fun at "gym culture," which has become easier to do with #FitSpo posts and wannabe "influencers" who encourage dangerous gym practices without concern for anatomy and physiology.[27] Perhaps that was the intent in the first place. But the road to hell . . .

Gender fluidity—while still a topic of debate, for some reason, as if Marlene Dietrich and others like her didn't exist before the term was even coined—is something that's more openly discussed today, with people feeling more comfortable "coming out" as part of the nonbinary spectrum of their gender and sexuality. And while this *could* work if it were set up differently—if, perhaps, Vera was played by a gender-fluid or gender-queer actor—it doesn't work with today's audiences in its existing configuration and incarnation.

Follow-up "Vera DeMilo" sketches: "Vera DeMilo: Buffed, Beautiful, and Bitchin'" (season 2, episode 7), "Vera DeMilo: Veracosa, Mistress of Destruction" (season 2, episode 12), "Vera DeMilo: Pretty Buffed Woman" (season 2, episode 19), "Milk Commercial with Vera DeMilo" (season 3, episode 6), "Vera DeMilo: The Fist That Rocks the Cradle" (season 3, episode 19), "Vera DeMilo and Little Richard: The Stank of a Woman" (season 4, episode 12), "Vera DeMilo: Breasts of Fury!" (season 4, episode 31), "Vera DeMilo: I Need a Buffneck" (season 5, episode 11).[28]

Roseanne Sings America

SEASON 2, EPISODE 2

This sketch doesn't air on Aspire, which airs *In Living Color* in syndication as of this writing. It's unclear why this is so, because it's not that the sketch is offensive either through twentieth-century or twenty-first-century eyes. (It's crude, sure, but it's not "Bolt 45" by any stretch.) Perhaps it's a way to not give *any* attention to Roseanne Barr (even in the form of her comedic avatar)—whose racist comments in 2018[29] caused the reboot of her popular eponymous show to be canceled by ABC[30]—and not airing a sketch that parodies her, by extension, continues to "shun" her as she rightly deserves. Perhaps it was because they couldn't get the clearance for the songs, even though the patriotic music is in the public domain and royalty free.[31]

Regardless of the reasoning, the sketch was initially written to poke fun at Roseanne's infamous performance of the National Anthem back in 1990,[32] which caused quite the uproar. Coffield portrayed Roseanne in all her crude glory—complete with crotch grabbing, spit hocking, and out-of-tune singing—and it was determined that there was, in fact, nothing worse than Roseanne singing "America the Beautiful" (or, if there were, it was a very short list).

Objectively, the sketch is funny. It was then, it is now, and it probably will be in the future as long as the American experiment continues to work.

Subjectively, though, when taking other things into consideration, it makes sense why it would be considered too raw for TV today.

The Head Detective

SEASON 2, EPISODE 13

While "The Head Detective" sketches were certainly a fan favorite series of sketches, the inaugural sketch gets partially cut off at the end of the so-called "hospital scene" because of offensive depictions of Mexicans.

The premise of "The Head Detective" is a police detective (played by Damon Wayans) who has a Mr. Potato Head–like look thanks to a terrible accident that rendered him as nothing more than the "head."[33]

And in the inaugural sketch, "The Head Detective" and his rookie sidekick (played by Marlon Wayans in one of his first, and most hilarious, roles[34]) happen upon a drug deal, which is what causes "Head" (as he's referred to in the sketch) to lose his tiny limbs. He survives, and they go back to the warehouse where they first happened upon the drug deal to kill the dealers. The upshot, of course, was

When Marlon Wayans was cast in *Requiem for a Dream*, he became one of the only members of the Wayans family—if not *the* only Wayans family member—to successfully cross over into more dramatic fare. *Artisan Entertainment/Photofest © Artisan Entertainment*

that they were able to overpower the rookie and Head just by kicking Head out the window. (And how was he going to fight back, really? He had no limbs . . .)

While *In Living Color*'s strength was in depicting Black issues with an authentically Black voice, its weakness—or, perhaps more accurately, its blind spot—was depicting issues faced by other races.[35] and the sketches often veered into the realm of stereotypes and caricatures rather than biting social commentary. And while it must be made clear, once again, that malice wasn't intended, it was still a problematic depiction—so much so that the latter half of the sketch doesn't appear in syndication.

But the show's frequent depictions of Mexicans—under the monolithic "Latino" category, even though it's nowhere near the same thing[36]—including in the inaugural "The Head Detective" sketch is the perfect example of this "blind spot," and it's easy to see why depicting Mexican men as unilaterally violent drug dealers could be seen as offensive.

Oprah PSA

SEASON 2, EPISODE 18

For the past forty years, Oprah Winfrey has been very open—and public—with her weight loss struggles. She has publicly spoken[37] about the effects of crash dieting, fad dieting, and the pressure to live up to a body ideal that she would never live up to.[38] And in the 1990s, Oprah's weight was considered "fair game" for comedians to attack.[39]

And *In Living Color* was no exception. Though this sketch—which starred Kim as "Fat Oprah"—was cut from syndication, this is just one of many that took aim at Oprah's fluctuating weight.

In this sketch, Oprah makes fun of the old "this is your brain on drugs" PSAs[40] by cracking eggs, frying bacon, and then putting it all on a hard roll and devouring it nearly whole.

At the time, "fat shaming" (as it's known today) was completely acceptable. And it was something that was reinforced in our society as a whole, as well: WeightWatchers used fat-shaming techniques until the 1970s, countless jokes were made at the expense of fat people in both films and television shows, and there was even a popular soft drink on the market called Tab—its main ingredient, saccharin, was linked to cancer in lab rats[41]—whose popularity was based on the premise of heretofore impossible-to-achieve thinness.[42]

But that didn't mean that the people who were being made fun of didn't feel the fallout from these types of jokes. And this is especially true when they're the target of several types of jokes in the same vein.

In 2004, Oprah—whose show, by now, was merely going by *Oprah*—had the Wayans family on her show, and she had the opportunity to tell Kim how hurt she was by the "Fat Oprah" sketches (even though she can laugh about them now).

Kim was visibly distressed by Oprah's admission, and though she initially tried to play it off as a joke, she realized that it would have been far better to merely own her role in causing harm to someone—even though that wasn't her intent when she was telling the joke.

"Damon wrote those sketches!"[43] she started, before shifting gears. "It's not really okay though for me. The person that I am now wouldn't do a sketch like that. Funny doesn't trump being mean for me anymore, and I apologize."

Kim's response is worth noting, not only because it's gracious and kind, but because it's a marked difference from the typical response a comedian of today would give when confronted about his or her own jokes that either fell flat or caused anguish to another person.

Crown Heights Story

SEASON 3, EPISODE 1

This parody of *West Side Story* didn't tackle the conflict between two rival New York City gangs. It didn't tackle the *Romeo & Juliet*-style themes upon which the initial play was based. No, it chose to tackle something a *lot* more volatile.

It tackled the growing tensions between the Black community and the Jewish community (and, to put a finer point on it, the Hasidic community) that culminated with the Crown Heights riots of 1991,[44] which took place over the course of two *very* hot New York City summer days and nights, from August 19 until August 21 of that year.[45]

Tensions between the two groups were always evident, with each believing that "the other" didn't belong.[46] But on August 19, 1991, tensions boiled over and reached a flashpoint when twenty-two-year-old Yosef Lifsh was driving a station wagon as part of a motorcade for a prominent rabbi in the Hasidic community. While driving the car, Lifsh lost sight of the rabbi's motorcade, and began speeding all over the Crown Heights district of Brooklyn, New York, trying to find it.[47] When he reached Utica Avenue—a main artery in Brooklyn—he struck a car, veered onto the sidewalk, crashed into a building pillar, and pinned two Black children underneath the pillar. Angela Cato, seven, survived but was severely injured, but her seven-year-old cousin, Gavin, wasn't as lucky; he died almost instantly.

Lifsh claimed he was trying to help the children when he got out of the car, but the privately commissioned EMS—which arrived only three minutes after the incident happened, and which strictly catered to the Hasidic community in the area—reported that Lifsh was being beaten viciously by the gathering for the offense. When Lifsh was whisked away by the EMS, several teenagers turned their anger onto the first responders who were whisking him away[48] because they seemed to be ignoring the two Black children in distress.[49] The long and the short of it, of course, was that this was the flashpoint that ultimately started the riots.[50] And while Lifsh may not have meant to run the children over—and there's no evidence to suggest he did so intentionally—there was a lot more that could have been done on the scene that wasn't done for the Black children, and the tragedy could have been lessened had better measures been taken.[51]

So, how do you handle such a powder keg?

Well, if you're *In Living Color*, you tackle the subject head-on. Who better than a Black man to "speak" (in a manner of speaking) on the racial tensions between Black people and Hasidic people?

And for what it was worth, he tackled it as well as one might be able to in the circumstances given. Unfortunately, even though he was fair and reasonable in his depiction of Black men and women, his depiction of Hasidic men left much to be desired, to put it mildly.[52]

"So, the Blacks and the Jews are gonna rumble tonight," says the "head" Hasidic man, played by Carrey, referencing the Crown Heights riots. "They bring knives—we bring lawyers. They bring guns—we bring *more* lawyers. They bring Uzis—we bring Alan Dershowitz."[53]

And the stereotypes got far worse from there.

The upshot, of course, was that Carrey's Hasidic character and Kim's Black character fell in love after seeing one another in the middle of the riots, as a callback to the meet-cute in *West Side Story*.

But from the problematic depictions of the Hasidim to the song about Carrey and Kim going together like "Manischewitz and Mandela," to everyone dancing the *hora* like they were at a wedding, one can easily see how this sketch would get cut from the DVD.

The Al Sharpton and Louis Farrakhan Comedy Hour: Jews on First

SEASON 3, EPISODE 2

Season 3, episode 2 is an episode that does not air in syndication *at all*, so it's pretty evident that the episode is filled with sketches that don't pass muster by any modern standard. But of all the sketches, this one is perhaps the most problematic, and its name alone is all the evidence one needs as to where it ends up going.

On its face, it's a brilliant modernization of the classic Abbott and Costello sketch, "Who's on First." Even in its execution—which featured Grier as Al Sharpton[54] and Damon as Louis Farrakhan—the sketch was brilliant: Grier and Damon were a powerhouse team on the show, and they clearly knew how to play off one another better than most other cast combinations[55] on the show.

But the subject matter . . . well . . . let's just say it was *controversial.*

As shown in the "Crown Heights Story" sketch, tensions between Black people and Jewish people—and, to put a finer point on it, Hasidic Jewish people—were at an all-time high in the late 1980s and early 1990s, especially in New York City and its surrounding boroughs. And *In Living Color* certainly wasn't going to let an opportunity to tackle the issue pass them by. Let's recall, after all, that comedy is a "social lubricant," and if you can't laugh at your own trials and travails, what *can* you laugh at? You can't blame *In Living Color* for trying to bring levity to a tense situation—if only so they could make sense of it all—even if they went about it in a less-than-perfect way.

The show was also keenly aware of how non-Black people view the likes of the Reverend Al Sharpton and Minister Louis Farrakhan: as violent insurrectionist leaders, as "race baiters," and as scary-looking Black men who hate white people.[56]

And it took aim at all of it—and landed right on the mark.

Since most, if not all, are familiar with the setup of "Who's on First," here's what you need to know about the player lineup: Say What is over in right field, Jews are on first, the owner is Whitey, The Man is on second, Mr. Charlie is the short stop, and A Conspiracy is at third. Preach On is the pitcher, and My Brother is the catcher. And as for Amen? He's playing center field.

"The Conspiracy is between My Brother and The Man," says Farrakhan.

"According to who?" asks Sharpton.

"According to Whitey and Jews," replies Farrakhan. "See, this is all the work of Whiteys and Jews."

And while, certainly, it's easy to understand why Jewish people felt slighted by the sketch, it must be made clear that the sketch wasn't necessarily complimentary to either Farrakhan[57] or Sharpton by any measure. At one point, Sharpton states that "Jews on First" is "more confusing than the Tawana Brawley case!"[58]

Despite this sketch living up to Keenen's claims that "nobody was safe" from his critical comedic eye, there are some instances where it's best to err on the side of caution after all. Certainly, this *In Living Color* sketch—like nearly every other—is to be credited for critiquing all sides with equal measure.

But it's perhaps best to say that this sketch is guilty solely of being released at the wrong time. Doing a sketch about "Jews on First" featuring the Reverend Al Sharpton and Minister Louis Farrakhan at a time when tensions between Black people and Jewish people were at an all-time high is—to put it politely—not the best of ideas.

The David Duke Show

SEASON 3, EPISODE 9

It should be noted that this sketch is impossible to find—it's been cut from the DVD, it hasn't appeared in syndication, and nary an enterprising YouTuber has been able to upload it in secret to the video-sharing site.

It's easier to find "Bolt 45: The Lost Sketch" than it is to find "The David Duke Show," and the former hasn't hit the airwaves since its first and only airing on May 5, 1990.

And, perhaps, this is for the best. This book does not object to making fun of Klansmen—in fact, it is almost every comedian's bounden duty to neuter bigots at every turn, and Keenen wasn't afraid to tackle such types of folks with his brand of humor[59]—but, in light of recent events, and in light of the rise of white supremacist groups being a genuine domestic terror threat to the United States,[60] the last thing anyone needs is to humanize a "charming bigot" like David Duke through comedy.

To be clear, this isn't the fault of *In Living Color* in the least. How were they supposed to know? In the 1990s, the internet wasn't omnipresent, which meant that it took a while for ideas to foment and spread. And, whether rightly or wrongly, many viewed the threat of white supremacists like the Ku Klux Klan as a "Southern" problem, one that was worthy of derision by big-city folks in New York and Los Angeles. Things like "microaggressions" weren't recognized, and the nuances of race relations were such that if it didn't involve someone screaming an epithet in your face or burning a cross on your lawn, it wasn't racism per se.

The twenty-first century, however, is a very different—and, arguably, more dangerous—place, and if nothing else, it's a place where white supremacist ideals can spread like wildfire thanks to the power of the internet and social media. And, if nothing else, Americans have seen with their own eyes that these violent, racially motivated thugs don't need much provocation to cause genuine harm and destruction.

And that, therefore, brings us to this consideration: knowing that these groups have a natural propensity for violence, it stands to reason that seeing one of their beloved figures—in this case, David Duke—held up for ridicule on a comedy sketch show (and a comedy sketch show wholly imagined and executed by a Black man, no less) would provoke them to further, unnecessary violence.

It was simpler when racists and bigots were easier to identify—when they merely wore white hoods and were seen as a regional problem concentrated solely in the American South—and most of all, were powerless . . . or, to put a finer point on it, they weren't openly validated by members of the government. But since these times are very different than those, it's best for all involved, then, to leave this sketch lost to the annals of time.

Darnel Bond: Agent 006

SEASON 3, EPISODE 14

As its name suggests, "Darnel Bond: Agent 006" is a parody of James Bond—aka Agent 007—with Grier purporting to serve in Her Majesty's Secret Service. As was standard of *In Living Color*, however, "Darnel" Bond had uniquely Black American characteristics about him: a swagger instead of a debonair,[61] wearing Nike Quantum Force IIs instead of wing-tipped Bruno Maglis, and a slick humor instead of a "dad humor."

Everything else about the sketch featured references to James Bond—including Darnel's request for a malt liquor (shaken, not stirred, of course) and the action going down in a casino (or, at least, in an illegal gambling house).

Where the sketch got problematic, though, is when Bond went up to the villain (portrayed by Steve Park, who adopted one of the best Marlon Brando in *The Godfather* accents on television), and his girl. Both, naturally, are of Asian descent, and their names were Lo Phat and Phat Ho, respectively. The punchline, of course, was that Darnel had difficulty remembering their names (calling the villain "Lo-Jack" at one point), and fetishizing their Asian names.

It's not hard to see how this could be seen as a problem—and why it was cut from the DVD.

Me Want Maury

SEASON 3, EPISODE 15

As hard as it is to believe now, Maury Povich—he of the "You are *not* the father!" fame—was once a serious journalist. And at this point in history, his eponymous show *Maury* was not the breeding ground for baby daddy drama, cheating drama, and lie detector tests that it has since become. Instead, in 1992, *The Maury Povich Show* covered topical fare, *à la Donahue* and *The Oprah Winfrey Show*. One notable episode recounted a woman who fought "the battle of the bulge" and got down from her six-hundred-pound weight to a respectable, and more manageable, two hundred pounds. Oftentimes, too, he'd have Jack Hanna—the American answer to Steve "The Crocodile Hunter" Irwin—and his menagerie of exotic animals as guests to fascinate the audience.

In other words, if you would have told anyone in 1992 that the mild-mannered journalist turned mild-mannered talk show host with ill-fitting suits and a dapper Ted Koppel–style haircut would have become the host of a three-ring circus featuring cheating men, the women they impregnate, and marathon sprints of running off the stage after the true paternity of the father was revealed (and it was almost never, ever who the woman thought it was, even though the baby and the presumptive father inevitably had the same nose), they'd have told you that you were out of your mind. *Not our Maury!*

As disparate as Povich's persona is from then to now, there was one constant in Povich's life no matter if he covered DNA tests or duckbilled platypuses: his wife, fellow journalist Connie Chung,[62] with whom he shares a son named Matthew.[63]

The "Me Want Maury" sketch first aired in 1992, at a time when Povich and Chung were actively trying to conceive a child—and Chung was being very open about her fertility issues.[64]

She wasn't, however, being open about what she was doing with Povich to get from the proverbial Point A to Point B—which was probably for the best—but *In Living Color* decided to show us all *anyway*.

In this sketch, Steve Park—a Korean American comedian who had become a featured player on the show—brought Chung to life in naughty red lingerie, thigh-high fishnets, and stiletto heels who moaned and orgasmed her way through the parody of "Me So Horny" by 2 Live Crew[65] as she not-so-politely asked for Povich—played with hilarious abandon by Carrey—to impregnate her, and use whatever position she could think of to make that miracle pregnancy happen.[66]

Depictions of Asian women as dragon lady[67] stereotypes are harmful on its face—but depicting a woman like Chung, who overcame seemingly insurmountable odds to pave the way for every other Asian journalist in her wake, as a dragon lady stereotype is a bit beyond the pale. And while it cannot be overstated that malice and harm wasn't intended in this sketch—they were mocking the ubiquity of Chung's presence in the media talking about her fertility issues and her desire to conceive a child with Povich, not her Asian heritage—it's important to recognize how so many stereotypes are ingrained in our collective consciousness, then and now, so we can identify our blind spots and do better by one another going forward.[68]

Nevertheless, between the problematic depiction of Chung, the licensing issue inherent in getting clearance for "Me So Horny," and the uncomfortable thrusting while sitting atop a collection of Chippendales dancers, it's not hard to see why this sketch got cut from the *In Living Color* DVD.

Other sketches that got cut from syndication, DVD, or both, include "Marlee Matlin Sings and Raps Deaf Def Jams," a sketch from the post-Keenen era (season 5, episode 15), which poked fun at hip-hop *and* deaf people (a bold choice—and not in a complimentary way—considering how many hip-hop acts got a performance slot on the show before and after Keenen was in charge, and to say nothing of the less-than-complimentary way the hearing impaired were depicted); "Rap Masterpiece Theater," another post-Keenen-era sketch (season 5, episode 17) that once again took aim at hip-hop and turned it into caricatures and stereotypes; and "Risky Business II: The Menendez Brothers"[69] (season 5, episode 19), which was more ghoulish than edgy and lacked even the most basic humor.

What is interesting to note is that regardless of the reasons *why* the sketches were cut from syndication, the DVD, or both, no one on *In Living Color* felt like they were being "canceled" in any way for the decision—especially as time went on. To the contrary: even at the height of Keenen being at loggerheads with the censors, they all were quite aware that they had more freedom than most to "do what they wanted to do," and it served no one—least of all them, as a collective—to get hit with fines because they were playing too fast and too loose with standards and decency.

And while, in later years, some of the cast—including the Wayanses—vocalized that they wouldn't be able to get away with many of the things they got away with on the show were *In Living Color* on the air today, that's mostly because society's standards for what's acceptable, and what isn't, have changed considerably—and more cultural sensitivities are necessary when telling a joke (or seven).

This isn't to say comedians *can't* make jokes, say, about gay people, or about Asians, or about whichever group of choice they prefer to use as their comedic whipping post. It's just a question of *who* is telling the joke more than it is about the joke itself. For example, as was mentioned previously, telling trans jokes as a trans person is empowering, because it reclaims the offensive words and ideas from the oppressors. On the other hand, a cis person telling a trans joke may—however unintentionally—be punching down and making a joke at the expense of the trans community . . . which isn't funny by any standard, except a bigoted one.

Perhaps, then, Keenen's idea—made at the Tribeca Film Festival in 2019—is the correct one: were *In Living Color* to air today, he'd create an even more diverse lineup, one that includes gay people and multiracial people (as a for-instance) to further tackle sketches that were too raw for TV, either then or now.

But even if that ship has, sadly, sailed—even if *In Living Color*'s more halcyon times are behind us all—that still didn't stop them from making history in ways most people don't even realize today . . . like they did with the Super Bowl.

CHAPTER 5

The Super Bowl Halftime Show That Changed History

On January 16, 1992, Keenen Ivory Wayans—dressed in an oversized suit, shaking hands politely with both Carson and his sidekick, Ed McMahon, and laughing awkwardly at sterile jokes—stopped by *The Tonight Show Starring Johnny Carson* to promote his show's proposed Super Bowl halftime show.

But before he could get into the full-fledged promotional aspect of his appearance, he had the opportunity to engage in some gentle banter with Carson—a touching tale about Keenen's grandmother's affection for Carson stemming from Carson's willingness to help Stevie Wonder off the stage, a humorous tale of protests from a poultry group that also had an issue with Carson's show for some reason, a chuckle and a smirk shared about "mistaken identity" when Keenen was mistaken for Keenen Wynn, the son of vaudevillian legend Ed Wynn.

And then, in the last few minutes of his segment, Keenen finally had the opportunity to tell the audience to tune in to Fox during the *Super Bowl Halftime Show* on January 26, 1992, because *In Living Color* was going to have a special treat in store for everyone.

Carson was polite but hardly sanguine about Keenen's chances. "Mmph," Carson mumbled. "Well, good luck with that."[1] He then announced his next guests—Jimmy Brogan, followed by Siskel and Ebert—as the Doc Severinsen-led band played Keenen off to commercial.

Carson's skepticism was well rooted. Since its debut on television in the 1960s, the Super Bowl was a ratings juggernaut—and, to this day, it still is—and any show that dared to go up against the biggest football event of the year was bound to be demolished in the ratings.

But the sole exception to that rule was the *Halftime Show*—an anemic, boring spectacle featuring "family friendly" fare like marching bands, Elvis impersonators, and (in 1992) Dorothy Hamill and Brian Boitano performing an ice-skating routine around people in snowflake costumes as Gloria Estefan caterwauled her way through her latest hits.

"All of them were the same," Keenen Ivory Wayans told ESPN back in February 2021.[2] "It was just the cheerleaders, it was just a lot of, like, batons dropping, and bands."

And that audience who "got up to pee" during the *Halftime Show* were the ones that *In Living Color* wanted to attract. So, they struck up a plan to put on a show featuring five sketches—just enough to get people through the boring *Halftime Show*—and get a few ratings.

They sensed an opportunity.

They ended up changing the course of history.

Homeboyz Shopping Network

Keenen and Damon kicked off the live show with a bang—by doing a live version of the first-ever sketch on *In Living Color*. They knew they had only one shot to get it right—and when they ran out onto the stage to greet the audience, the energy between the brothers—and the audience—was kinetic enough to knock down a building.

Damon, as Iceman, was in rare form, kicking off the sketch by announcing that he had some "super slick, smashing with a brick, and if you don't like it, you can suck my . . . sorry, censors, that's merely a display item."

The crowd went wild.

The wares that the Homeboyz had to offer were Super Bowl themed as well—everything from passes that promised to get the patron "on the field" to a football uniform (with the blue-and-white colors of the New York Giants, who were *not* playing that evening) that promised to get the patron "in the game."

They even had credit cards belonging to the players—Mastercard, Visa, American Express—with one gold card belonging to Thurman Thomas.[3] When Iceman informed The Whiz (Keenen) that Thomas had just signed a multimillion-dollar "get a ho and a couple of yachts and be lovely for life type deals," The Whiz informed the audience that the gold card was "just a display item" and tossed it back into his locker, presumably for his own personal use.

As usual, the Boyz offered "jewelry, jewelry, jewelry," which included a Super Bowl ring—and the steroids that will make your hands grow to fit the oversized rings.

They even kidnapped a football player to autograph footballs for the kiddies.[4]

And the coup de grace for the Boyz was a "widescreen TV" that was actually a big-screen projector they'd stolen from the Metrodome—with the "MVP"—

Most Valuable Perpetrator—getting the option to bring home a classic sports car that they'd also swiped for the occasion.

Fire Marshall Bill at the Sports Bar

After a brief commercial break, "the ladies" of *In Living Color*—Keymáh, Coffield, and Kim—introduced the next sketch featuring Carrey as Fire Marshall Bill.[5] They advised the audience to pay attention, because the information he'd provided "just might save their lives."

The sketch opened in a bar, where patrons were slogging through the *Super Bowl Halftime Show*, and someone had ordered a round of flaming kamikazes.

No sooner did the bartender—replete with stereotypical Nu Yawk accent—light up the refreshing alcoholic drink than he was hit with a blast of foam putting out the flame. At that point, Fire Marshall Bill appeared, blowing a whistle, and tossing a yellow flag, ready to warn unsuspecting patrons about "football and alcohol—a *deadly combination!*"

And so began the next five minutes of some of Carrey's most brutal, and hilarious, physical comedy. Carrey would later remark that by the end of the sketch—after having been hit with everything from darts to Gatorade, to electrical shocks that singed his hair off—his "face-scape" felt a little rougher. (In fact, if you look at Carrey's face by the end of the sketch, it's all but evident that he's in physical pain.)

Sugar Ray's Celebrity Interviews

Celebrities loved stopping by *In Living Color*, and Davidson—who portrayed a pitch-perfect Sugar Ray Leonard[6]—took the time to "interview" them as part of a brief interlude while the "Million Dollar Giveaway" and the "Men on Football" sketches were being set up.

First up for an interview was Phil Buckman.[7] "I'm having the time of my life, man," he said into the microphone. "This is absolutely the best thing I've ever done in my life."

Up next was a baby-faced Blair Underwood, who was thrilled that the Redskins were winning. The ladies in the house, meanwhile, were thrilled to be in the same room as a baby-faced Blair Underwood. And who could blame them, really?

Then came Pauly Shore, the iconic stoner-dude of the 1990s, who clearly thought he was on the MTV set and couldn't understand a word "Sugar Ray" was saying. "Excuse me, sir?" he asked in all earnestness when "Sugar Ray" asked him if there were enough "nugs" (chicken nuggets) for him.[8] Shore also had a predilection for the Fly Girls, who had "plenty of moisture," which is not exactly the visual one wants conjured up when discussing Super Bowl activities—or, at least, Super Bowl activities featuring Pauly Shore.

And finally came Corin "Corky" Nemec, a sometime "teen dream" heartthrob of the 1990s, who was having a great time—and politely asked if "Sugar Ray" was also having a good time as well.

And he was. He most definitely was.

Men on Football

For the penultimate part of the live show, Grier and Damon performed as Antoine Merriweather and Blaine Edwards giving their commentary on the Buffalo Bills against the Washington Redskins.[9] Of course, Blaine would have preferred to see the Oilers and the Packers face off against one another, and it had nothing to do with the quality of their game play on the football field.

The double entendres were at an all-time high on the live sketch, from the Wilson's Sporting Goods sponsorship—who provided the "Official Balls of the NFL"—to Blaine and Antoine catching "blue balls" as they learned how to play the game. And of course, they had far too much fun with players' names—Antoine was thrilled to pieces that "Dick Butkus" (which he pronounced "Dick Butt-Kiss") was a real player, while Blaine's favorite was Bob Griese ("Greasy").

But, as with most live shows, there were more than a few times when Grier and Damon struggled to stay in character—and there were a few times when both broke character and laughed, such as when Blaine referred to the cheerleaders as "old fish,"[10] (and, of course, they "hated 'em!"[11]) or when Antoine asks if Griese was a tight end and Blaine snaps, "Well, he *was*."

Grier then completely broke character and said, "you need to stop!" in between fits of laughter when Blaine/Damon said that he thought the numbers on the back of the players' jerseys were meant to represent the number of men they'd been with in their lifetimes.

"I saw one with the number 78 on the back—child, I almost fainted!" Blaine said, adopting a demure tone, which was the sentence that got Grier to break character—though, in fairness to both Grier and Damon, neither one had very much luck keeping a straight face throughout the sketch.

And it was evident that the audience couldn't get enough of Blaine and Antoine—because the live studio audience screamed louder with each punchline, each double entendre, and each smart remark.

But that said, this was another "you had to be there" sketch, because subsequent airings of the sketch—including on DVD and in syndication—edit out ad-libbed lines implying that Richard Gere[12] and Carl Lewis ("Well, you know why Carl Lewis runs so fast—you can run, but you can't hide from your true self, Miss Lewis," said Blaine) are homosexuals. And, according to Keenen, it's for the best in the latter case.

"Carl Lewis was *livid*," Keenen later told the Television Academy in 2013, when recounting why the references to the latter's homosexuality were, ultimately, cut out. "And he wanted to sue. I think there was an apology letter that went out to him, and ultimately, it got resolved. But, for me, years later—I mean, many years later—I saw a documentary on Carl Lewis. And he actually spoke about that, and how—I guess he was going through a lot of things during that time, and was under a lot of scrutiny, and his sexuality was being questioned. And it really upset him. And I felt bad that he was so hurt by that. Because, again, that was not the intention—and it wasn't even written. It was just something that came off the cuff. And it was hilarious. But, again, you don't know . . . that's the thing about comedy. Your intention is to be funny. Once it goes out to the world, you don't know how it's received. And that's sort of the . . . downside of the comedian, you know?"[13]

As an aside, it's interesting to note that both Keenen and Kim weren't above apologizing to those to whom they caused harm in their comedy—especially since the harm wasn't intentional—and both felt terribly when they realized harm had been caused to the targets of their comedy. This proves that no matter how raw Keenen and *In Living Color* were—and no matter how raw every subsequent Wayans family production has been—cruelty was never, ever the point.

But the conclusion of the "Men on Football" sketch is notable because it included a line that will sound familiar to fans of *RuPaul's Drag Race*, years before VH1 debuted the legendary drag queen's hit show: "the books have been read,[14] and the library is closed."[15]

Background Guy: Super Bowl Interview

Carrey's "Background Guy" character appeared doing increasingly outrageous physical acts with each interview.

The show closed out with Keenen giving thanks to everyone who participated in the show—and even had Sam Kinison standing next to him, of all people—before tossing the show over to Color Me Badd closing out the show with "I Wanna Sex You Up" as the Fly Girls danced along.

The *In Living Color* Super Bowl halftime show was only five sketches long, and its total run time was just a hair under thirty minutes. But in terms of impact, the show may as well have been the Chicxulub asteroid.[16]

By several estimates, this episode drew nearly 30 million pairs of eyes[17]—which included people who both did and did not watch "the big game." But worse yet, the NFL had lost ten points off their ratings after the halftime show was over. That meant that at least 10 percent of the people who were previously watching the Super Bowl *did not* turn back to the game after *In Living Color*'s special episode was over.

And it was at that moment that the NFL executives realized that the numbers didn't lie, and if they wanted to keep all eyes on them, they had to do something drastic.

"The Super Bowl halftime is one of my proudest moments of the show," Keenen told the Television Academy in 2013.[18] "Because we're responsible for halftime at the Super Bowl being this huge event. We realized that we were going to be up against the Super Bowl. And the Super Bowl dominates television—and at that time, *really* dominated television. Anything that ever went up against the Super Bowl would die. But we saw a window, which was halftime, when people normally got up to pee. And so, Doritos wanted to do something with us, and that was the event which we chose to do. We would put our half-hour from the time the play stopped until the time the play started. And we put a clock up so people would know when to turn back. And when halftime came, the entire audience for the Super Bowl turned their channel to *In Living Color*. And it was this little show that took on this giant and *crushed*. And the next year, they hired Michael Jackson to do their Super Bowl, and every year since, they've had a humongous star at Super Bowl halftime . . . because of *In Living Color*."

CHAPTER 6

"Men on Film"

FROM LGBTQIA+ PARODY TO ACCEPTANCE

List of "Men on Film" sketches: "Men on Film" (season 1, episode 1), "Men on Art" (season 1, episode 4), "Men on Books" (season 1, episode 7), "Men on Films II" (season 2, episode 1), "Men on Vacation" (season 2, episode 9), "Men on Television: Blaine Becomes Hetero" (season 2, episode 24), "Men on Film: Straight Man Out" (season 3, episode 2), "Men on Film Festival" (season 3, episode 10), "Men on Football" (season 3, episode 16—the live Super Bowl halftime show), "Men on Videotape Rentals" (season 3, episode 23), "Men on Cooking" (season 4, episode 29[1]), "Men on Fitness" (season 4, episode 15).[2]

In Living Color was uniquely qualified to speak about Black American life, and that's exactly what it did best. But were they uniquely qualified to speak about a *particular* subset of Black American life—specifically, *queer*, and Black American life?

That question is one worth exploring when considering the "Men on Film" series. One of the best-known *In Living Color* sketch series (if not *the* singular defining sketch of the series), "Men on Film" features Damon as Blaine Edwards and Grier as Antoine Merriweather, two film critics who tackled the popular films of the day "from a male point of view"—think of an effeminate Siskel and Ebert, or a template for today's Miss Lawrence and Derek J. Though the sketch would later expand into other areas—including "Men on Vacation," "Men on Fitness," and, notably, "Men on Football" during the *Super Bowl Halftime Show*—"Men on Film" flexed its muscle (*tee hee!*) the hardest when Blaine and Antoine focused on films.

The premise of the sketches was simple: Blaine and Antoine hated everything that was stereotypically "feminine" and loved everything that was stereotypically "masculine." (In the inaugural sketch, for example, *Dangerous Liaisons* was praised by Blaine for casting Glenn Close in a "feminine" role; when Antoine reveals that Close is a woman, Blaine giggles and praises the film for being

David Alan Grier (left) and Damon Wayans as Antoine Merriweather and Blaine Edwards, respectively, the hosts of "Men on Film." *Fox/Photofest © Fox*

"sneaky," then awards the film "two snaps up." But *Miss Firecracker*, a largely forgotten film that starred Holly Hunter in the lead role as an ultra-*femme* woman, was simply dismissed with a "hated it!")

If intent follows the bullet, both in comedy and the law, the reason there isn't such virulent hatred for Blaine and Antoine in the twenty-first century is because both Grier and Damon have said, in different ways, that it was never their intention to depict gay men—especially gay, effeminate Black men—in a harmful way.

For Grier, he'd merely imitated what he'd seen throughout his career. As a child of the stage and theater, Grier was surrounded by gay men—especially effeminate gay Black men—throughout his career, and he was privy to their culture, customs, and language. When he spoke to NPR in 2012[3] about the origins of Antoine Merriweather's mannerisms, he spoke with quite a bit of affection for many of his former theater colleagues.

"Being in a musical and working with other performers who were gay, I was privy to that vocabulary backstage," he said. "They were being themselves. So, a lot of it was hijacked from what I heard in the theater and what was permeating around. Now at that time, if a gay person was going to read you—to tell you off—it was always accompanied by snaps. Now I don't know if it was a gay thing, but it was also a very Black thing."

Whether it was a "gay thing" or a "Black thing" or a "gay *and* Black thing"—and it was all of the above—the fact is, *In Living Color* got pushback for the "Men on . . ." sketches. Back in 1990, the *Los Angeles Times*[4] was privy to Keenen's travails about the pushback, which ramped up shortly after he'd won the Emmy Award for Best Comedy-Variety Show. The newspaper noted that Keenen was reading a *Time* magazine article about the show, and the magazine mentioned that the sketches were being boycotted by prominent gay and lesbian groups like GLAAD (Gay and Lesbian Alliance Against Defamation). Keenen took offense to this characterization, and he felt the reports were greatly exaggerated.

"This article is just trying to create controversy," Keenen said to the *Times* at the time. "It's dwelling on the bad things too much."[5]

And while, certainly, that may be true,[6] the sketches *did* receive some critical pushback. Marlon Riggs,[7] a prominent and outspoken gay Black activist, had the sharpest words for the "Men on Film" sketches, and took exception to Grier and Damon's depiction of gay Black men as "sissies, ineffectual, ineffective, womanish in a way that signifies inferiority." For Riggs, being gay came in many different shapes and sizes, and not all gay men—let alone gay Black men—acted effeminate.[8]

Writing for *Vulture*, Carleton Atwater summed it up a bit more succinctly. The problem with "Men on Film," he said, was not the fact that the characters were gay, nor was it the fact that the characters were flamboyant in their gayness. The issue was that there were no other jokes they had to tell outside of their gayness—or, in modern parlance, their queerness—and the characters were, therefore, one dimensional.

"It's not that Grier and [Damon] Wayans are being mean-spirited with their depiction of gay characters, it's just that there is little to their jokes beyond the fact that they are gay," he wrote.[9]

Interestingly, in what can only be described as a serendipitous turn of events, "Men on Film" found an ally in the most unlikely of places: John J. O'Connor of the *New York Times*,[10] the same critic who could barely contain his confusion and microaggressions for *The Richard Pryor Show* almost fifteen years prior to his review of *In Living Color*. While O'Connor pointed out that Damon and Grier seemed detached from the reality of AIDS in the gay community (they were straight men, after all, and it's all but impossible that they would have experienced the crisis the way a gay Black man would have at the time), "they have become two of the more likable regular characters on the show. [He also presciently called Keenen 'a man not to be underestimated.'] There is no venom here in the manner of an Andrew Dice Clay."

To be clear, the 1980s and 1990s was far from an enlightened time for "different" groups, but even a less enlightened—or, if you prefer, less politically correct—time had its limits. Clay's 1987 comedy special *One Night with Dice* got virulent pushback—and rightly so—for its vile rhetoric. A sample "joke" from Clay involved a remark about how there are no gay people in Brooklyn "because they're all dead" (bearing in mind that this disgusting "joke" was told at the height of the AIDS crisis). And that was the *least* offensive thing that Clay said.

So, as has been mentioned before, "intent follows the bullet," and while Clay, Kinison, and the like had an intense and psychologically unhealthy hatred of gay men, Grier and the Wayans brothers clearly did not.

All the criticisms—and the compliments—are valid. The summary of it all is that "Men on Film" was funny for its time—and in many ways, it's still funny today—but it's not a sketch series without its issues. In other words, it's not perfect—but it works because it's very real, and it did the best it could with the information it had at the time.

And while Keenen—and the rest of the cast—were a bit testy about any pushback they received at the time the show was on the air, time—as it's often wonted to do—has softened the blow, and the cast members all take a different, and more deferential, approach to the sketch.

In 2019, Grier was asked whether he'd do "Men on Film" today if he were approached to do so—and whether it was even advisable to tackle such a sketch in the twenty-first century.

"I don't think you can," Grier replied. "And this is my own personal opinion. But that was 1990. My personal politics—my knowledge of [the community]—is different. You know, I have evolved from then. But, back then, what I would say is, there was never any malice in our portrayal of these gay men—at least from my perspective at that time. But it was very much of its time."[11]

Keenen, for his part, agreed with Grier's assessment. "I agree [about] the characters, but I think that the sketch *could* be done today. I think that we have more information about gay culture. So, we could make it even funnier."[12]

"Maybe we could have gay cast members," opined Grier.[13]

"Yeah, that would be the thing," agreed Keenen. "But the whole intent of the show was to include *everybody*.[14] You can only be as good as the time period that you live in . . . with the information that you have. And so, that's what we tried to do."[15]

It's clear from their statements both then and now that neither Grier nor the Wayans brothers had an intense and virulent hatred for the queer community—and that, perhaps, is why they are still beloved, however problematic or "of its time" their jokes are at any given moment. The fact that both are willing to acknowledge—especially as elder statesmen of comedy—that their choice of words can, and should, evolve with time proves that they have the grace and the maturity to stay relevant while still staying true to themselves and their characters.

Compare these comments from the *In Living Color* cast in 2019 to Andrew Dice Clay's most recent comments about a similar subject. In August 2021—after he was diagnosed with Bell's palsy, no less—he claimed that he had "no regrets" about any of the things he'd said, then or now; that he was still "edgy" (which is pretty incredulous, considering he was sixty-four years old in 2021—one year older than Keenen Ivory Wayans is—making him all but eligible for being fully vested for his social security check); and that he was "the greatest comic on Earth" (which is stretching it, to put it mildly).[16] Yet, Clay was the first to take offense when people in the *TMZ* comments were making fun of his Bell's palsy, proving that those who dish it out most often can't take it when the proverbial shoe is on the other foot.

It's interesting to note that, even for its time, the response to the "Men on Film" series was very generational. According to Keenen and Grier, the younger gay community in the 1990s—who were slowly, but surely, starting to make their way to the forefront of pop culture—was very much in favor of the sketches and found them hilarious, while the older, more conservative gay community—who had survived such things as the Stonewall riots and the AIDS crisis—was not as welcoming about the sketches.

And to be clear, this is not to paint either community with a broad brush—certainly, there were outliers who fell into both categories—but this is to suggest that, as with everything else, what's considered funny, and appropriate, is always on a sliding scale. Our greater understanding of the queer community, and all its different intersections, is much greater now in the twenty-first century thanks in no small part to social media, but also thanks to the increased exposure of society at large to such concepts . . . which has, in turn, led to more acceptance of differences (even if the laws haven't quite caught up with the rest of America's acceptance of intersectional cultural diversity).

For many Gen Xers—especially those who didn't live in or near a culturally and ethnically diverse city like New York City or Los Angeles, and as such, had limited exposure to people who didn't look like them—"Men on Film" was the first time they'd seen *any* sort of depiction of gay Black men. And whatever the problems (deliberate or accidental) that existed with the creation, it went a long way in showing a whole lot of people that there was a whole different world out there than the one they'd been exposed to growing up. If nothing else, "Men on Film" deserves credit for showing the more sheltered a new community, one they may not have seen represented otherwise.

Could the "Men on Film" sketches be done today? In the format they were in, with the cast that they had, and the way the sketches were presented, they cannot. As Grier correctly stated, the "Men on Film" sketches as we know them on *In Living Color* were a product of their time, and while they were irreverent and—to a great degree—funny, they were also reductionist in their depiction of queer Black men, and as a collective society, we all know that *now*, even if we didn't know it back then. And when you know better, you do better.

This is not to suggest that we can't—or shouldn't—laugh at "Men on Film." Everything else aside, Grier and Damon have amazing chemistry, and both men have stated on different occasions that they enjoyed working with each other the most . . . and it's evident each time they team up, both for this sketch and for others. But this *is* to suggest that we do so with the knowledge that it was a product of its time, and that comporting oneself in such a way in the twenty-first century—or, worse yet, reducing the broader gay community to a narrow scope such as this one—is unacceptable.

And if given the opportunity to recreate "Men on Film" with broader parameters—if Grier's suggestion of increased cultural sensitivity, combined with Keenen's suggestion of holding space for both queer writers to write the sketches *and* queer actors to reprise the roles, thus giving both a character depth and an authenticity to Blaine Edwards and Antoine Merriweather that didn't exist before—then *In Living Color*'s creators *absolutely* should take it on.

When asked about rebooting the "Men on Film" sketch by *The View* in 2017, Damon summed it up succinctly: "We *should* do it. America needs to laugh at itself again."[17]

CHAPTER 7

Keenen's Departure

If you believe the 1993 reports detailing Keenen's departure from *In Living Color*, the words used to describe him are problematic, at best. *Entertainment Weekly*[1] was one of the first to report on Keenen's departure from the show, and it sounded like something out of a pulp fiction novel or the *National Enquirer*— nowhere near the celebrity fluff pieces and exclusive interviews the outlet is known for today.

Describing a Black man as a cross between Martin Luther King Jr. and Benito Mussolini would *never* fly in modern newsrooms—not even before Black Lives Matter became the cause célèbre and diversity, equity, and inclusion (DEI) efforts have been made (at least on the surface level) in modern-day newsrooms—and calling him a "fella" (when he was, at the time, a grown man of thirty-four) is downright insulting and infantilizing. But writing for the publication, Alan Carter had no problem doing either one.

And why?

Because Keenen had the temerity to criticize Fox as he stormed out the door. "This is a shell of a company making desperate moves," he said to the outlet at the time.[2] "They're collapsing, and they don't care who they offend or what shows they ruin."

Now, admittedly, those are very strong words. And, certainly, Keenen's assertion of the channel collapsing was a misguided one, at best, considering the global juggernaut that Fox has become since he uttered those words.

There's also no question that there are things Keenen may—or may not— have done at the time that could have been better. Success—especially when it's sudden, seemingly overnight success that makes a lot of money for its recipient—can make one act in a way that one wouldn't otherwise do.[3] There are always three sides to every story—his side, her side, and the truth—and much like *Rashomon* (or, if you prefer, Obi-Wan Kenobi), the truths that people cling to often depend greatly on their own points of view.

But even if we assume the worst—even if we assume that Keenen developed a big head and became an out-of-control egomaniac who regularly kicked puppies and beat up babies as a result of his seemingly overnight fame—there was absolutely no excuse for Fox to do what they did to a show that was Keenen's singular vision, and that made untold amounts of money for a network that was, at the time, struggling to find its footing against the "Big Three" of CBS, ABC, and NBC.

Imagine, if you will, an alternative scenario, with a different creator and director.

When Martin Scorsese created *The Irishman*—a laborious and overbearing film that clocks in at more than four hours long—he was excoriated by the critics for his use of de-aging technology. And that was one of many criticisms that pop culture commentators had about the film, especially since Scorsese was creating the film for Netflix (which meant he could have turned it into a four-part miniseries, thus making it easier on the viewer and the critic alike). Yet, when confronted about the criticism, Scorsese's response was a smirk and an "I don't know," and he said that he received encouragement from his cast and crew indicating they believed that everything he did was "the best, state of the art."[4]

Scorsese even managed to make Robert De Niro—perennial tough guy—look obsequious and fawning.

And what did Scorsese change? What feedback did he take? What changes did he implement to make his film better?

None. Zero. Zilch. *Bupkis*.

One might argue—successfully—that Scorsese was a true maestro of a director, creator, and producer at the time *The Irishman* was released, which had earned him the right to do whatever he wanted when it came to his creations. And one also might argue that Scorsese—unlike Keenen—has an Oscar on his mantel to prove his worthiness of exercising the auteur theory[5] if he so wishes.

But if Scorsese's works are definitive auteur masterpieces, then certainly, the creations of Keenen Ivory Wayans deserve that same deference. For what it's worth, too, Keenen also has been nominated for six Primetime Emmys, and won one (for Outstanding Variety, Music, or Comedy Series for *In Living Color*) in 1990. So, he's quite the force to be reckoned with, and to suggest otherwise because he doesn't have an Oscar on his mantel—yet—is again the height of folly.

A true auteur creation bears—among other things—the "unmistakable personal stamp of the director," and as his subsequent creations have proven, Keenen's creations are all, unmistakably, his own.

So, why would he be required to overhaul a show that was almost exclusively his singular vision—and a show that was a proven moneymaker—when a white director of *any* stripe would have been given infinitely more deference?

Keenen's brother, Damon, hinted that the brothers' relationship with Fox was messy—to put it mildly—in his 2015 interview with *The Breakfast Club*. The hosts asked Damon about the rumored "beef" between the two brothers—and referred to the TV Land special about *In Living Color* in 2012, which Damon was notably absent from[6] and refused clearance on clips featuring his classic characters (Homey D. Clown, Blaine Edwards from "Men on Film")—and Damon's words suggested that the reasons for his absence were multilayered and complex.

"I never want to make my brother look bad," Damon said to the syndicated radio show.[7] "But, at a certain point, when you feel disrespected . . . there's something in me that can't allow that disrespect."

Although the popular gossip suggests that Damon and Keenen are at perpetual loggerheads—with *Deadline*[8] pointing out that Damon is not part of the production company that Keenen formed with Shawn and Marlon, and the outlet citing "sources" that claim there was "friction" between the two brothers—Damon's own words make clear that this is not the case.

"I apologized to my brother, but everyone else can kiss my ass," he said to *The Breakfast Club* hosts. "We're good. Family's fam, you know? You get your feelings hurt, and then you laugh about it."

When Charlamagne Tha God pressed the issue, Damon again repeated that he and Keenen are brothers who love one another, and then recounted the story of how his mother, Elvira, used to make her sons kiss one another on the mouth when they were at loggerheads to prevent the "beef" from continuing.

As journalists in the entertainment industry know, "sources" cited in major publications are unreliable and are, often, publicists who are more interested in getting their clients that much-coveted press coverage than they are about the veracity of the scenario. Simply put, the "truth" is often boring in the world of publicity. While this book doesn't claim to know the most intimate of details about the Wayans brothers' relationship—only they can know that, after all, and it's not only irrelevant to the cultural history of *In Living Color*, but it's also really no one's business at the end of the day—it's hard to believe that the brothers are at loggerheads when *both* have made clear on several occasions that this isn't the case. The TL;DR (too long, don't read) answer, then, is to take the *primary* source as the gospel truth. In other words, if it didn't come directly from Damon's mouth—or any of the other Wayans brothers' mouths—it's to be taken with a *pillar*, let alone a grain, of salt.

From a business standpoint, when someone works overtime to create a television show—a television show that, it should be noted, all but printed money for what was then a fledgling network—only to then watch that television show get unceremoniously ripped from his hands and turned into something he doesn't recognize, and watch the value of his once-great creation take a nosedive in value . . . well, that's about as nice as one could be, given the circumstances.

It's worth breaking down, at this point, why Fox's decision to repackage episodes of *In Living Color* and air them on different nights before Keenen could negotiate a syndication deal had such a negative impact on the bottom line.

The definition of a *syndicated* show is one that runs on a different network than the one it was initially made for and broadcast on in its original run. Popular syndicated shows that everyone is most likely familiar with include *The Golden Girls* (which initially aired on NBC, and now airs on TV Land as of 2022), the original *Law & Order* (which initially aired on NBC, and now airs on WE TV in reruns, while new episodes air on NBC as of 2022), and *Dr. Phil* (which initially—and currently—aired on CBS, and now airs in reruns on OWN and on its own channel on Pluto TV). These types of shows are called *off-network syndicated programs.*

There are some shows that are explicitly made for syndication because they are aired on different networks in different markets. Long-running game shows like *Jeopardy!* and *Wheel of Fortune* fall into this category, and these types of shows are called *first-run syndicated programs.*

Typically, a show must have at least eighty-eight episodes—but ideally, one hundred episodes is the magical number—before syndication interest is generated. In the twenty-first century, syndication options are more plentiful for shows thanks to the rise in streaming services like Amazon, Netflix, Hulu, and Apple+. In fact, there are some shows that were unsuccessful in their initial network run that find a "second life" on a streaming network, and sometimes, the streaming network orders new episodes of the previously unsuccessful series. An example of this is the show *Designated Survivor*, starring Kiefer Sutherland, that ran for two seasons on ABC before getting canceled, then finding a "second life" on Netflix in 2019. But at this point in history, streaming networks weren't even a glimmer in a computer engineer's eye—so Keenen either had to make the show sink or swim if he wanted a shot at syndication.

Regardless of the minutiae, once syndication is achieved, a show—and its participants—can make more money than ever before. Not only do the actors make money from residuals, but the creator of the show makes money, *and* the investors make their money back and then some.

Here's an idea of how lucrative syndication can be: as of this writing, *Seinfeld*—which ran for nine seasons and ended in 1998—generates $400 million *each* for cocreators Jerry Seinfeld and Larry David *just* from its airing in syndication.[9] Even more gobsmackingly, *I Love Lucy*—which hasn't been on the air since 1957—continues to generate a salary for CBS executives,[10] even though Lucille Ball (the last surviving *I Love Lucy* star) died in 1989.[11]

Understanding these few numbers, then, it's easy to understand why Keenen would want the show to be primed for syndication—and why that value would be diluted by repeats of the show airing before the magical one hundredth episode could be aired.[12] Put simply, Fox was over-priming the pump—they were turning a show that families looked forward to watching every Sunday night into something they could catch on any night of the week—and the excitement about, and interest in, the show was dwindling as a result.

And it's also no surprise, then, that Keenen was more than a little taken aback at Fox's callous approach to the value that *In Living Color* brought to Fox as a network. "To tell you the truth," he said to *Entertainment Weekly* back in 1993,[13] "I was so stunned, I kept saying, 'You're joking, you're joking.' They were so sneaky about it. Then they said they were only going to show reruns from the first season. But they're not even doing that—they're editing shows from all different seasons. I was supposed to have that control, and even that was usurped. The years I put into the show were being robbed from me."

And so, it seems, the more things change, the more they stay the same. The phrase "the nerve of this Black man" is once again being said—but this time, it's *out loud*. How dare Keenen want creative control of his own television show? How dare he want the value of the show to be as high as possible so he makes as much money as he can from a brilliant, groundbreaking show? *How dare he?*

Eventually, it became a battle of wits and wills. Keenen wouldn't relinquish the tapes, the network wanted full control, and they went back and forth until, finally, Keenen gave up and walked away from the show completely.

"It was absolutely the most difficult thing I've ever had to do," he said to *Entertainment Weekly* in 1993.[14] "But I had to. I couldn't condone what they did, and how they did it. No one wanted me to leave, but I couldn't continue in good conscience. I couldn't give them a show that was a certain quality and not have them return that quality."

In response to Keenen's departure, Damon and Marlon followed their brother out the door.[15] Kim, who had a multiyear contract with the network, ended up in litigation when she wanted to get out of her contract. Ultimately, Shawn and Kim stayed on until the end of the fourth season—but as Shawn told the *Hollywood Reporter* in 2019,[16] it was horrible for them.

"Kim and I were contractually obligated to be there. It was hell. I knew we were on the *Titanic* without the captain, and the iceberg was up ahead, and I was shackled to the banister. Not one sketch would work without Keenen's touch," he said—and time would prove him correct.

Carrey, on the other hand, took a very different approach.

In 1993, the *Los Angeles Times* reported that Carrey became a soldier—whether deliberately or not—in the war being waged by the network on Black shows. The *Times* reported that Carrey burst into the offices of the new *In Living Color* brass—who were almost all white and male—and wanted, literally, to whitewash everything.

"Listen, guys, I gotta talk to you now!" he was reported to have said.[17] "You know, guys, seriously, you gotta lose the whole Black thing on the show. Here's how I see it. Hear me out, hear me out! We're beating a dead horse here. What we gotta do here is get everything white. The cast is white, the dancers are white, I'm white. White, white, white, white, white!"[18]

Mr. Carrey was apparently under the impression that white people were struggling to get their shows on the air thanks to *In Living Color* and were it not for the profundity of Carrey's infamous one-liners like "Sma-hokin'!" and "Lah-hew-hew-zer!" the entire white race stood a chance of perishing thanks to Keenen Ivory Wayans and his Blacker-than-Black machinations on a then-fledgling network. *Yikes.*[19]

One can only wonder how Pam Veasey—a Black woman, and one of the producers who was in this meeting that Carrey made these tone-deaf, disgusting, and borderline racist (if not outright racist) comments—felt when all this was going down, although the *Times* claimed that Veasey reportedly only replied "gee, thanks Jim," which garnered peals of laughter from the rest of the white men in the room—though it's not clear what's funny about this scenario at all. This complete lack of humor—and the seeming delight that the white men took in making the Black people in the room feel uncomfortable—would permeate into the subsequent *In Living Color* sketches, which took a nasty, vile turn after Keenen's last episode.

But according to the *Los Angeles Times*, the producers were quite all right with Carrey's newfound "white is right" attitude,[20] even though the show was called *In Living Color* (with "color" being the operative word). Not hesitating to say the quiet part out loud, the *Times* reported that the producers were finding it easier to "laugh, breathe a sigh of relief, and congratulate each other for surviving the most difficult season since the show's debut three years ago."[21]

Les Firestein, one of the producers in the room, couldn't wait to get the new version of *In Living Color* on the air. Now that The Problem was out of the way, and the Black Man relinquished control of the show,[22] they could put on the show that *they* wanted to put on. There was "Life after Wayans," as the white men so infamously told the *Los Angeles Times*, and *their* humor was going to see the light of day. Gone was the predominantly Black cast and the legendary characters—and in its place was Borscht belt humor, stereotypes of Black Americans, and a show that was a shell of its former self.

But it was fine! It was all going to be *totally* fine.

Keenen, himself, couldn't believe what he was seeing.

"It always was comedy from an African American point of view," Keenen told *Entertainment Weekly* in 1993,[23] "but now they have all white consultants. There's a fine line between African American humor and making fun of African Americans. Fox didn't even have the good taste to bring in that other voice, and that's offensive not only to the show but to a large segment of the population."

Keenen's last comment hits differently in 2021, and there's a much stronger chance it would have been heeded, especially in the wake of such movements as #OscarsSoWhite and the subsequent success of such Black power players as Ava DuVernay and Shonda Rimes.

Alas, Keenen uttered this prescient statement in 1993, so many viewed it as him bleating on about nothing—it happens all the time in television, after all, so why didn't he just get used to it?

None of it made a difference, however, because the producers were going to do what the producers were going to do. You might say they were going to "do what they want to do," but *certainly not* "in living color." Steve Bell, who was the head of network television for Twentieth Century Fox, assured the viewers that the network and the Wayans family were totally fine with one another—and that it was "hurtful" that Keenen would insinuate otherwise. In this context, Bell is using "hurtful" to make the reader feel like the "Big, Scary Black Man" (Keenen stands six foot three and is very muscular and broad) is hurting the scared white man with a dad bod's feelings. But the reality is, Bell was using "hurtful" to describe Fox's bottom line—in other words, Keenen wasn't doing the network brass any favors by letting the press know what was really going on, and his refusal to keep quiet about their flagrant disrespect to him and his creation was costing them money.

One truth of the entertainment industry is that it's always, *always* about business and money—it's never personal—and Keenen could have stood on the corner of Sunset and Sepulveda Boulevards in the middle of Los Angeles and called Bell every name under the sun, and Bell wouldn't have cared so long as it didn't cost him a buffalo head's nickel for Keenen to do so. Nevertheless, the double meaning was meant to conjure up racist images in the minds of the white audience Bell was hoping to target with his "new and improved" vision of *In Living Color*, and he knew it.

But Bell did the usual "LA Shit" (as it's derisively called in the industry) and delivered a fluffy, publicist-approved soundbite. "It was a very amicable parting," Bell said to the *Los Angeles Times*.[24] "We are still in negotiations with Keenen's people about certain things—possible projects that could include members of the Wayans family." (It goes without saying that these "projects" never materialized.)

Bell also insisted that the show's ratings were still the same, which was proof to him that the show was a "franchise" that was going to go on no matter who left the show, and any suggestion to the contrary was treasonous, because Bell was *certain* that he—and the rest of the white brass—knew more than Keenen about his own creation.

"This has been a tough year, to be sure," Bell said.[25] "You can't lose the creator and spiritual father of the show without causing problems. The fact that Les, Greg and Pam have come through so successfully, and that the ratings have held on, is just great news. This is a franchise, which, like *Saturday Night Live*, will go on despite people leaving."

But this wasn't *Saturday Night Live*.

This was *In Living Color*.

And Steve Bell could not have been more wrong in his assessment.

CHAPTER 8

The End—and the Beginning— of an Era

"They didn't understand that the show was a vision," Keenen told the *Hollywood Reporter* in 2019.[1] "And once you remove the visionary, all you have is a sketch show."

Under Keenen's tutelage, *In Living Color* certainly took aim at sacred American cows—Bill Cosby, *I Love Lucy*, various pop stars. And, certainly, there are things that were said in 1990 that would *never* fly in 2021 and beyond and were problematic at best. But there was never a maliciousness about Keenen's brand of comedy, and—perhaps most important—while Keenen had a field day with the adults, children were never, ever fair game. Even in the "Homey D. Clown" sketches that were meant to feature "children," the *adults* played children—proving that even when there was no real threat to a child's physical or emotional safety, Keenen et al. stayed away from even the intimation of impropriety.

But under the new white management—with a new and predominantly white writer's room—malice was the name of the game, and the cruelty was the point.

Under the "new management," *In Living Color* took a dive in the ratings—and in the quality of the sketches. Gone was the good-natured ignorance of Frenchie and the affable charm of Anton Jackson—in its place were sketches like "Go on Girl, with Barbara Bush and Hillary Clinton" (season 4, episode 2), which featured the two First Ladies (portrayed by Coffield and newcomer Alexandra Wentworth, respectively) trading nasty insults with one another as a Black woman (Keymáh) moderated the show and interjected various stereotypical affirmations ("I know that's right!" "Mm-hmm!"). The sketch barely got a few forced laughs from the studio audience and seemed out of place on a show like *In Living Color*, belonging more on *Saturday Night Live* and with its almost-exclusively all-white cast. Viewed through 2021 eyes, the sketch isn't funny at all, especially given what Americans know about what Secretary Clinton went through in 2016 and beyond. In fact, in hindsight, not one of the sketches that aired in season 4 or season 5 falls in the "classic" category, and not one is funny when viewed through 2021 eyes—something that cannot be said for the first three seasons of the show.

Then there were some sketches that were completely vile and violated all bounds of decency. The season 4, episode 3 sketch "Woody Allen for Date the Children" is one such sketch. This sketch, which was meant to depict Allen as a lovable *nebbish* who just happens to like 'em a little young, aired in October 1992, less than two months after Dylan Farrow—Allen's adoptive daughter with actress Mia Farrow—first accused the disgraced filmmaker of sexually assaulting her in her mother's Bridgeport, Connecticut, home.

Dylan Farrow was seven years old in 1992.

Even granting that the United States in the 1990s was less than complimentary to rape victims—there was no Lieutenant Olivia Benson on *Law & Order: SVU* every week painting sympathetic pictures of rape victims and changing minds one solved case at a time, after all—pedophilia is a taboo subject at best in comedy, and it was a topic that Keenen knew better than to *ever* broach in his own work on *In Living Color*. Even the edgiest of comedians take aim at the *pedophiles*—not their victims—because the sacred rule in comedy is "don't punch down," and making light of victims of predators, alleged or actual, isn't funny . . . not then, not now, and not ever.

The cast must have *also* noticed that the quality of the material was taking a sharp downturn—and they continued to let their distaste with Keenen's departure be known. The most infamous example was the "Christmas performance," when Jamie Foxx performed "This Christmas" at the close of episode 11 of season 4. Foxx, then as now, had an unparalleled musical talent—more so, in fact, than any other *In Living Color* cast member—but Coffield, Grier, and the other cast members stood behind him wearing sunglasses and straight faces, reminiscent of the common dress of the Nation of Islam.

While Carrey and Keymáh did not join their fellow castmates in wearing sunglasses and straight faces, their mood during the performance was far from jovial. Keymáh was visibly distressed, and Carrey awkwardly tried to get into the spirit but to no avail. While the animus from the cast was almost to be expected, it was a shame that Foxx's performance—which was very well done, from both an objective and a subjective point of view—was overshadowed by such a somber event, because this performance was a harbinger of things to come in Foxx's own career. The only one who really got into Foxx's performance was Jennifer Lopez—and given her subsequent diva reputation, it's perhaps unsurprising. But it also makes Foxx's post-*In Living Color* stand-up routines—in which he referred to his former castmate as "Hey, Ho"—seem a little catty, to put it mildly.

In any event, Keenen's last on-screen appearance on *In Living Color* was the same day as Foxx's first-ever live television performance, so this explains the funeral-like atmosphere on the set. But while the cast's distress was palpable and to be expected, this was unfair to Foxx—it wasn't, and still isn't, his fault that things went down the way they did. In the same breath, the cast members had to do what they thought was right, even if it meant someone getting caught in the crossfire and becoming collateral damage as a result.

And it kept getting worse. There were the nasty depictions of Mexican Americans, such as "Edward James Olmos Does Yardwork" (season 4, episode 1) and "Magnifico Lets Himself Go" (season 5, episode 7). There's a difference between performing a sketch that has a few offensive elements (vis-à-vis "The Head Detective" and their problematic depiction of Mexican Americans, which was written and performed during the so-called Keenen era) and performing a sketch that depicts certain ethnic groups with deliberate stereotypes—and these problematic, late-era *In Living Color* sketches that didn't have Keenen's "magic touch" fell into the latter category.

Then there were the depictions of gay men that were beyond the pale even by 1990s standards, such as what was seen in "Gays in the Military" (season 4, episode 10). Certainly, this is by no means meant to "woke-check" *In Living Color*, but when it's offensive even by its own time's standards, there's unquestionably a problem.

The sketch featured two men—presumably soldiers—talking effeminately and with a lisp, slap-fighting with one another, and even dusting each other's butts with feather dusters. And of course, the sketch was replete with double entendres about "standing up straight" and "spit polishing my helmet." It was meant to make fun of the Clinton administration policy—first proposed in 1993, and formally adopted in 1994—about gay men and women in the military, in which officials were not permitted to ask recruits about their sexual orientation in a policy that became colloquially known as "Don't Ask, Don't Tell." The fear of being discharged if their sexual orientation was revealed was real—and the fact that the writers could take aim at the American armed forces, regardless of the soldiers' sexual orientation, demonstrated nothing but cowardice on their parts. "Don't Ask, Don't Tell" was ultimately repealed in 2010, which means that, today, gay men and women could now openly serve in the United States armed forces without fear of being discharged.

And then there were sketches that simply had no place on a show called *In Living Color* (with, once again, the word "color" being the operative word).

The new writer's room (which had, inexplicably, "white consultants"—because white sensibilities had to be protected at all costs, proving that the more things change, the more they stay the same) had an inexplicable fascination with Ross Perot.

Henry Ross Perot, often known merely as Ross Perot, can be thought of as a prototypical Elon Musk (but, presumably and allegedly, without the apartheid-era levels of racism against his Black workers). In 1962, Perot quit his job at IBM to create his own company, Electronic Data Systems, and became a billionaire when he sold the company to General Motors in 1986. That deal *netted* him $1.5 billion—nearly $4 billion in twenty-first-century money—and he netted another $800 million when he sold Perot Systems to Dell Computer for $3.9 billion in 2009. But when he ran for president, he was seen as an eccentric, especially because he ran as an independent and took out half-hour-long info-mercials in which he would regale the American people—in his folksy, Foghorn Leghorn–style Texarkana accent—on all the ways he planned to fix the economy.

While Perot sketches did well on *Saturday Night Live*—and that's thanks in no small part to the comedic genius of Dana Carvey, who had a pitch-perfect impersonation of him—they fell flat on *In Living Color*. How many Black men and women *really* wanted to see *yet another* good ol' Southern boy being depicted in a humorous light? When was the last time *that* worked out well for Black men and women?

Yet, the new *In Living Color* brass thought the audience would enjoy not one but *two* sketches featuring the former presidential candidate in a humorous light (the who-the-hell-even-thought-this-was-a-good-idea "Ross Perot at an NAACP Meeting," season 4, episode 1; "Ross Perot Buys Up Airtime," season 4, episode 10). Presumably, after the second sketch fell flat, the dense writer's room finally got the message and gave up the ghost.

And when they weren't trying to make Black Americans see an eccentric billionaire with a deep Southern accent in a positive light—so much so that *he even went to an NAACP meeting! Isn't that hilarious? Laugh, people!*—they were throwing constant shade at President Bill Clinton—a president who was nearly universally beloved by the Black voters who helped put him into office, and who Toni Morrison infamously (and controversially) called "the first Black president."[2]

While the "first Black president" statement by Morrison was seen as an assessment of "Big Willy's" soulfulness—he played the saxophone on Arsenio Hall, after all, and in the collective white mind-set, that made him "down with the brothers"—her comment was actually an indictment of the American power structure and the inherent, built-in systemic racism. As Ta-Nehisi Coates brilliantly explained, "Clinton isn't black, in Morrison's rendition, because he knows every verse of 'Lift Every Voice and Sing,' but because the powers arrayed against him find their most illustrative analogue in white supremacy."[3]

Morrison's comment aside, Clinton was a president who was well-loved by the Black community in the 1990s, so it's really not clear why the new brass at *In Living Color* thought it would be a good idea to have "Bill Clinton" parodying

Bobby Brown's "Humping Around" (season 4, episode 6)—in which not one, but *two* beloved figures were butchered mercilessly; Brown was the "bad boy of R&B," and at the time, he was married to Whitney Houston, who was nothing short of a modern pop goddess—or to depict the Clinton family as "The Capitol Hillbillies" (season 4, episode 13).

Then there were "Ugly Wanda" sketches, as portrayed by Jamie Foxx. The first appearance of the character was in season 3, episode 18, while Keenen was still at the helm. "Ugly Wanda" was very much a Sapphire[4] caricature, and certainly contained punchlines that would never make it on the air today. But there was something genial about her, something that endeared her to the audience, something that made her relatable and funny—all characteristics that made her one of the most popular characters on *In Living Color*. But subsequent sketches—sketches without Keenen's "touch," as Shawn infamously put it— depicted Wanda as an ape-like barbarian, to the point that her facial expressions were more reminiscent of a pre–civil rights era minstrel show instead of any modern Black woman in the 1990s.[5]

Consider the season 5, episode 1 sketch "Ugly Wanda: Wanda Gives Birth," which features Foxx's character wearing an exaggerated pregnancy belly and engaging in all the horrid stereotypes of Black motherhood—questions of the father's paternity, the doctor donning a "toxic waste" suit when stepping between her legs to deliver the child, Wanda snapping off at anyone within a five-mile radius. This sketch would be carried through to the end of the final season, and it was treated less like a running joke (à la Homey D. Clown's "Homey Sells Out") and more like a bad *Maury* episode.

To be clear, this is not to suggest that Foxx lacked the talent to pull this character off effectively. To the contrary—as his subsequent career trajectory has proven, Foxx had (and has) both the talent *and* the drive to pull off anything he sets his mind to. But this *is* to make clear that Foxx—like any other actor—can only work with what a writer gives him or her, and even the best improvisation will fall flat if the setup is flawed. And it's very evident that the disparity in quality between what Keenen gave Foxx to work with, and what the "new management" gave Foxx to work with, is separated by country miles.

It was evident—and painfully so—that the new writers were *trying* (and failing) to do what came naturally to Keenen. And not only were the sketches decidedly *not* funny, but they all seemed to have a vicious, and cruel, undertone that was thankfully lacking in the first three seasons. The warmth, charm, and inclusion were replaced by "othering," tired stereotypes, and one-liners that simply were *not funny*.

The magic was gone. *In Living Color* had become decidedly monochrome. And people—especially the Black audiences that once tuned in *en masse*—were changing the channel, almost embarrassed at the shell their once-beloved show

Jamie Foxx, as "Ugly Wanda," giving a massage to a hapless Tommy Davidson. *Fox Broadcasting/Photofest © Fox Broadcasting*

had become. They knew it wasn't Keenen's fault—they knew that he had done everything in his power to save his beloved show, even taking extraordinary measures[6] to keep the tapes from falling into the wrong hands, to no avail—but they couldn't, in good conscience, continue to support a show that had strayed so far from its original mission (and its original audience) that it had become something they didn't even recognize.

Because contrary to the executives' assertion, the show was not *Saturday Night Live*, and it wasn't going to survive regardless of the cast changes. The show was *In Living Color*, and without the original formula—without Keenen at the helm discovering, developing, and nurturing Black talent, and telling Black stories to a Black audience while also making his non-Black audience feel "in on the joke"—it simply was (as Keenen would succinctly put it in 2019) just another sketch show, and the sketches and their players were—simply put—lacking in the heart and the soul to keep the audience's once-rapt attention.

Would *In Living Color* have lasted forever if the circumstances were better? Probably not. No show on television does. But would it have gone out ignobly had it not burned the brainchild of the operation? Definitely not.

When the show finally got canceled in 1994, the Wayans family felt—rightly—vindicated. While promoting *Blankman*, Damon spoke to the *Baltimore Sun* about the show's cancellation, and he was almost giddy in his celebration of its demise. (And who can blame him, really?)

"When we were there, you laughed with us," Damon said to the outlet.[7] "When we left, you started laughing *at* us as Black people. A lot less TLC was put into the sketches. It's a testament to my brother's genius that the show got canceled because they thought they could do without him."[8]

For a while, *In Living Color* completely faded from memory, save for a few reruns on Fox's sister networks FXX and FX.[9] The animosity left a bitter taste in many mouths, and Damon's sense of vindication when the show got canceled was far from an outlier.

But it wasn't *all* bad.

The original cast members went on to have successful careers all their own.

Carrey (who, by then, was being billed as "Jim Carrey") broke into the mainstream with *Ace Ventura: Pet Detective*—the film that was the bane of David Alan Grier's existence—which was released in 1994. That same year, Carrey appeared in the films *The Mask* and *Dumb and Dumber*. That would mark the first of many films that played upon his slapstick comedic prowess, though he did earn accolades for his dramatic undertakings in such films as *Man on the Moon* (in which he played Andy Kaufman, opposite Courtney Love, Danny DeVito, and Paul Giamatti). Unfortunately, though, Carrey has also been embroiled in several controversies, including the circumstances surrounding an ex-girlfriend's death,[10] vaccine skepticism,[11] and lying about carrying certain STIs

The cast of *In Living Color* would work together, periodically, throughout the years. Here, Jamie Foxx (left) and Tommy Davidson can be seen together in the 1997 film *Booty Call*. *Columbia Pictures/Photofest ©️ Columbia Pictures*

and passing them on to his deceased ex-girlfriend.[12] These days, Carrey's acting credits are far more limited—his role as Dr. Robotnik in the *Sonic the Hedgehog* films came after a four-year hiatus from films—though he's known for his artwork, which he periodically shares on social media.

Coffield (who later became Kelly Coffield-Park after 1999 when she married her fellow *In Living Color* castmate Steve Park—the pair have two children) remained a working actress, getting roles in such films as *Jerry Maguire* and *Bride Wars*, and in such television shows as diverse as *Law & Order* and *The Young and the Restless* to *30 Rock* and *Hope & Faith*. Proving, however, that the Wayans family is loyal to those who are loyal to them, she worked with the family on a few occasions after *In Living Color* went off the air. In 1998, she appeared in *The Wayans Bros.* sitcom, which starred Shawn and Marlon. Then, in 2000, she had a role in the Keenen-created and directed blockbuster *Scary Movie*, and followed that up with a role in the 2006 Keenen-created and directed comedy vehicle *Little Man*.

Tommy Davidson voiced Oscar (center) on *The Proud Family*, introducing his talents to a whole new generation of children who weren't even alive when *In Living Color* was on the air. *Photofest*

Davidson followed up his success on *In Living Color* with a series of bit parts in films like *Booty Call* (which also starred his fellow *In Living Color* castmate Jamie Foxx) and *Woo* (which starred Jada Pinkett, later Jada Pinkett Smith). But he really found his groove in voice-over roles. He loaned his voice talents to the cartoons *Duckman: Private Dick/Family Man*, *The Ren & Stimpy Show*, and—most notably—*The Proud Family*.

Grier, for his part, returned to his first love—the stage. A Yale graduate, Grier certainly dabbled in subsequent comedic roles post–*In Living Color*—with his most infamous role being in the hit television series *Martin*, as the Reverend Leon Lonnie Love. On film, he flexed his comedic muscle in the classic comedies *Boomerang*, *Blankman*, and *In the Army Now*—but he was always most "at home" in the theater. His 2012 performance in *Porgy & Bess*—alongside Audra McDonald and Norm Lewis—got him his first Tony Award nomination for Best Performance by a Featured Actor in a Musical. Ultimately, though, he wouldn't win a Tony Award until 2020, when he took home the win as Best Featured Actor in a Play for his role as Tech Sergeant Vernon C. Waters in *A Soldier's Play*, reprising the role originated by the legendary Adolph Caesar.

David Alan Grier always had a love for the stage and theater, and after ***In Living Color*** **went off the air, he would demonstrate that love when he'd take such roles as the Cowardly Lion in** ***The Wiz Live! NBC/Photofest © NBC***

Keymáh had a different type of career after *In Living Color* went off the air. She had a few notable acting roles in such TV shows as *Cosby* (where she stayed for four years) and *That's So Raven* (where she stayed for two years). But she also became known just as much for her lifestyle—as a vegetarian and an active gardener who self-published three books about meditation, self-care, and natural hair—as she was for her acting career. Overall, Keymáh seems quite content with the way things transpired in her career, and that's really all one can ask for in life.

And though he wasn't an original cast member—he only joined *In Living Color* in the third season—Foxx deserves a special mention here, as well, for he is certainly a prime example of *In Living Color*'s talent pool, and a testament to Keenen's ability to identify, cultivate, and nurture prime talent.[13] After Foxx finished his run on *In Living Color*, he got an eponymous show of his own, which ran for five seasons from 1996 until 2001. He also continued to cultivate his musical career, releasing four albums—2005's *Unpredictable*, 2008's *Intuition*, 2010's *Best Night of My Life*, and 2015's *Hollywood: A Story of a Dozen Roses*—and taking home several Grammy awards for his work. But he made history when he was cast as Ray Charles in the 2004 biographical film *Ray*, and his performance was lauded by none other than Mr. Ray Charles himself.[14] Foxx's incomparable performance as the musical legend earned him a Golden Globe,

Jamie Foxx with Barbara Walters on Oscar night, February 27, 2005. Foxx would make history that night when he became the first cast member from *In Living Color* to take home an Oscar. *ABC/Photofest © ABC*

a Screen Actors Guild (SAG) Award, a BAFTA Award, a Critics Choice Movie Award, and an Academy Award for Best Actor[15] in 2005.

Incidentally, Foxx's Oscar win meant that a cast member from *In Living Color* took home the coveted trophy before any cast member of *Saturday Night Live* ever did. As of 2022, no *Saturday Night Live* cast member has ever won an Oscar, though several—including Eddie Murphy, Bill Murray, and Dan Akroyd—have been nominated.

And Foxx continues to be a formidable, multitalented entertainer—and now, his eldest daughter Corinne has begun to wade her way in the industry, too. In fact, in 2016, Corinne was named Miss Golden Globe, an honor given to the daughters and sons of celebrities and chosen by the Hollywood Foreign Press Association (HFPA). The title, however, has since been adjusted to "Golden Globe Ambassador" to be more gender inclusive. Just one year after being crowned "Miss Golden Globe," Corinne Foxx walked the New York Fashion Week runway for fashion designer Sherri Hill, with fellow industry legacy model Nala Wayans—daughter of none other than Keenen Ivory Wayans and his now ex-wife, the former Daphne Polk.

As for the Wayans family, they banded together—as they'd learned to do all those years ago—and created an entertainment juggernaut all their own. And with the rise of their new, self-made empire came a rediscovery of the old *In Living Color* sketches thanks to DVDs and, later, YouTube, the syndication that they deserved a long time ago, and—ultimately—a whole new generation of Black content creators looking to the family (with Keenen as the patriarch) and their success as a template for their own.

In the twenty-first century, Black ownership of content was tantamount—the recognition of Black talent would no longer be silenced or sidelined—and *In Living Color* took on a whole new tenor.

CHAPTER 9

Black Ownership in the Hour of Chaos

The global COVID-19 pandemic opened up several cans of proverbial worms. It exposed the best of us, and it exposed the worst of us. But one of the biggest things that the global COVID-19 pandemic opened up was a larger discussion about the ravages of systemic racism and how to start setting the scales of justice right.[1]

And while the larger discussion of legal systemic racism is beyond the scope and purview of this book—though it's certainly worth mentioning that approximately 95 percent of the nonsense that Keenen et al. went through was part and parcel of a larger issue involving systemic racism—the topic of Black equity and ownership in the media, and in Hollywood as a whole, is certainly worth discussing vis-à-vis *In Living Color*.

There's a common misconception in American society that racism merely involves white people using the N-word, donning a white sheet on their face, and burning a cross on a front lawn. While those extreme examples are certainly racist, those aren't the only forms of racism that manifest in American society. And if recent times have taught us nothing else, it's that if we don't heal what's hurt us, we'll bleed all over people who didn't cut us.

Systemic racism is the cancer that not only rots America from the inside out but also has cost us *all* some of the greatest contributions to society of all time. *In Living Color* is just one casualty of many of this cancer—and more casualties will follow unless we, as a nation, face the cancer head-on.

There's no question that there has been an undercurrent of racism that has permeated every aspect of American culture—and at the height of the global COVID-19 pandemic, both the *Los Angeles Times* and the *Kansas City Star* issued a public mea culpa for their decades of racist coverage.

Even looking at these media within the microcosm of *In Living Color*, one can see how the coverage was problematic at best. Describing a Black man who created the show as a cross between Benito Mussolini and Martin Luther King Jr.—as *Entertainment Weekly* did—is just the beginning of it all.

What makes this past coverage of Keenen—and *In Living Color*—even more galling is that Keenen's reputation in the entertainment industry is a near-impeccable one. To this day, his colleagues enjoy working with him to the point that they campaign to work with him *and* his family on several productions more than thirty years after *In Living Color* went off the air. On a personal note, both his ex-wife *and* his most public ex-girlfriend have nothing but good things to say about him. The entertainment industry is a small one, and people talk. If Keenen had skeletons in his closet—literally or figuratively—they would have come out a *long* time ago.

This is by no means meant to suggest that the man is a saint on Earth—certainly, he has plenty of flaws, and Pope Francis isn't going to canonize a Saint Keenen anytime soon—but this is to say that comparing him to Benito Mussolini isn't just a reach . . . it's an *over*-reach.

One only must wonder if *In Living Color* would have faced the same type of resistance—and experienced the same ousting of its Black majordomo—if its creator was a white man. (And one needn't wonder for too long—because it's almost a universally accepted truth that the answer is *no*.) And when you consider that the media's depiction of a Black man as an Italian dictator is "not that bad" compared to other depictions in even the most recent past—just pick up a copy of the *New York Post* and make a mental note of how many times the word "animal" or another dehumanizing descriptor is used to describe non-white criminal suspects—it's safe to say that change is not only going to come but also that it's long overdue.

Writing for the *Hollywood Reporter*, activist Alicia Bell was much blunter in her assertion of how culpable media is in the lack of Black ownership in media. "The United States must come to terms with the ways racist media policies have excluded the Black community from owning and controlling our nation's media infrastructure or having access to it," she said.[2] "We must sow the seeds for a more just and equitable media and dismantle media's role in supporting a white-racial hierarchy over content and control."

Had *In Living Color* been on the air in the twenty-first century—had their authentically Black voice been on a major network like Fox in March 2021, and available for streaming the next day on Hulu or Netflix—there'd be no question that Keenen wouldn't have to wrestle with the Powers That Be to retain control of his own creation. Or, if he did, he'd have the backing of social (media) justice warriors, whose outcry would have disturbed the apple cart of advertisers, thereby forcing the network to comply with Keenen's (reasonable, to be frank) demands of creative control and ownership. He would not be a man alone, a

A promotional shot from the 2009 film *Dance Flick*, directed by Damien Wayans (Keenen's nephew), featuring Keenen Ivory Wayans in a prominent role. *Paramount Pictures/Photofest © Paramount Pictures*

David facing a Goliath he would ultimately be unable to fell, and a man who ultimately abandoned his creation after he'd been left with no other choice.

But more than disrupting the apple cart of advertisers, the audience for an *In Living Color* of today would be powerful in another way: with its purchasing power. In August 2021, McKinsey reported that the Black American consumer had a purchasing power of more than $300 *billion* (with a B).[3] The Fox executives of yesteryear clearly didn't view *In Living Color* as valuable—no matter how many pairs of eyes Keenen et al. brought to Fox on Sunday nights—because they didn't believe that the Black audience had the power to spend that type of money. Keenen proved he could bring eyes to the screen with the Super Bowl halftime show that changed history—but what he *couldn't* prove, in one of those rare moments where his then-lack of industry savvy cost him more severely than he'd ever could have bargained for, was that those eyes were attached to fat wallets.

The dollars, in other words, didn't make sense to the Fox executives.

But this shortsightedness on the part of the Fox executives proved to be a grave mistake: per McKinsey, Black audiences are more brand aware and—especially in the twenty-first century and beyond, but just as much in the twentieth century—more plugged in to emerging trends than their white counterparts. They also are more acutely aware of authenticity than their white counterparts—

which is why they averted their eyes elsewhere when *In Living Color* no longer spoke to them in an authentic voice.

Racism—white supremacy—and microaggressions cost Fox the equivalent of *billions* in revenue when it dared tamper with the winning formula of *In Living Color*.

But in the same breath, *In Living Color* also created space for Black creators to use their voices in other authentically Black spaces in the future. Forget the subsequent success of the Black cast—although, certainly, *In Living Color* is to be commended for it—but, instead, consider how many of the Black writers in the writer's room went on to create authentically Black shows and give a larger platform to Black content creators. Pam Veasey went on to *The Gregory Hines Show*, and Larry Wilmore went on to executive produce *Black-ish* and cocreate *Insecure*—and that's the short list.

Whether modern media consumers realize it or not—and whether American media realize it or not—Keenen Ivory Wayans was just a candle in the dark, but his was the spark that lit a million fires. Think of how many Black content creators of all stripes have gotten their flowers with just those three shows alone—*The Gregory Hines Show*, *Black-ish*, and *Insecure*. And think of

Kim Wayans (left) and Shoshana Bush in Damien Wayans's 2009 production *Dance Flick*, proving that even the next generation of Wayanses have learned to stick together. *Paramount Pictures/Photofest © Paramount Pictures*

how many more Black content creators will cite those works as inspirational and aspirational in the future.

"Parity in representation is important, but TV isn't always about reflecting reality. It's often a way to escape it," wrote the Nielsen Company.[4] "This makes the expansion of the stories, themes and roles Black women and Black men inhabit, both in front of and behind the camera, just as critical. Not just for the thrill that being seen has on Black audiences, but for the potential that full inclusion in the creation and distribution of TV content will have in shaping the hopes and dreams of Black families, our country and the world."

Whether you like his brand of comedy or not—and that, too, is subjective—Keenen Ivory Wayans certainly deserves his flowers for being, if nothing else, the man to knock over the first domino in a ripple effect that is still being felt today . . . a ripple effect that has helped other Black content creators share their hopes and dreams in a bold and authentic way.

And Keenen is long overdue to receive his proverbial flowers as a pioneer, as a Black content creator, and as a television revolutionary—and his long-overdue flowers shouldn't just be handed to him by other Black creatives, but by creatives *as a whole*.

Conclusion

In 1990, Keenen—who, at that point, had been overwhelmed by both the show's seemingly overnight fame and the constant demand for information from the media—told the *Los Angeles Times* that he wasn't sanguine about the show's legacy. In his opinion, he was just doing a sketch show, and all the rest of it was much ado about nothing.

"People expect miracles in the wrong places," he said to the outlet at the time. "This show isn't going to change the world. It may have an effect, but . . ."[1]

Keenen could not have been more wrong in that assessment.

In Living Color is ingrained so deeply into the pop culture consciousness that few, if any, realize it's there. It has changed the way we watch television, it has changed the way we view diversity, and it has even changed the way the Super Bowl has done business.

It also opened a larger conversation—what's funny? What do we find funny? *Why* do we find it funny? And most of all, can something be funny even if it's offensive—and if it can, why are some things still funny, while other things aren't?

What's most remarkable about *In Living Color* is that it's so integrated into the pop culture consciousness—and its impact is still felt in popular media today—yet it's hardly been acknowledged as the juggernaut that it was. A show that didn't make it to 150 episodes has had more impact on today's pop culture—a pop culture that goes above and beyond what we watch on television, and how—than shows that have lasted twice as long. And it deserves the recognition—and the accolades—as such, and it's almost criminal that more people don't recognize the show's impact on the American zeitgeist.

Did it singlehandedly change media? Was it singlehandedly responsible for the rise in Black entertainers and the rise in demand for equity in ownership?

No, it was not.

In Living Color, however, *was* the proverbial straw that broke the camel's back. It was the final blow that burst the dam open. And it was the first salvo in a war for equity and equality that continues to be fought today, on all fronts. Once *In Living Color* rang the bell, there was no un-ringing it anymore—not that anyone wanted to anyway, because they just happened to like the sound.

In Living Color was the forefather of Black sketch comedy shows like *The Chris Rock Show, Key & Peele, A Black Lady Sketch Show,* and *Chappelle's Show.*

Thanks to *In Living Color,* "Middle America" got used to welcoming Black men and women playing authentically Black characters—and speaking to authentically Black issues—into their homes via their television—so much so, in fact, that seeing non-white men and women on our television screens is the norm, not the exception. In fact, shows *without* diversity like *Friends* and *Girls*—considered by white media critics as the standard bearers for comedy—stand out in the twenty-first century for all the wrong reasons.

Leaving aside the experience that *In Living Color* alumnus Park had with the show, *Friends* is considered a modern-day sacred cow among the white critical *intelligentsia*—but even if you don't want to "woke-test" *Friends,* and consider it a product of its time like *In Living Color* was, it's worth noting that *In Living Color* had two white cast members in a sea of Black cast members, whereas *Friends* had exactly *zero* Black cast members in a sea of white cast members. Consider, too, that *Friends* was set in New York City—one of the most diverse cities on planet Earth—and yet, throughout the show's ten-year run, there were only *two* actors of color who got a story line or acted as more than "the help" in the Central Perk coffee shop: Lauren Tom's Julie and Aisha Tyler's Dr. Charlie Wheeler.

HBO's *Girls,* which is another modern-day sacred cow among the white critical *intelligentsia,* also has—among countless other problems—a problem with the lack of diversity in the show. Like *Friends, Girls* is set in New York City—in Brooklyn, no less—which is one of the most diverse cities on planet Earth, yet the core cast was all-white, and Black people were scattered throughout later episodes but never had a permanent story line.

Put simply, *In Living Color* got column space, in part, because it was a Black sketch comedy show—and because it was done at a time when such things were an anomaly. In the twenty-first century, when a show of *any* stripe lacks diversity, it causes an outcry among people on social media—even among those who *don't* live in diverse cities like New York City or Los Angeles—because today's television watchers grew up in a time where they were used to seeing Black—and Asian, and Latino, and Native/First Nations—people on television.

You can thank *In Living Color* for that.

The *Super Bowl Halftime Show* has become a spectacle—more people tune in to the halftime show than they do the actual game itself, even if they're sports fans. In 2017, 117.5 million people tuned in to watch Lady Gaga perform at the *Super Bowl Halftime Show*, compared to 111.3 million people who tuned in to the actual Super Bowl.

The game, itself, is considered the biggest television event of the year, which generates millions of dollars—and, as of 2019, *billions* of dollars—in ad revenue for what amounts to a little under one hour of actual airtime in commercials. In 2021, it was revealed that NBC was commanding $6 million for a thirty-second commercial. That was a 9.1 percent increase over CBS's demand for $5.5 million for thirty seconds. The 2021 Super Bowl also generated a record-breaking $545 million in revenue.

You can thank *In Living Color* for all of that.

Hip-hop is no longer a "niche" musical sound—it's an integral part of our everyday life. It's used to sell everything from vegetables to automobiles, and its vernacular has been adopted by children and adults alike.

You can, in part, thank *In Living Color* for all of that.

And even in the rare instances when *In Living Color* was too raw for TV—even when they offended the status quo with their tackling of such touchy subjects as date rape, race, microaggressions, queer issues, disabilities, and the fight for equality *and* equity—they still managed to be funny by *all* standards, even if the sketch would never make it to air today.

And the reason *In Living Color* was funny, even when it was too raw for TV—and the reason *In Living Color* is funny today, thirty-three years to the day after its initial broadcast on network television—is because, despite the strides we *think* we have made in social equity and equality, we still have a long way to go before things can truly be the way they should be.

If *In Living Color* is still funny more than thirty years after its initial broadcast, it's because *In Living Color* is still true more than thirty years after its initial broadcast.

Ultimately, *In Living Color* is more than just a sketch comedy show—it's a cultural touchstone, it's a watershed moment in pop culture, and it's the butterfly effect that forever changed the look, the feel, and the face of television.

But there's also a larger lesson to be learned here throughout the critical exegesis and the celebration of all the contributions *In Living Color* has made to the American zeitgeist as we know it: the importance of family and loyalty, the strength of never compromising yourself and your values, and the value of persistence and believing in yourself and your dreams.

When Keenen first lighted out to California, his goal was a singular one: "getting his family out of the projects," in his words. He knew that comedy would be the vehicle by which this goal would be achieved—and though he initially thought he would make his fame and fortune in films, he took a little detour to get there, and that detour changed the world. But it also changed his family's life: four of his siblings followed him out west and established careers of their own in the entertainment industry, but they always "came back home" in a manner of speaking, consistently working together on projects in some way or another. And were it not for their big brother laying the groundwork—well, they *might* have been successful, but statistically speaking, it would have been highly unlikely. But thanks to their big brother's efforts, they had financial and career stability, and today, the Wayans family is a legacy show business family— an honor previously only given to white families like the Barrymores and the Fondas—whose work is instantly recognizable and profitable, and whose next generation can enjoy the fruits of their forefathers' labor. To date, Keenen alone has generated more than $1 billion in gross box office receipts and has created an overall net worth of $300 million for his family—an impossible feat to conquer by every standard, made even more remarkable by Keenen's origin story and the subsequent challenges he overcame.

During the battle for the soul of *In Living Color*, Keenen tried everything in his power to hold on to the show he created. He knew it would, eventually, be a losing battle—but he also knew his moral compass wouldn't allow him to simply take it lying down. And when he ultimately lost the battle, he knew the only way to win the war was to leave, take his family with him, and let the show die the ignoble death it deserved—and that's exactly what it did. He never

The inaugural cast of *In Living Color* (left to right): Jim Carrey, Kim Coles, Keenen Ivory Wayans, Damon Wayans, T'Keyah Keymáh, David Alan Grier, Kim Wayans, Tommy Davidson, Kelly Coffield. *Fox/Photofest © Fox*

once considered the possibility of bowing down before people who didn't have his, or his family's, best interests at heart—even if it meant the downfall of his once-mighty show. Sacrificing *In Living Color* was worth it, to him, as long as he and his family were okay—and that willingness to protect his family at all costs is remarkable in a business where men and women, in equal measure, seem all too happy to sacrifice their most vulnerable family members to the fickle god of fame.

But most important, the lesson to be learned here—a lesson to be learned regardless of one's color, but a lesson that's especially pertinent to historically marginalized races—is that when the doors you're knocking on won't open despite your best efforts, when everything you've ever worked for falls flat, and when you're not invited to a seat at the table . . . you build your own table, and then you invite your family and true friends to feast with you.

And that's exactly what Keenen did . . . and in so doing, he invited all of us to do the same thing: to be authentic in our method of expression, to remain true to ourselves and our belief systems, to never surrender—even when the tide has turned against you—and, above all else . . .

To do what you want to do . . . in living color.

Ladies and Gentlemen, the Musical Performances

By the second season of *In Living Color*, it had become one of the hottest shows on television. Celebrities of all stripes would stop by the set—everyone from Irish rebel-rock singer Sinead O'Connor to action star Bruce Willis and *Cheers* star Kirstie Alley[1]—to hang out with the cast and crew, enjoy the show, or even participate in the sketches.

But it was only when the show began inviting musical guests to close out the show that *In Living Color* took on a completely different dimension. The musical guests were all—at the time—rising superstars in the hip-hop world, and they would go on to become legends in the game.

The live musical performances on *In Living Color* were nothing like the live musical performances on *Saturday Night Live*, which were—at the time—chock full of nostalgia acts and nowhere near as exciting as what was offered on *In Living Color*.

But by bringing these hot, talented acts to prime time, hip-hop continued to make its way into the mainstream, and it wouldn't be long before other sketch shows—including *Saturday Night Live*—would eventually follow. If you know one—or more—of these names, and recognize them as legends in the game, you can thank—in no small part—*In Living Color* for pumping them into your parents' and grandparents' living rooms every Sunday night on Fox.

Queen Latifah feat. Flavor Flav
Season 2, Episode 1
"Mama Gave Birth to the Soul Children"

Monie Love
Season 2, Episode 4
"Monie in the Middle"

Heavy D and the Boyz
Season 2, Episode 6
"Theme from *In Living Color*"[2]

3rd Bass
Season 2, Episode 9
"Product of the Environment"

D-Nice[3]
Season 2, Episode 10
"Scott Made Me Funky"/"Call Me D-Nice" Medley

Nikki D[4]
Season 2, Episode 11
"Lettin' Off Steam"

Rich Nice[5]
Season 2, Episode 13
"Outstanding"

Leaders of the New School[6]
Season 2, Episode 16
"Case of the PTA"

Another Bad Creation[7]
Season 2, Episode 18
"Iesha"

KRS-One
Season 2, Episode 19
"The Bridge Is Over"[8]

Public Enemy[9]
Season 2, Episode 22
"Security of the First World"/"Black Steel in the Hour of Chaos"/"Buck
Whylin'"/"Fight the Power"/"911 Is a Joke" Medley

The Afros
Season 2, Episode 23
"This Jam's for You"

Leaders of the New School
Season 3, Episode 2
"Teachers, Don't Teach Us Nonsense!"

Nice & Smooth
Season 3, Episode 6
"Hip Hop Junkies"/"How to Flow" Medley

Big Daddy Kane
Season 3, Episode 8
"Ooh, Aah, Nah-Nah-Nah"

Queen Latifah
Season 3, Episode 9
"Latifah's Had It Up 2 Here"

A Tribe Called Quest
Season 3, Episode 14
"Check the Rhime"

Eric B. and Rakim
Season 3, Episode 19
"Know the Ledge"

Shabba Ranks feat. Maxi Priest
Season 3, Episode 20
"Housecall"

Black Sheep
Season 3, Episode 22
"The Choice Is Yours"

Kriss Kross
Season 3, Episode 23
"Jump"

Jodeci
Season 3, Episode 26
"Xs We Share"

Heavy D and the Boyz feat. Tupac Shakur and Flavor Flav
Season 3, Episode 28
"You Can't See What I Can See"

MC Lyte
Season 3, Episode 29
"Poor Georgie"

Redman
Season 4, Episode 1
"Blow Your Mind"

Gang Starr feat. Nice & Smooth
Season 4, Episode 3
"DWYCK"

A.D.O.R.
Season 4, Episode 4
"Let It All Hang Out"

Grand Puba
Season 4, Episode 5
"360 Degrees (What Goes around Comes Around)"

Wreckx-n-Effect with Teddy Riley
Season 4, Episode 7
"Rump Shaker"

Pete Rock & CL Smooth
Season 4, Episode 8
"Straighten It Out"

Mary J. Blige
Season 4, Episode 9
"Reminisce"

Jamie Foxx
Season 4, Episode 11[10]
"This Christmas"

Digable Planets
Season 4, Episode 12
"Rebirth of Slick (Cool Like That)"

Father MC
Season 4, Episode 13
"Everything's Gonna Be Alright"

Arrested Development
Season 4, Episode 17
"Mr. Wendal"

Naughty by Nature
Season 4, Episode 21
"Hip Hop Hooray"

Heavy D and the Boyz[11]
Season 4, Episode 22
"Truthful"

Prince Markie Dee & the Soul Convention
Season 4, Episode 24
"Typical Reasons (Swing My Way)"

Da Youngsta's
Season 4, Episode 25
"Crewz Pop"

Showbiz and A.G. with Dres
Season 4, Episode 27
"Bounce Ta This"

Onyx
Season 4, Episode 29
"Slam"

The Pharcyde
Season 4, Episode 31
"Passin' Me By"

Guru with N'Dea Davenport
Season 5, Episode 6
"Trust Me"

Leaders of the New School
Season 5, Episode 7
"What's Next"

Lords of the Underground
Season 5, Episode 8
"Chief Rocka"/"Here Come the Lords" Medley

Us3
Season 5, Episode 11
"Cantaloop (Flip Fantasia)"

Patra feat. Lyn Collins
Season 5, Episode 12
"Think (About It)"

Simple E
Season 5, Episode 20
"Play My Funk"

Eazy-E with Dresta and B. G. Knocc Out
Season 5, Episode 21
"Real Compton City G's"

Souls of Mischief
Season 5, Episode 22
"93 Til Infinity"

Boss
Season 5, Episode 23
"Progress of Elimination"

Meshell Ndegeocello
Season 5, Episode 25
"If That's Your Boyfriend (He Wasn't Last Night)"

To Be Continued
Season 5, Episode 26[12]
"One on One"

Notes

Introduction

1. Pew Research Center, Journalism and Media Staff, "The American Newsroom," Pew Research Center's Journalism Project, Pew Research Center, May 30, 2020, https://www.pewresearch.org/journalism/2006/10/05/the-american-newsroom/.

2. John J. O'Connor, "TV: Pryor's Art Is Strong Stuff, 'Soap' Weak," *New York Times*, September 13, 1977.

3. Shalwah Evans, "United States House of Representatives Passes the CROWN Act," *Essence*, September 23, 2020, https://www.essence.com/beauty/house-of-representatives-passes-crown-act/.

4. William Manning Marable, "Rediscovering Malcolm's Life: A Historian's Adventure in Living History," in *The Portable Malcolm X Reader*, ed. Garrett Felber (New York: Penguin, 2013), 580–83.

5. *Message to the Grassroots* was also sampled by Living Colour in their hit song "Cult of Personality."

6. This sort of "armchair liberalism" was explored to great effect in Jordan Peele's 2017 award-winning horror flick, *Get Out*. Bradley Whitford, who played Dean Armitage, told Daniel Kaluuya's Chris Washington that he would, indeed, vote for Barack Obama for a third term if given the opportunity—as if a third-term vote for Obama would have somehow precluded the fact that Armitage harvested Black bodies hoping to obtain eternal youth.

7. Given the current situation in the United States regarding abortion—and *Roe*—it will be interesting to see if things do, indeed, revert back to the 1970s when the states determined whether a woman had a right to bodily autonomy—and how many states will actually grant women that right. With the 2022 overturning of *Roe* in a 6–3 ruling by the Supreme Court, many states have already threatened to severely restrict, if not outright ban, abortion—even in the extreme cases of rape, incest, and/or a credible threat to the mother's life.

8. Andrew Kohut, "From the Archives: 50 Years Ago, Mixed Views about Civil Rights but Support for Selma Demonstrators," Pew Research Center, July 28, 2020, https://www.pewresearch.org/fact-tank/2020/01/16/50-years-ago-mixed-views-about -civil-rights-but-support-for-selma-demonstrators/.

9. Laura Santhanam, "How Has Public Opinion about Abortion Changed since *Roe v. Wade?*," PBS, July 20, 2018, https://www.pbs.org/newshour/health/how-has-public -opinion-about-abortion-changed-since-roe-v-wade.

10. Micah Sierra "Katt" Williams earned an audience almost overnight when he appeared as "Money Mike" in *Friday after Next*, and he was the obvious choice for the voice of A Pimp Named Slickback on *The Boondocks*. But with his hilarious depictions of Black life—first seen in *Let a Playa Play*—he seemed remote and inaccessible to most of white America, unlike, say, Kevin Hart (whose comedy dealt in more topical mainstream matters) or Chris Rock (who took frequent aim at the political establishment, which was easy pickings at the time his career was at its peak).

11. America seemed perfectly okay with *The Flip Wilson Show*, however. Though largely forgotten today, *The Flip Wilson Show* aired from 1970 until 1974, and was once one of the highest-rated shows in the Nielsen ratings. It was also the first successful variety show hosted by a Black man. But just two years after its debut, *The Flip Wilson Show* was knocked out of the top spot by *The Waltons*, with CBS VP of Programming Fred Silverman remarking that he was glad that happened because the audience for *The Flip Wilson Show* was very "urban," whereas *The Waltons* appealed to "rural America." Given the subject matter of the respective shows, Silverman's euphemisms were hardly thinly veiled. But, in contrast to *The Richard Pryor Show*'s subversive humor, *The Flip Wilson Show* was family-friendly fare, with the most "controversial" (and popular) character being "Geraldine Jones," a Sapphire caricature that went on to inspire Martin Lawrence's "Sheneneh Jenkins" on *Martin*, Tyler Perry's "Madea Simmons" in countless plays and films featuring the meddling matriarch, and of course, Jamie Foxx's "Ugly Wanda" on *In Living Color*.

12. James Boyd, "Nixon's Southern Strategy," *New York Times*, May 17, 1970, https:// www.nytimes.com/1970/05/17/archives/nixons-southern-strategy-its-all-in-the-charts .html.

Chapter 1

1. "Keenen Ivory Wayans," Television Academy, accessed August 30, 2021, https:// www.emmys.com/bios/keenen-ivory-wayans.

2. Founded in Harlem, New York, Drake's manufactures baked goods that are a popular snack food among children raised in the Five Boroughs of New York City. Drake's was an exclusive staple to the Northeast market until 2016, when it also began being introduced to the Mid-Atlantic and Southeastern regions. Yodels, Ho-Hos, Funny Bones, and Devil Dogs are just a few of the many delicious confections offered by the company.

3. "Keenen Ivory Wayans."

4. Harry DiPrinzio, "At NYCHA's Fulton Houses, a Bitter Divide over the Future of the Development," City Limits, August 27, 2019, https://citylimits.org/2019/08/21/at-nychas-fulton-houses-a-bitter-divide-over-the-future-of-the-development/.

5. NYPR Archive Collections, "Statement on Harlem Riot: WNYC," WNYC, July 22, 1964, https://www.wnyc.org/story/statement-on-harlem-riot/.

6. "Keenen Ivory Wayans."

7. Although often used interchangeably, "the projects" and "the hood" are colloquialisms that refer to two different things. "The projects" refers to the actual subsidized housing provided by the city or the state. "The hood," on the other hand, is shorthand slang for "the neighborhood," but in common parlance, it's become a derogatory term to refer to the poor, ethnic minorities and "undesirables" who live in said projects, and the accompanying lifestyle characterized by poverty, violence, scholastic truancy, illegal business dealings, and teenage pregnancy/unwed motherhood. When describing his childhood, it's important to note that Keenen Ivory Wayans never uses the phrase "the hood" to describe himself, his family, or his surroundings.

8. Nicholas Dagen Bloom and Matthew Gordon Lasner, Affordable Housing in New York: The People, Places, and Policies That Transformed a City (Princeton, NJ: Princeton University Press, 2016), 2.

9. Bloom and Lasner, Affordable Housing in New York.

10. "Keenen Ivory Wayans."

11. The full quote, which is from a 1957 Cosmopolitan interview with Allen, reads as follows: "Man jokes about the things that depress him, but he usually waits till a certain amount of time has passed. It must have been a tragedy when Judge Crater disappeared, but everybody jokes about it now. I guess you can make a mathematical formula out of it. Tragedy plus time equals comedy" ("'Comedy Is Tragedy plus Time,'" Quote Investigator, February 17, 2020, https://quoteinvestigator.com/2013/06/25/comedy-plus/).

12. Alexandra Michel, "The Science of Humor Is No Laughing Matter," Association for Psychological Science, March 31, 2017, https://www.psychologicalscience.org/observer/the-science-of-humor-is-no-laughing-matter.

13. "Keenen Ivory Wayans."

14. Dacher Keltner and George A. Bonanno, "A Study of Laughter and Dissociation: Distinct Correlates of Laughter and Smiling during Bereavement," Journal of Personality and Social Psychology 73, no. 4 (1997): 699, https://doi.org/10.1037/0022-3514.73.4.687.

15. "Keenen Ivory Wayans."

16. Psychology Today Staff, "Humor | Psychology Today," Psychology Today, accessed November 6, 2021, https://www.psychologytoday.com/us/basics/humor.

17. "Keenen Ivory Wayans."

18. "Keenen Ivory Wayans."

19. "Keenen Ivory Wayans."

20. "History of the Improv," Improv, accessed December 9, 2021, https://improv.com/history/.

21. "Keenen Ivory Wayans."

22. By no means is this meant to imply that Keenen denied his Blackness when he stepped onstage. To the contrary: then, as now, Keenen was—and is—unapologetically

Black. Rather, this is meant to show how the audience—especially its white members—didn't view him as someone speaking solely to the Black audience members, but to *all* audience members regardless of their background.

23. "Keenen Ivory Wayans."

24. Based on the true story of Diana Ross and the Supremes, *Sparkle* also starred *Miami Vice* star Philip Michael Thomas and *A Different World* star Mary Alice, with Curtis Mayfield serving as the composer and producer of the film's score. Though the film was a box office disappointment, it eventually developed a cult following and remains popular to this day. It was also remade in 2012, with Jordin Sparks taking over Irene Cara's role, and featuring Whitney Houston in her final film role.

25. The episode also guest-starred Dominique Dunne—daughter of journalist Dominick Dunne and sister of acclaimed actor Griffin Dunne—who was best known for her role in *Poltergeist*, and who was murdered by her abusive ex-boyfriend, John Thomas Sweeney, less than one month after the episode aired.

26. "Keenen Ivory Wayans."

27. Mickey Rose, writer, *The Tonight Show Starring Johnny Carson*, season 21, episode "Sean Connery / Keenen Ivory Wayans / Tania Maria," aired October 5, 1983, on NBC, https://www.imdb.com/title/tt5340482/?ref_=ttep_ep139.

28. "Keenen Ivory Wayans."

29. In 2014, shortly before Keenen would join the rest of the Wayans brothers on a world tour, he'd met a man who had a copy of his first-ever appearance on *The Tonight Show Starring Johnny Carson* and showed it to him. At that point in his life, Keenen said he'd "lost sight" of the joy of making people laugh. Seeing his debut performance on *The Tonight Show Starring Johnny Carson* reminded him that he needed to be "that guy" again ("Keenen Ivory Wayans").

30. "Keenen Ivory Wayans."

31. "Keenen Ivory Wayans."

32. While the late John Witherspoon was revered in comedy circles, his appearance in *Hollywood Shuffle* wasn't his "big break." That wouldn't come until he appeared in the *Friday* film franchise created by rapper/actor Ice Cube and DJ Pooh, whose first film was released in 1995. In mainstream media, Witherspoon is known for voicing Robert Jedediah "Granddad" Freeman in the hit 2005 cartoon series *The Boondocks*, opposite Regina King's Huey and Riley Freeman.

33. "Keenen Ivory Wayans."

34. Rita Kempley, "*The January Man*," *Washington Post*, January 13, 1989. Writing for the *Washington Post*, Rita Kempley called *The January Man* "a damp sock of a movie that makes you wish for a leap year."

35. Writing for the *New York Times*, Janet Maslin said, "*I'm Gonna Git You Sucka* is a lively but uncertain mixture of nostalgia, silliness and genuinely unpredictable humor" (Janet Maslin, "Review/Film; *Sucka*, a Sendup," *New York Times*, January 13, 1989).

36. Writing for the *Chicago Sun-Times*, Roger Ebert compared the film to Townsend's *Hollywood Shuffle*, and pointed out that while Townsend was funny, Keenen is "not half as funny, and not half as acute in the way he skewers black stereotypes" (Roger Ebert, "*I'm Gonna Git You Sucka* Movie Review," RogerEbert.com, December 14, 1988, https://www.rogerebert.com/reviews/im-gonna-git-you-sucka-1988).

37. "Keenen Ivory Wayans."

38. Mara Reinstein, "'We Were Warped Out of Our Minds': *In Living Color* Stars Recall Fox Censors, Spike Lee's Disdain in Dishy Oral History," *Hollywood Reporter*, July 10, 2019, https://www.hollywoodreporter.com/movies/movie-features/living-color-oral -history-fox-censors-spike-lees-disdain-1219192/.

39. "Keenen Ivory Wayans."

Chapter 2

1. "Homey don't play that!"

2. In addition to starring in *Hollywood Shuffle* and *I'm Gonna Git You Sucka*, Damon had a breakthrough role in the Eddie Murphy comedy vehicle *Beverly Hills Cop*, which was released in 1984. He played the "Banana Man," an effeminate gay man, elements of which could be seen in his subsequent depiction of Blaine Edwards in the "Men on Film" sketches on *In Living Color*. He also starred in *Roxanne*, opposite Steve Martin, and in *Earth Girls Are Easy*, costarring Jim Carrey.

3. On March 15, 1981—with Griffin Dunne as the host, and Roseanne Cash as the musical guest—he performed the sketch that got him fired: "Mr. Monopoly," which was supposed to be a send-up of *Miami Vice*. The premise of the sketch was that "Mr. Monopoly," played by Jon Lovitz, was bailing out a presumptive drug dealer, and Damon—who played opposite Randy Quaid—improvised his Ricardo Tubbs–like character as an effeminate gay man in the vein of Blaine Edwards of "Men on Film." It was the last sketch of the evening—and more's the better, because the sketch was sophomoric and juvenile—and after it was over, Damon reportedly got harangued by *SNL* head honcho Lorne Michaels, before he was unceremoniously informed that he was fired.

4. Mara Reinstein, "'We Were Warped Out of Our Minds': *In Living Color* Stars Recall Fox Censors, Spike Lee's Disdain in Dishy Oral History," *Hollywood Reporter*, July 10, 2019, https://www.hollywoodreporter.com/movies/movie-features/living-color-oral -history-fox-censors-spike-lees-disdain-1219192/.

5. Micaela Hood, "The New Damon Wayans," *South Florida Sun-Sentinel*, November 10, 2013, https://www.sun-sentinel.com/entertainment/events/sf-go-damon -wayans-improv-111013-20131107-story.html.

6. Grier had a voice-over role in the 1981 radio adaptation of *Star Wars*, where he played a small role as a nameless X-wing pilot.

7. "*In Living Color* 25 Year Reunion," YouTube, 2019, https://www.youtube.com /watch?v=QQSM7ltyFfY.

8. Shortly before Davidson auditioned for *In Living Color*, he appeared as the warm-up comedian for Robert Townsend's HBO comedy special.

9. "*In Living Color* 25 Year Reunion."

10. Coles only lasted on the show for one season. In 1993, shortly before she signed on to a Fox show called *Single Life* (which would eventually become *Living Single*), she flat-out denied rumors that her tenure on *In Living Color* ended due to an affair gone wrong with Keenen. She did, however, claim that Keenen had a "narrow-minded" vision,

and that he was very "male-oriented." Coles also claimed that Keenen would deny her roles, preferring instead to give prime parts to his sister Kim and Coffield. Keenen never commented on Coles's claims at the time, and to this day, he has not spoken one word about her to the press.

11. From 1957 until 1963, NBC's tagline was "NBC: Living Color." Unlike other networks, NBC was at the forefront of the color TV revolution because its parent company, RCA, was the number one manufacturer of color televisions at a time when black-and-white televisions were the norm.

12. Reinstein, "'We Were Warped Out of Our Minds.'"

13. Under Chernin's tutelage, Fox went from a fledgling network to a multimedia powerhouse. By the time Chernin left the network in 2009, Fox and its various networks—including Fox News Channel, FX, Fox Sports Net, Fox Movie Channel, National Geographic Television, SPEED, and the Fox Reality Channel—were in more than 400 million homes. After Chernin left the network, he founded the Chernin Group, which is best known as the parent company of anime company Crunchyroll and the online dude-bro basecamp Barstool Sports.

14. The industry term is "development hell," and today, it's also used in the software industry about games and programs that never quite make it to production for a wide variety of reasons. When a project is abandoned after it has been in development hell, it's taken as a tax write-off by the studio and chalked up to the "cost of doing business." It's not immediately clear whether *In Living Color* was destined to meet that fate were it not for Keenen and his team's scrappiness and sheer force of will, but it wouldn't be out of the scope of possibility.

15. This concern by white executives for the welfare of their Black audiences was progressive, even for its time. But considering what Fox would eventually become infamous for—and considering the noxious "alternative truths" their news division is known for promoting today—this concern was downright *revolutionary*.

16. "*In Living Color* 25 Year Reunion."

17. Emma Dibdin, "*In Living Color* Creator, Cast Reflect on Show's Impact: 'America Needed Something New,'" *Hollywood Reporter*, April 27, 2019, https://www.hollywoodreporter.com/tv/tv-news/living-color-creators-reflect-shows-impact-25th-anniversary-1205371/.

18. Annie Flanders, ed., "*In Living Color*," *Details*, 1989.

19. After the third season, the song was remixed and called "Cause That's the Way You Livin' When You're in Living Color," and it was also by Heavy D and the Boyz.

20. DJ Twist (aka Leroy Casey) took over DJ duties in the show's third season, and Shawn moved up to "featured" player status.

21. Today, Carrie Ann Inaba is best known for being a judge on ABC's hit reality competition show *Dancing with the Stars*. But before she judged routines, she danced them: in addition to being a "Fly Girl," Inaba was a dancer for the likes of David Bowie, Prince, and Madonna. She also had a minor singing career in Japan and released hit singles like "Party Girl," "Yume No Senaka," and "Be Your Girl."

22. Monica Rizzo, "*Dancing with the Stars*' Carrie Ann Inaba," *People*, October 16, 2006.

23. Almost 23 million people tuned in to watch the premiere episode of *In Living Color*.

24. Not to be confused with the rapper and producer Andre "Dr. Dre" Young, Andre "Doctor Dre" Brown is a Long Island, New York, native who got his start as a radio DJ at Adelphi University before graduating to WQHT—aka Hot 97—in New York City and was Ed Lover's costar on *Yo! MTV Raps*.

25. There was also a Saturday morning edition of *Yo! MTV Raps*, which clearly got more viewers.

26. "Fly Girl" by Grandmaster Flash and the Furious Five, released in 1988, was infinitely more popular. But the "Fly Girl" was forever immortalized in hip-hop culture in 1990, between *In Living Color* and LL COOL J's megahit "Around the Way Girl," which peaked at number 9 on the *Billboard* Hot 100 charts and became LL COOL J's first top 10 single. "Around the Way Girl" also went to number 1 on the *Billboard* Rap charts in December 1990, where it stayed for four weeks.

27. "*In Living Color*: Back in Step with the Fly Girls," YouTube, 2004, https://www.youtube.com/watch?v=eMbgcdem8XU.

28. "*In Living Color*: Back in Step with the Fly Girls."

29. "*In Living Color*: Back in Step with the Fly Girls."

30. Reinstein, "'We Were Warped Out of Our Minds.'"

31. Michael Quintanilla, "*In Living Color* Fly Girls Start a Fashion Buzz," *Baltimore Sun*, August 7, 1991.

32. Quintanilla, "*In Living Color* Fly Girls Start a Fashion Buzz."

33. "*In Living Color*: Back in Step with the Fly Girls."

34. Nelson George, "How Rosie Perez Got Her Start on *Soul Train*," *Esquire*, March 24, 2014, https://www.esquire.com/entertainment/tv/a27953/rosie-perez-soul-train/.

35. Dvora Myers, "Diary of a Fly Girl: Rosie Perez Tells Her Story," *Elle*, March 25, 2014.

36. "*In Living Color*: Back in Step with the Fly Girls."

37. Tai Gooden, "The Lasting Impact of *In Living Color*'s Fly Girls," Nerdist, April 9, 2021, https://nerdist.com/article/fly-girls-in-living-color-impact-hip-hop-dance -fashion/.

38. In 1991, the Apple MacIntosh PowerBook—the first ergonomic laptop computer of its kind—cost $2,299. When adjusted for twenty-first-century inflation, the computer would cost more than $4,000 in today's money. By 2015, the Apple MacBook had dropped to a measly $1,299.

39. Reinstein, "'We Were Warped Out of Our Minds.'"

Chapter 3

1. Firestein would become best known for his work on *The Drew Carey Show*.

2. Veasey is best known for her work on *CSI*, including *CSI: Cyber* and *CSI: NY*. She also served as the executive producer for *The Gregory Hines Show*.

3. Before he died in 2002, at the age of forty-six, Greg Fields was known for his work on such shows as *Full House.*

4. After his tenure on *In Living Color,* Wilmore went on to write for shows like *The Simpsons* and *The PJs.* He died on January 30, 2021, in Pomona, California.

5. Larry Wilmore would go on to become an executive producer for the hit ABC comedy *Black-ish* and the cocreator of the super-smash HBO series *Insecure,* the vehicle that rocketed Issa Rae into superstardom.

6. Bahr went on to work extensively with comedian Jamie Kennedy, penning the vehicle *Malibu's Most Wanted* and subsequently becoming the head writer on *The Jamie Kennedy Experiment.*

7. Small went on to write for *Lopez Tonight* (starring George Lopez) and *In the Flow with Affion Crockett*; he also wrote the script for the film *Bad Grandpa.*

8. In addition to being one of the head writers and comedians on *The Richard Pryor Show,* the late, great Paul Mooney was instrumental in cocreating some of *In Living Color*'s most memorable skits, including skits featuring "Anton Jackson" and "Homey D. Clown." But perhaps his most memorable skit was the "Duke & Cornbread Turner" skit, which featured Jamie Foxx as Cornbread Turner and a dead dog named Duke auditioning for the police force. The skit was so funny that Foxx himself consistently broke character and laughed throughout the skit.

9. At the time that Keenen and Damon did the "Do-It-Yourself Milli Vanilli Kit" skit in 1990, the scandal involving the band's lip-synching hadn't yet hit the news wires. In 1997, however, Fabrice Morvan told VH1's *Behind the Music* that both he and his Milli Vanilli bandmate, Rob Pilatus, caught the skit—with the punchline, "so act now, because we are almost out of style!"—and realized the "clock was ticking for them" from that point forward (Gay Rosenthal, writer, *Behind the Music,* season 1, episode 1, "Milli Vanilli,"aired August 17, 1997, on VH1, https://www.imdb.com/title/tt0394380/full credits/?ref_=tt_cl_sm). Depending on your point of view, this skit is either hilarious and prescient, or it's hilarious and extremely problematic—because this skit was the first domino that fell in a series of tragic events that would ultimately culminate with Rob Pilatus's death of an accidental overdose in 1998, at the age of thirty-three. To be fair to both Keenen and Damon, *and* Milli Vanilli, there was absolutely no way the Wayans brothers could have possibly known the extent of the scandal—they were merely poking fun at a pop group that had grown ubiquitous and annoying—and it's doubtful that either Keenen or Damon would have performed the skit if they knew it was going to be the first domino in a series of events that culminated in tragedy.

10. White rappers wouldn't gain respect from their Black peers until Marshall Bruce Mathers—better known as Eminem—dropped *The Slim Shady LP* in 1999, and even *he* garners his fair share of critical fire. (And to be fair, he deserves both praise and criticism in equal measure.)

11. Sanders Greenfield, dir., *The Black List: Volume One* (New York: HBO, August 2008).

12. In the 1990s, "portable car phones" came as optional equipment in luxury cars. Cell phones as we know them today were nonexistent, save for in the hands of a white-collar worker who would only turn them on in the event of an emergency because the cost to use them was so exorbitant. Most found in BMWs and Mercedes-Benzes, the

portable car phones broadcast in 800 mHz, and the cost ran anywhere from $1,000 to $3,000 for the equipment. When adjusted for inflation, the phone equipment would cost upward of $10,000 in twenty-first-century money. That cost was exclusive of the phone contract, which charged callers by the minute, and the starting price was 50 cents a minute for a domestic call (almost $4 a minute in twenty-first-century money, when adjusted for inflation).

13. In the early 1980s, satellite dishes cost upward of $10,000. If you could afford one, you would get every single channel it could pick up and subsequently transmit—including HBO—for free thereafter. By the time 1990 rolled around, though, HBO and other movie channels had scrambled their channels, so they couldn't all be picked up by satellites. Subscription services (including most of the movie channels), however, were available on both satellite and cable, but such services were cost prohibitive for the average working-class family at the time.

14. In 1992, at the height of his *In Living Color* fame, Damon wrote a film called *Mo'Money*, which starred himself alongside a pre–Fox News Stacey Dash, *The Rockford Files* actor Joe Santos, and his little brother Marlon. Although the film was critically excoriated, it debuted at number one at the box office, bringing home more than $12 million in box office receipts in its opening weekend, and eventually finished with more than $40 million in box office receipts.

15. Later, when Davidson would temporarily leave the show to enter rehab, Grier would serve as the "host" of the skit.

16. *Hidden Figures*, the film that featured theretofore unknown Black women who were instrumental in NASA's inaugural space launch, didn't come out until 2017. That same year, classrooms slowly began integrating lessons about women—both white *and* Black—and other marginalized groups who worked at NASA, often without credit and certainly without anywhere near the pay that their white male counterparts received. This skit took place seventeen years before that film—and one can't help but wonder how many Black astronauts tried out for the inaugural space flight and were summarily rejected based on the color of their skin.

17. Christine Winter, "Credit Cards Charge into the 90s," *Orlando Sentinel*, December 27, 1989.

18. Bill Rogers, in what would be his first PGA win.

19. Coffield's character is referencing Title 47, Section 223 of the United States Code, which states that anyone who knowingly "initiates the transmission of any comment, request, suggestion, proposal, image, or other communication, which is obscene or child pornography, with intent to abuse, threaten, or harass another person" is subject to a fine and up to two years of imprisonment. One would be hard-pressed to find anyone who enforces that law in the twenty-first century, given the nature of most communications today. But then again, it wouldn't be the first time that the law was unjustly applied to a Black man—especially since it's highly likely a white man in that same situation would escape prosecution altogether (how long did the Zodiac Killer evade justice?). Also, this reference is a testament to the sheer intelligence of the *In Living Color* writer's room, who had to know—and otherwise research—things like this without the benefit of Google or the internet.

20. Marion Barry was originally a key figure in the burgeoning civil rights movement, and his political star continued to rise as he became the second, and subsequently the fourth, mayor of Washington, DC. But in January 1990, his career took a turn for the worse when he was caught on camera smoking crack cocaine in a Ramada Inn hotel room and was arrested on federal drug charges as a result.

21. Hall's show consistently performed well in so-called urban markets, like Baltimore and Miami—and no one took Letterman or Leno to task for discussing the same topics.

22. This sketch featured Ellen Cleghorne, before she starred on *Saturday Night Live*, as a courtroom observer.

23. This sketch featured "scream queen" Danielle Harris as a teenage drug addict.

24. It's unclear how a movie about a Black man—and not just *any* Black man, but *Morgan Freeman*—performing in a role of a quasi–"Magical Negro" and a white woman performing a *grande dame* trope is supposed to be a watershed moment on par with Martin Luther King's march on Selma and the election of Barack Obama to the United States presidency, but that's late 1980s/early 1990s "race relations" logic for you.

25. Marlow Stern, "Spike Lee Blasts *Selma* Oscar Snubs: 'You Know What? F*ck 'Em,'" *Daily Beast*, July 12, 2017, https://www.thedailybeast.com/spike-lee-blasts-selma-oscar-snubs-you-know-what-fck-em.

26. Damon breaks character after he says this and starts chuckling lightly.

27. Wayne M. Blake and Carol A. Darling, "The Dilemmas of the African American Male," *Journal of Black Studies* 24, no. 4 (June 1994): 402–15, https://doi.org/10.1177/002193479402400403.

28. In the 1990s, one researcher noted that approximately 44 percent of all Black men in the United States were functionally illiterate, which meant that at the time that *In Living Color* was on the air, nearly *half* of all Black men watching the show lacked the literacy necessary for coping with most jobs and everyday situations. And because they lacked that basic ability to both read *and* comprehend what they were reading, it created a ripple effect of lower-paying jobs, which led to increased crime rates—since they needed money that they didn't have, and couldn't get, to survive—which led to increased incarceration rates.

29. Blake and Darling, "The Dilemmas of the African American Male," 402–3.

30. This sketch aired on Damon Wayans's last episode as a full-time cast member.

31. Damon Wayans was no longer a cast member at the time this sketch aired, so he was billed as a "special guest star."

32. Damon Wayans's last episode as a regular cast member was on May 17, 1992, at the end of season 3. When he appeared as Anton in this sketch, for what would be the final time, he was billed as a "special guest star."

33. Located south of downtown Los Angeles, Compton is best known, today, for birthing the "West Coast" sound of so-called gangsta rap thanks to N.W.A. But contrary to popular belief, Compton isn't just known for being the birthplace of prominent Black entertainers—and more specifically, Black rappers. Actor James Coburn and Krist Novoselic of Nirvana were both born and/or raised there. Even the Bush family—President George H. W. Bush, First Lady Barbara Bush, and President George W. Bush—lived in Compton in 1949, and Robin Bush (the eldest Bush daughter, who died from leukemia in 1953, just months before her fourth birthday) was born in Compton in

1949. That said, Compton also has a large Black American community, which is why the British press lobbed the "straight outta Compton" racially charged insult at Meghan Markle, Duchess of Sussex, when she began dating Prince Harry (even though Markle was born in Canoga Park, which is in the San Fernando Valley, and raised in Hollywood, which is one hour north of Compton *without* traffic—and as any SoCal native knows, there's *always* traffic).

34. Named for Robert William "Jheri" Redding and popularized when Comer Cottrell founded a company that manufactured at-home products that created the look, the Jheri Curl was a popular hairstyle among Black men in the late 1980s and early 1990s. The Jheri Curl was a "wash-and-wear" hairstyle, and easier to maintain than a hairstyle that was achieved by a chemical relaxer. But it gave the user a "glossy" and loosely curled look, and maintenance required the daily application of a "curl activator" spray and moisturizers, which were expensive and easily depleted—hence the "addiction." Michael Jackson wore a Jheri Curl on the cover of the *Thriller* album, and Samuel L. Jackson's character of Jules Winfield wore a Jheri Curl in the 1994 film *Pulp Fiction*. In the *In Living Color* universe, Keenen's character of Frenchie also had a Jheri Curl hairstyle. And one of Keenen's characters on *Hollywood Shuffle* was also called, fittingly enough, "Jeri Curl," and Townsend's character gets him to tell what he knows about a murder by withholding access to the activator.

35. This casting was a very interesting choice, because Davidson would end up leaving *In Living Color* in the middle of the show's fourth season to get treatment for ongoing substance abuse. Davidson credits Keenen, and other cast members of *In Living Color*, for "pulling him aside" and urging him to get help. "If it wasn't for me having good people around me, I'd be where Elvis [Presley] is, John Belushi is, [Chris] Farley. I'm grateful. I don't even trip," he said (Erika Marie, "Tommy Davidson Left *In Living Color* for Rehab, Says He Would Be Dead If He Hadn't," HotNewHipHop, January 30, 2020, https://www.hotnewhiphop.com/tommy-davidson-left-in-living-color-for-rehab-says-he-would-be-dead-if-he-hadnt-news.102336.html). Davidson would ultimately return to *In Living Color* in the show's fifth and final season.

36. The Jheri Curl products were notorious for staining everything they encountered, including pillowcases, furniture, and clothing. To prevent staining, Jheri Curl users would have to wear silk wraps or shower caps to "absorb" the oils.

37. This was a reference to a tragic fire that happened on January 27, 1984, while Michael Jackson was shooting a Pepsi commercial. At the time, Jackson had the infamous "Jheri Curl" hairstyle, and the subsequent burns on his scalp and face—which easily caught fire thanks to the products—left him permanently scarred.

38. John Voland, "Turner Defends Move to Colorize Films," *Los Angeles Times*, October 23, 1986.

39. "Because they're *mine*, and I can do what I want with them. Nyah nyah nyah!"

40. It's a play on Bogart's infamous line in the film, "of all the gin joints in all the towns in all the world, she walks into mine."

41. This was a send-up of the Charlie Chaplin classic film *The Kid*, which was released in 1921, and was Chaplin's first film as a director.

42. He came in third, behind Gary Hart and Walter Mondale, who ultimately won the Democratic nomination. Mondale would ultimately get decimated in the 1984

presidential election, after choosing Geraldine Ferraro as his running mate—and Mondale's campaign for president was bludgeoned to smithereens not due to him choosing a woman, but due to him choosing a woman whose husband had ties to the Mafia. This isn't to say that the 1980s were a progressive time for women in politics—to the contrary—but it is to suggest that the Mondale/Ferraro ticket may have had a fighting chance if Ferraro's husband didn't have less-than-savory connections to organized crime. One also can't help but wonder how much further along the United States would be, as a society, if the first woman vice president was elected in 1984 instead of 2020, when Kamala Harris would finally assume the mantle.

43. Steve Kornacki, "1984: Jesse Jackson's Run for the White House and the Rise of the Black Voter," NBC News, July 29, 2019, https://www.nbcnews.com/politics /elections/1984-jesse-jackson-s-run-white-house-rise-black-voter-n1029596.

44. This feels like a direct hat-tip to Richard Pryor's sketch about the first Black president.

45. Eerily, Obama's campaign slogan in the 2008 general election was, simply, "Hope." Lord Jamar probably has a few things to say about *In Living Color*'s "predictive programming," though if we're talking about Fox shows involved in "predictive programming" efforts, *The Simpsons* has *In Living Color* beat by a country mile. Maybe Obama was an *In Living Color* fan?

46. In real life, that title would go to Ronald Reagan.

47. In the Arab-speaking world, this "call and response" is a form of greeting, and the phrases mean "peace be upon you" and "peace be upon you as well," respectively. It was also the standard greeting between members of the Nation of Islam. In colloquial Arabic, *salaam* is sufficient in a greeting between familiars.

48. John J. O'Connor, "TV: Pryor's Art Is Strong Stuff, 'Soap' Weak," *New York Times*, September 13, 1977.

49. Jackson's platform featured an American infrastructure plan, reversing the Reaganomics plans of tax cuts for the rich, giving reparations to ADOS (American Descendants of Slavery), creating single-payer universal health care, applying stricter enforcement of the Voting Rights Act, and officially supporting Palestine as a sovereign nation—among other things. So, contrary to the vitriolic spewings of the "Bernie Bros," Bernie Sanders wasn't the first candidate to propose this platform, and assuming the American experiment continues to work, he won't be the last.

50. The depiction of the residents of the American South as slow and subliterate is a common trope in American popular media—so much so that there are several subtropes within the genre. Keenen portrayed Jackson as a combination of two American South tropes: the "Southern-fried genius," whose hayseed name and exaggerated drawl belies his intelligence, and the "Simple Country Lawyer," who talks in simple metaphors to make people think he's an idiot—only to bludgeon said people over the head with his above-average intelligence.

51. Erika Neddenien, "We Tracked down the Kid Vice President Dan Quayle Made Misspell 'Potato,'" BuzzFeed News, September 12, 2019, https://www.buzzfeednews .com/article/buzzfeednews/dan-quayle-potato-spelling.

52. The Mirage was notable because it was the first hotel developed by Steve Wynn, who would go on to become one of the most powerful hotel magnates in Las Vegas. In

January 2022, it was announced that it would be demolished as part of a larger renovation plan. As of this writing, the Hard Rock Group is poised to take over the spot, and a guitar-shaped, rock-themed hotel will stand in the place of the formerly luxurious hotel and casino.

53. This was Keenen Ivory Wayans's last episode as a cast member.

54. In *patois*, a "rude boy" is a teenager of lower- or working-class status who was also a juvenile delinquent that listened to ska music all day—basically, a synonym of a "bum," a "loser," and a "flop-about." The American analogue is the "greaser" of the 1950s, popularized by James Dean in *Rebel without a Cause*, who was a teenager of lower- or working-class status who was also a juvenile delinquent that listened to rock music all day.

55. Pronounced "bloodclot," this is a *patois* colloquialism for a menstrual pad. Used in this context, *bloodclaat* implies that the receiver of the insult is a despicable, unpleasant, worthless person—a piece of excrement, basically. Alternatively, "what di bloodclaat" is also commonly used as an expletive and is the equivalent of saying "what the [f-word]" in American English.

56. Maybe this should serve as motivation in Hollywood to have more diversity in their hiring process—if only so the Powers That Be could avoid getting proverbial egg on their face *and* the inevitable fines from the FCC when one too many *patois* swear words get through the gates.

57. It was only when West Indians began writing into the network—remember, this was before the internet and social media, so criticism wasn't in real time—to inform the Fox censors about what the Hedleys were really saying that the Powers That Be began getting stricter with what could, and couldn't, be said in Jamaican *patois* or any other language. It's highly implied that had the community not started "snitching," the *In Living Color* cast would have gotten increasingly raucous with their use of *patois* insults—which would *definitely* have been "too raw for TV." But Grier hilariously parodied the Fox censors and their consternation at the Tribeca Film Festival in 2019.

58. Sam Machkovech, "The Best Game-Breaking Speedruns of Summer Games Done Quick 2020," Ars Technica, August 24, 2020, https://arstechnica.com/gaming/2020/08/the-best-game-breaking-speedruns-of-summer-games-done-quick-2020/.

59. Machkovech, "The Best Game-Breaking Speedruns of Summer Games Done Quick 2020."

60. This is the most unrealistic part of the sketch, because everybody knows white people don't season their food, and Homey would not have had an enjoyable culinary experience at all. It would have been hilarious, however, for Homey to recount the story of getting into the white establishment, only to find that while the Anglo-Saxons conquered nearly the entire physical world to get their hands on spices, their descendants found salt "too spicy," thus resulting in the culinary equivalent of passing off prison food as *haute cuisine*.

61. It's not immediately clear if the hassling came because of Homey's ridiculous clown costume, the maître d's racism, or both.

62. Damon using "snowflake" in this context and at that time is a bit of a curiosity, considering that in modern parlance, "snowflake" refers to a person who has an overinflated sense of uniqueness, is easily offended, and has an unwarranted sense of entitlement. But whether used to snark on the maître d's whiteness—as it was in the 1990s—or

on his lousy personality, as it is in modern parlance, the reference has several layers that work, and is a further testament to Damon's genius as a comic.

63. The sketch was called "The Angry Black Comic," which began, "Good evening, white people. On my way down here tonight, I killed three white people. Oh, you ain't laughing? Then you would have been dying."

64. "Damon Wayans on the Inspiration behind Homey D. Clown, 'Men on. . .' and More," *UPROXX*, April 15, 2015, https://uproxx.com/hitfix/in-living-color-damon -wayans-on-the-inspiration-behind-homey-d-clown-men-on-and-more/.

65. Damon had already left the show by the time this sketch aired, so he was billed as a "special guest star" for this episode.

66. The Smothers Brothers consisted of Thomas and Richard (aka "Tom and Dick"), folk singers and comedians (though their brand of humor was decidedly "country," which is as polite of a way of saying "vanilla" and "white" as possible). But that all changed as the Vietnam War escalated, because their tenor went from being folksy and "good ol' boy" to highly charged and political, which ultimately led to them being fired from their own variety show that aired on CBS. Keenen and Damon were clearly sending up the former—and not the latter—incarnation of the Smothers Brothers.

67. It's entirely unclear, to this day, how the Fox censors either didn't catch—or completely ignored—the "Uncle Tom" reference in this sketch, though it's probably safe to say that the white censors had no clue about the reference, much like the Jamaican *patois* in the Hedleys sketches. In common parlance, an "Uncle Tom" refers to a Black man who is excessively servile, especially to white people, and until recently, it was an epi- thet used exclusively in the Black community to insult a Black man who "acted white." Named after the main character in Harriet Beecher Stowe's *Uncle Tom's Cabin*, the titular "Uncle Tom" in Stowe's book was beaten and slaughtered—Christ in cruciform style—by his white masters because he *refuses* to betray the whereabouts of Black women who had escaped slavery. This was seen as commendable at the time, and many literature classes taught that the titular "Uncle Tom" was a hero in the fight against racism and in favor of abolitionism. But it was only after the publication of James Baldwin's 1949 book *Everybody's Protest Novel* (which took straight aim at Stowe's depiction of the character and broke down how the depiction was racist in itself) that "Uncle Tom" became a racial epithet. In recent years, it's become an epithet that's evolved into common parlance in *other* languages, as well. In Latino American communities in New York City (especially in the Nuyorican and Colombian communities), a "Tio Tomas" (literally, "Uncle Thomas," or "Uncle Tom") is a man of Latino descent who is excessively obsequious, especially around non-Latino white men (because there's a delineation between a "white Latino" with more European/Spaniard roots, and an "Afro-Latino" with more native/ African roots), with characteristics including Anglicizing his name, refusing to speak the Spanish dialect he grew up with, marrying outside his race, and snitching on members of his community to the police.

68. The "White-Out" reference in the *In Living Color* sketch may not make sense to modern audiences, but a 1990s audience would understand the reference. Though computers have rendered Wite-Out obsolete, it was a correction fluid that would liter- ally "white out" a mistake on a sheet of white paper and was commonly used to correct typewriter errors. The inventor of Wite-Out (sometimes called Liquid Paper, after its

first commercial name) was a woman by the name of Bette Nesmith Graham, who was working as a bank secretary at the time she invented the product. Nesmith Graham sold the rights to Wite-Out to the Gillette Corporation for $47.5 million in 1979. She was also the mother of Michael Nesmith of the Monkees, who inherited $25 million when she died in 1980 thanks to his mother's invention.

69. Of all the lyrics in the sketch, this one doesn't work in the twenty-first century, given what we know about Bill Cosby's behavior. (Or maybe it does because it's unintentionally ironic.) Additionally, it's quite interesting that Damon's "Tom" made reference to the Cosby kids being "good kids who don't get knocked up," because according to Lenny Kravitz, his then-wife Lisa Bonet—who played Denise Huxtable on *The Cosby Show*—was fired from the show after she revealed she was pregnant with their child, the actress Zoë Kravitz. It's also quite interesting that Lisa's pregnancy—which happened in a marital bed when she was twenty-one years old, a legal adult by every definition of the word—was viewed as a "bad" thing by Cosby, especially since he was purporting to showcase a Black family that didn't engage in stereotypes such as teenage and unwed pregnancies (and Bonet was neither at the time she got pregnant with Zoë).

70. According to blues legend, Robert Johnson took his guitar to the crossroads of Highways 49 and 61 in Clarksdale, Mississippi. There, he encountered none other than Satan himself, who gifted him with a mastery of the blues guitar in exchange for his soul. Apparently, he agreed to the terms, because he only recorded one album of music before his untimely death in 1938 at the age of twenty-seven (becoming yet another member of the infamous "27 Club") and lived a life that could only be described as tumultuous, at best. Such legends often fall under the larger umbrella of "Faustian bargains"—named after Doctor Faustus, a character created by Christopher Marlowe who was based on the alchemist Johann Georg Faust (who sold his soul to Mephistopheles in exchange for worldly pleasure and knowledge)—and are common motifs in Christian literature. Most often, however, supernaturally talented musicians and entertainers were often accused of being part of a larger Faustian bargain. To bring it back to *In Living Color*, Damon and Keenen—through their characters, Tom and Tom Brothers—were making it clear that not only were they not interested in "selling out" for Hollywood fame but also they thought that people—especially Black people—who did so were servile and intellectually challenged, to put it mildly.

71. Stepin Fetchit was a persona created by a Black actor named Lincoln Perry back in the 1920s. As an actor, Perry started out in the minstrel shows that were popular in the day—but which, it almost went without saying, were flat-out racist in their depictions of Black people. The running gag about Stepin Fetchit was that he was a caricature of being "the laziest man in the world," which only further fueled the racist stereotypes of Black Americans as held in the white American pop culture consciousness. Thanks to his Stepin Fetchit character, Perry was the first Black actor to earn $1 million in Hollywood, but that money came at a very steep price. When he died in 1985, he was universally reviled by Black America, his son Donald met with a violent end thanks to the FBI's COINTELPRO counterintelligence program, and he was buried in a pauper's grave since he died penniless.

72. Bernadette Giacomazzo, "Inside the Controversial Life and Career of Stepin Fetchit, the First Black Movie Star," All That's Interesting, August 9, 2021, https://allthatsinteresting.com/stepin-fetchit.

73. Danette Chavez, "David Alan Grier on *The Carmichael Show*, the Prescience of *Blankman*, and Repeatedly Turning down *In Living Color*," *A.V. Club*, August 31, 2018, https://www.avclub.com/david-alan-grier-on-the-carmichael-show-the-prescience-1828686418.

74. As of this writing, the most recent film is *Being the Ricardos*, an Amazon Studios original that was released in 2021. It was directed by Aaron Sorkin and featured Nicole Kidman as Ball and Javier Bardem as Arnaz.

75. Later episodes of *In Living Color* would feature "What If" sketches that would blatantly pose the question—such as "What If Archie Bunker Was Black?," which eventually became "All Up in the Family," as seen in season 4, episode 22—but didn't pack the same punch as "I Love Laquita," because—as we will later learn—the creative control of *In Living Color* was wrested away from its creator and put in the hands of a new, predominantly white writer's room, which didn't understand the same nuances that came naturally to Keenen.

76. Pig's feet, as Laquita/Kim are referencing them here, are a staple of "soul food," which has its origins in Georgia, Mississippi, and Alabama. At the height of the Transatlantic Slave Trade, Black slaves were given meager portions and "undesirable" parts of meat that white people wouldn't eat. To prevent starvation, the slaves would incorporate their traditional African recipes—which were replete with spices and fragrances, both of which grew in abundance in the humid Gulf states—into the food that was available, and a whole new cuisine was born, with pig's feet being one of the most common, and beloved, staples of the cuisine. Interestingly, pig's feet are also a common staple in other "poor" or agrarian nations. Sicilians, for example, incorporate the feet into a *ragou*, or sauce, that's often eaten together with lentils on New Year's Day in the hopes of having a prosperous year. Other variations of the *ragou* are eaten in Haitian and French Canadian cultures as well.

77. While female rappers were present in the hip-hop genre at this point in history, they were nowhere near as mainstream or ubiquitous as they are today. But the 1990s would ultimately prove to be the "golden era" for female rappers, and many of them—including Queen Latifah, MC Lyte, Bahamadia, Foxy Brown, Lady of Rage, and more—were influential in shaping the way we view the genre today.

78. This is a reference to a cheap wine made famous on *Sanford and Son*, which was both fortified and carbonated. It also had a much lower alcohol-by-volume (ABV) content than typical table wine and was most popular in the 1960s and 1970s. Though it was cheap—and thus seen as "low class"—in its prime, bottles of ripple (if you can find them) retail for more than $200 each today.

79. Though the concept of the "casting couch" exploded in the late 2010s with the indictment, trial, and conviction of Harvey Weinstein, it was by no means an anomaly in the 1990s. But this was a different time, in terms of the collective American consciousness—there was no #MeToo movement, victims were blamed for the fallout, and there was no social media support—which is why the joke of the casting couch worked well at the time. Arguably, it might be cringe worthy today. As a counterpoint,

however, while there's no question this skit with these references couldn't be pulled off in the modern era, by no means was the skit any less funny, no matter how uncomfortable it may make a 2020s audience.

80. It's this desperation for fame that makes aspiring entertainers easy targets for the "casting couch."

81. *Showtime at the Apollo* was an American variety show that ran from 1987 until 2008; it returned for a brief revival in 2018 with Steve Harvey as the host. Taking place at the legendary Apollo Theater in New York City, *Showtime at the Apollo* featured both established and up-and-coming artists, many of whom got their "big break" on the show if they were able to pass the notoriously difficult-to-please audience's muster. In New York City, *Showtime at the Apollo* aired at 1:00 a.m. on Saturday, right after *Saturday Night Live*. The juxtaposition of what was then (and probably now) the whitest show on television with what was then, unquestionably, the Blackest show on television garnered more than a passing chuckle from pop culture commentators.

82. From 1989 until 1992, Byron Allen hosted a late-night talk show that had a moderate amount of success. Today, though, Allen is known as one of the wealthiest Black men in the entertainment industry, with an estimated net worth of $450 million, and whose media group owns more than thirty television stations across the country.

83. In October 2020, nearly thirty years after the character's debut, Kim revived the Benita Buttrell character in a public service announcement that urged people to get out and vote in the general election. As usual, she referred to her beloved Ms. Jenkins and filled in the viewer on the latest neighborhood gossip, but she also had decidedly more political interest than in years past—for what are, perhaps, obvious reasons, chief among them being that she "knows where things are heading, and I don't know about you, but I'm allergic to cotton"—and remarked that democracy was "collapsing faster than a fake woody on Viagra."

84. "*In Living Color* 25 Year Reunion," YouTube, 2019, https://www.youtube.com/watch?v=QQSM7ltyFfY.

85. For what it's worth, you need a license to hang a clothesline in New York City. It's safe to say Ms. Benita didn't have said license, not that it would have mattered or that she would have cared in either case.

86. "Keenen Ivory Wayans," Television Academy, accessed August 30, 2021, https://www.emmys.com/bios/keenen-ivory-wayans.

87. Much like *Hollywood Shuffle* is Townsend's magnum opus, and *I'm Gonna Git You Sucka* is Keenen's magnum opus, *Delirious* is considered Murphy's magnum opus. Though *Raw* was the stand-up comedy film that made Murphy a worldwide sensation, *Delirious* is considered the critical darling. The stand-up portion of the film features Murphy in a leather suit that would, eventually, become his signature style. In *Raw*, the suit was purple with a black stripe across the bottom of his butt cheeks, but in *Delirious*, the suit was red.

88. "Keenen Ivory Wayans."

89. Protégés of James himself, the Mary Jane Girls were a popular R&B, soul, and funk group whose career was at its peak in the 1980s. Their best-known mainstream hit was the October 1984 single "In My House," which was released on Gordy Records. But

they had other popular songs, including "All Night Long," a cover of the Four Seasons classic "Walk Like a Man," and "Candy Man."

90. In a subsequent sketch, Frenchie would pour chitlins onto a serving tray filled with duck foie gras.

91. At this point in history, it was perfectly legal to get someone's private information from the DMV if you had their license plate number. That changed in 1994, when Rep. Jim Moran (D-VA) introduced—and subsequently received bipartisan support to pass—the Driver's Privacy Protection Act (also known as the DPPA). Moran introduced the law because antiabortion activists were obtaining private information from both patients looking to obtain abortions and doctors who performed the procedure, which they were then using to subsequently harass them, threaten them, and cause them harm. (In other words, it was "doxing" before doxing was a thing.) But thanks to the law, no one—except for law enforcement or another government agency—is allowed to obtain your private information unless you give him or her expressed permission to do so in writing. But one year before this joke was made, the actress Rebecca Schaeffer was murdered at her home by a stalker named Robert John Bardo who obtained her information in this exact way, so there was still a *yikes* factor to it all—even though Frenchie was a well-meaning, and clearly nonthreatening, man.

92. This may have been a nod and a wink to Sho'Nuff, the Shogun of Harlem, from the 1985 film *The Last Dragon*—or it may have just been done to illustrate how Frenchie was so ignorant that he referred to every Asian man as "Bruce Lee." Either way, while it's made clear that Frenchie is clearly lacking in intentional malice, it's certainly not a joke that Keenen—or any other comedian, for that matter—could make without getting blowback today.

93. While the terms "cold duck" and "champagne" are often used interchangeably by those who don't know better, they're two very different things. Champagne is a sparkling wine that originates from the Champagne region of France. A sparkling wine that does *not* come from the Champagne region of France cannot, legally, be called "champagne." Cold duck, on the other hand, is a mixture of champagne, sparkling burgundy, and sugar. Its roots trace back to Bavaria—which is not to be confused with Germany, as it's a free state of its own—where the practice originated to prevent unused champagne from going to waste. It was initially known as "cold end" but over time became "cold duck," because the Bavarian words for "end" (*ende*) and "duck" (*ente*) are remarkably similar.

94. The seven original members of the Justice League were Green Lantern, Flash, Superman, Batman, Wonder Woman, Aquaman, and Martian Manhunter. Carrey's character was wearing a costume that was meant to look like Superman's (skin-tight suit, cape) but sported the colors of The Flash (red and yellow). It's probably safe to say that *In Living Color* didn't get license clearances from the DCEU to outright call Carrey "Superman," so this was the closest they could get without getting a cease and desist order from the comic book giant.

95. Cyborg, a humanoid Black man, was first teased in 1980 but wasn't formally introduced until 2011, when the DCEU ordered a reboot of their comic series. At that time, Cyborg replaced Martian Manhunter—which was for the best, given the quality of Martian Manhunter's story lines—and was billed as a founding member of the Justice League of America. Interestingly, Cyborg is considered a remarkable superhero in

the DCEU because he's both Black *and* disabled, which seems relevant to mention in a sketch about a Black *and* disabled superhero that was seen as an outlier in 1990.

96. Kitty Pryde—who was introduced in *X-Men No. 129* in July 1980—was an X-Men recruit who wore a Star of David necklace, so many comics enthusiasts suggest that she's the first "openly" Jewish superhero. But there was also the mention of Colossal Boy's Jewish heritage (as he celebrated Hanukkah) in DC Special Series #21, released in 1979.

97. "Oriental" is a term that is, at best, antiquated—but opinions on its level of offensiveness vary. Chrissy Teigen, whose mother is from Thailand, doesn't find the term offensive, and neither does Korean American comedian Margaret Cho, but Steve Park—a later *In Living Color* cast member who, like Cho, is Korean American—does. Far be it from this writer—or any other non-Asian person—to tell an Asian person what is, and isn't, an offensive word. The stereotype of Asians being preternaturally superior at mathematics seems to be more universally offensive than the term "Oriental." That said, "Asians" are not a monolith, so regardless of the offensiveness, or lack thereof, of the term, President Barack Obama signed a federal law in 2016 banning the use of the terms "Oriental" and "Negro" from federal documents. And in newsrooms, journalists are advised that "Oriental" is a term to be used to describe a rug (or another inanimate object), not a person.

98. Interestingly, at this point in history, Shang-Chi—a character from China, recently brought to life on the big screen by actor Simu Liu—was already part of the Marvel Universe, having first been introduced in 1973.

99. In 2019, the first Black feminist lesbian superhero hit the small screen when Nafessa Williams portrayed Thunder on CW's *Black Lightning* television series, which ran from 2018 to 2021.

100. This was obviously an error on Carrey's part, but the sketch worked anyway, so it was worth leaving it in.

101. This is the most recognizable disability symbol and features a white stylized stick figure of a person in a wheelchair against a blue background.

102. DJ Envy, Angela Yee, and Charlamagne tha God, hosts, *The Breakfast Club*, episode "Damon Wayans Interview at *The Breakfast Club* Power 105.1," YouTube, September 4, 2015, https://www.youtube.com/watch?v=n52uSXCKdLs.

103. For what it's worth, the YouTube comments on "Handi-Man" videos seem to back Damon's claim up—not that this should be taken as empirical evidence, but it's at least something worth noting.

104. Luaine Lee, "Wayans Started Making People Laugh at Early Age," *Baltimore Sun*, April 3, 1995.

105. Damon Wayans was no longer on the show at the time this sketch aired, so he was billed as a "special guest star."

106. It was *very* much a 1990s style, thank you very much.

107. According to the National Fire Protection Association, the number one cause of domestic fires is cooking. That's followed by heating, which is followed by electricity. Smoking is the fourth cause of domestic fires and rounding out the top five domestic fire hazards is candles.

108. When asked if he was all right by Daughter, Fire Marshall Bill replied—rather matter-of-factly—that he'd been hit by lightning nineteen times. Mother then replied that it was horrible, to which Bill deadpanned, "Not really. I'm starting to enjoy it."

109. The sketch closed with him heading to the neighbor's house after he noted, out loud, that the neighbor had a wood shingle roof—which, it goes without saying, is a fire hazard.

110. Marc Maron, host, "Jim Carrey," episode 1140 of *WTF with Marc Maron* (podcast), July 16, 2020, http://www.wtfpod.com/podcast/episode-1140-jim-carrey.

111. When the show entered syndication, the line about Fire Marshall Bill and a man named "Abdul" being somewhat responsible for the 1993 World Trade Center bombing—which took place on February 26, 1993—was edited out due to the first World Trade Center attacks, which happened that same year. Officially, however, the offensive line is, "That's what they said about the World Trade Center, son. But me and my friend Abdul and a couple of pounds of plastic explosives showed them different." Recent airings of this particular installment of the sketch—which, it should be noted, falls into the post-Keenen era of the show, which meant that it lacked the cultural sensitivity that the Keenen era had—don't have the line in it, either; this most likely stems from 9/11, the attack that took down both towers of the World Trade Center.

112. Aside from the usual reasons of not wanting to play dive bars and being tired of the cleaning bills for all the suits, Les informs Wes that he's tired of Wes "passing gas and blaming me."

113. Tesh hosted *Entertainment Tonight* from 1986 until 1996, when he left to pursue his musical career. Gibbons was his cohost beginning in 1984, replacing Mary Hart.

114. Eagle-eyed fans will note that with this statement, Gibbons looks up at Tesh and can barely keep from laughing. Tesh, hoping not to break character, doesn't make eye contact with Gibbons—he just scratches his head and clears his throat, hoping he doesn't break.

115. Again, Gibbons could barely keep a straight face as she delivered the line.

116. Remember, cell phones are a luxury—not a ubiquitous necessity—at this point in history.

117. Each one of the Death Row Comic's appearances would end with him being wheeled away to his execution, usually with him whimpering in fear. But either he survived each execution, or he got a stay each time, because he appeared in at least three subsequent sketches.

118. This was the very last episode of *In Living Color*.

119. This was obviously in a time before the Supreme Court became a shining example of partisan rancor.

120. Ultimately, Hill's accusations did nothing to stop Thomas from being confirmed to the Supreme Court. In 2007, he gave an interview to ABC News about Hill's accusations, where he called her a "traitor" and "touchy." He also claimed that she resented him because he "preferred" light-complexioned women—what many in the Black community refer to as "light-skinned," as opposed to Hill's darker complexion, which is referred to as "dark-skinned"—and admitted that now-president Joe Biden voted against him because of what he believed, not on the basis of his character. Nevertheless, Thomas

also referred to all the senators who voted against him as "his enemies," and even implied that Hill's left-of-center politics made her mentally unstable.

121. Jan Crawford Greenberg, "Clarence Thomas: A Silent Justice Speaks Out," ABC News, September 30, 2007, https://abcnews.go.com/TheLaw/story?id=3665221 &page=1.

122. As of 2022, and especially in the wake of the January 6, 2021, insurrection and the overturning of *Roe v. Wade*, nothing has changed.

123. Daryl Gates was the chief of police for the Los Angeles Police Department (LAPD) from 1978 until 1992. As the cofounder of the failed DARE (Drug Abuse Resistance Education) program and the creator of the SWAT teams, Gates took a punitive approach to law enforcement that disproportionately affected Black and Latino residents of Los Angeles more than their white counterparts. He resigned in disgrace after the Rodney King arrest and the subsequent riots, and one study revealed that the LAPD was at its most racist and noxious under Gates's tenure.

124. Would it be that Thomas was even *somewhat* like Grier's character portrayed him to be instead of the servile conservative token falling in lockstep with the rest of the white establishment? *Would it only be, indeed.*

125. Code-switching is the practice by which people switch between the two languages they speak based on the situation they find themselves in. It can be as simple as a first-generation American switching between the English language and the language of their parents' country of origin, or it could be as nuanced as Black Americans switching between "white" English and AAVE (African American Vernacular English, which is a preferable term to "Ebonics").

126. Fox was the first network to air the first-ever condom commercial on national television. It was a fifteen-second commercial for Trojan condoms that aired on November 17, 1991. Its tagline was "to help reduce the risk," because at the time, condom commercials were only allowed to promote the prevention of STIs, not the prevention of conception. Yet, Fox was the only network that aired condom commercials—the "Big Three" continued to resist airing the ads because the commercials were deemed "in bad taste," even as a disproportionate number of gay men were dying of AIDS. CBS accepted its first paid condom commercial in 1998, and NBC accepted its first paid condom commercial in 1999. But as of this writing, at the end of 2021, ABC and its affiliate networks, UPN, and the WB continue to refuse to air paid condom commercials. And to this day, *no* condom commercial is allowed on the air if it suggests it can be used to prevent conception.

127. In 1997, Ennis Cosby—Bill Cosby's only son—was shot and killed near Interstate 405 in Los Angeles, California, in a robbery attempt gone wrong. He was twenty-seven years old. Mikhail Markhasev, who was eighteen at the time he committed the murder, tried to rob Ennis when he stopped on the side of the road to change a tire—and when that didn't work, he shot Ennis in the head, killing him instantly. Markhasev was sentenced to life in prison without the possibility of parole.

128. He either had something as minor as a urinary tract infection (UTI) or as major as chlamydia. Being that this is for a condom commercial, the latter is the more likely scenario.

129. Bill Cosby, *Childhood* (New York: Berkley, 1992).

130. Consent, or lack thereof, wasn't addressed in the insinuation. Rather, it was more implied that he cheated on his wife, and that all parties were consenting in the matter.

131. David Johnston, "Survey Shows Number of Rapes Far Higher than Official Figures," *New York Times*, April 24, 1992, sec. A.

132. Lucia Graves, "Hannibal Buress: How a Comedian Reignited the Bill Cosby Allegations," *Guardian*, April 26, 2018, https://www.theguardian.com/world/2018/apr/26/hannibal-buress-how-a-comedian-reignited-the-bill-cosby-allegations.

Chapter 4

1. "Keenen Ivory Wayans," Television Academy, accessed August 30, 2021, https://www.emmys.com/bios/keenen-ivory-wayans.

2. It's not clear to whom Keenen is referring in this particular context—at least not by name—but it seems like there's one particular censor whose frustration with *In Living Color*'s tendency to flout the "law of the land" was quickly becoming evident.

3. "Keenen Ivory Wayans."

4. This isn't an intuitive sex phrase (unlike, say, "do the horizontal mambo," which conjures up a very specific visual), which is probably why the censor didn't know what it meant. But though the actual origins of this slang phrase for anilingus are unclear, modern lexicographers first noticed the phrase in a gay slang dictionary in the early 1970s. Since the origins of Black ballroom culture—vis-à-vis *Paris Is Burning*—can be found somewhere between 140th and 141st Streets in Harlem (and, to put a finer point on it, at the Savoy Manor Ballroom) in the 1970s, it's safe to say that Keenen et al. heard the phrase somewhere in their travels, even though they didn't participate in ballroom culture. On the other hand, it's highly unlikely that the straight white male censor heard that phrase prior to Keenen's mischievous suggestion at that point in history, because it wouldn't enter common parlance until 1996. That year, HBO aired its frightening documentary *Prisoners of the War on Drugs*, which featured a frank description of prison rape and the perpetrator explaining—in all-too-graphic detail—how he liked to "toss the salads" of the "fresh meat" that had just entered the prison. And, for whatever reason, the act involved grape jelly, though the perpetrator also explained that he preferred to use pancake syrup when it was available.

5. This generated barely contained laughter from the interviewer at the Television Academy, who was clearly very familiar with the term as Keenen tried—in vain—to keep a straight face while explaining it to her in the most professional and delicate way that these sorts of things can possibly be explained (which is to say that there *is* no polite way of explaining all this in an academic setting).

6. The reason the musical parodies aren't included in this list, even though they were cut from syndication, is because they were cut due to licensing issues, not due to a censor taking offense with the parody.

7. In 2016, after a nearly twenty-five-year hiatus, Williams once again became the spokesperson for the Colt 45 brand.

8. Lauren Porter, "Billy Dee Williams Is a Colt 45 Spokesperson Again," *Essence*, March 29, 2016, https://www.essence.com/news/billy-dee-williams-colt-45-spokesperson -once-again/.

9. On March 7, 1978, the late scientist Carl Sagan appeared on *The Tonight Show Starring Johnny Carson*. At one point, Carson asked Sagan about his opinion on *Star Wars*—at that time, only "the original" *Star Wars* (which would eventually be renamed *Star Wars Episode IV: A New Hope* as more films that were part of the so-called Skywalker saga were added to the repertoire) had been in the theaters, and it was a cultural phenomenon. In a nutshell, Sagan felt that *Star Wars* was not only biologically inaccurate (specism, basically) but also had a bit of a racial problem (inadvertently, as it turned out, at least on George Lucas's part) because there were *literally* no Black people in space in the original *Star Wars*. There's some suggestion that Williams's character of Lando Calrissian was created in response to Sagan pointing out this lack of diversity in a galaxy far, far away—but one must wonder why Lucas, well-intentioned as he may be, had to make a space version of Willie Dynamite for *Star Wars Episode V: The Empire Strikes Back* and beyond.

10. Keenen as Billy Dee Williams: "What'd you expect? Whitney Houston?"

11. Many jurisdictions have public intoxication laws and, as a result, require alcohol be carried in brown paper bags if they're to be consumed publicly. Public intoxication, however, is a crime in many jurisdictions, so if you're going to drink publicly, don't get wasted in the process.

12. Travis M. Andrews, "Comedians Have Long Used Rape as a Punchline: The Me Too Era Is Changing That," *Washington Post*, November 9, 2018, https://www.washing tonpost.com/lifestyle/style/comedians-have-long-used-rape-as-a-punchline-the-me-too -era-is-changing-that/2018/11/08/54ffc888-dd5b-11e8-b3f0-62607289efee_story.html.

13. "Keenen Ivory Wayans."

14. While date-rape jokes have been a part of comedy—from *many* different cultures, not just the American culture—since time immemorial, their prevalence exploded in the 1970s and 1980s with the rise of the feminist movement. It violated the first rule of comedy—"don't punch down"—but it was quite evident that the more violent responses were those triggered by men who felt disempowered by women who wouldn't just lay down and have sex with them and their doughy dad-bods on demand.

15. The reason this explanation doesn't ring true is that Keenen is many things, but stupid is not on that list. Knowing that there would be a risk (however minute) of "the wrong cut" airing, why would Keenen (or any other producer, for that matter) take a chance like this? Why wouldn't he ensure that the broadcaster had the correct cut from the get-go?

16. Cosby was ultimately found guilty of sexual assault in 2018, but his conviction was overturned in 2021 by the Pennsylvania Supreme Court after it was revealed that a previous prosecutor's statement that Cosby wouldn't face charges (so he could testify in a civil trial without fear of prosecution) meant that he shouldn't have been charged in the first place. It should be noted that an overturned conviction does not presume innocence or guilt, especially when Cosby testified, under oath, to drugging and raping women during his civil trial.

17. It should be noted that rape jokes were still the premise of several films in the early twenty-first century as well. For example, 2007's *Superbad*'s premise focuses on teenage boys who go on a quest to buy alcohol so they can get their female classmates drunk enough to have sex with them. And in 2012, Daniel Tosh—who inexplicably had a "comedy" career in the early 2010s—told a female audience member that "it would be funny if you were gang-raped" after she criticized him. Though the #MeToo movement was initially founded in 2006 by Tarana Burke, it went viral in 2017 following the widespread sexual abuse allegations against Hollywood producer Harvey Weinstein—and it was only after *that* reckoning that rape jokes began becoming taboo.

18. It goes without saying that there would be a racial element to the "*really* not funny" depiction in this hypothetical scenario, too, especially in the 1990s. That said, the 2004 film *White Chicks*—another Wayans family production—played up a rape scene for laughs, but that was also a satire that played on resisting "the hegemony of the white gaze," so while it was certainly risky, it was a risk that paid off, at least for the time.

19. "Keenen Ivory Wayans."

20. This isn't to excuse the statement or the harm it may cause. No one is perfect, and it's clear that malice and harm wasn't intended. But the road to hell . . . you know the rest.

21. "*In Living Color* 25 Year Reunion," YouTube, 2019, https://www.youtube.com /watch?v=QQSM7ltyFfY.

22. Plus, she was "having trouble getting rid of those darn breasts! I mean, look at 'em! They just won't go away!" Yeah. *Yikes*.

23. Objectively, *The Closer* wasn't one of his best, and the low streaming Netflix numbers proved it. Even removing the transphobia from the stand-up routine couldn't do much to save its comedic value, or lack thereof.

24. According to a 2021 Gallup poll, less than 1 percent of the population—to wit, 0.6 percent—identify as trans. So, conspiracy theories about "the trans agenda" and "trans people taking over" are more than a little fallacious and, quite frankly, disingenuous. Also, it's unclear why such a small minority of people bothers such a large majority of people so much, and why it's so difficult to just respect one another, regardless of differences . . . but here we are.

25. Jeffrey M. Jones, "LGBT Identification Rises to 5.6% in Latest U.S. Estimate," Gallup, November 20, 2021, https://news.gallup.com/poll/329708/lgbt-identification -rises-latest-estimate.aspx.

26. Scottie Andrew, "What These Trans Comedians Have to Say about Dave Chappelle's Jokes at Their Expense," CNN, October 24, 2021, https://www.cnn.com /2021/10/24/entertainment/trans-comics-dave-chappelle-netflix-cec/index.html.

27. This isn't to suggest that there weren't these types of "influencers" back in the 1990s. To the contrary: with the explosion of the fitness revolution in the 1980s, these influencers were just as prevalent when *In Living Color* was on the air as they are today. The only difference between then and now is that there was no social media when *In Living Color* was on the air, which meant that the sole catharsis people had to get their laughs on about this ridiculous subculture was on their TVs on Sunday nights.

28. This sketch was cut from the *In Living Color* DVD, presumably because it was too offensive—but most likely because they couldn't get the clearance from MC Lyte, who recorded the original "Ruffneck" song back in 1993.

29. John Koblin, "After Racist Tweet, Roseanne Barr's Show Is Canceled by ABC," *New York Times*, May 29, 2018, https://www.nytimes.com/2018/05/29/business/media/roseanne-barr-offensive-tweets.html.

30. In 2018, Barr wrote a racist tweet about former Obama adviser Valerie Jarrett, and the tweet was so offensive that it can't be repeated here. Suffice it to say that it played into the worst stereotypes of both Black people and practicing Muslims, so the firing from her show was quite merited.

31. It's entirely possible that Aspire doesn't air the sketch out of respect to America's armed forces and veterans, for whom patriotic music takes a different, and much deeper, meaning.

32. On July 25, 1990, Barr (who was, at the time, known by her married name of Roseanne Arnold) was invited to sing the National Anthem at Jack Murphy Stadium before a San Diego Padres game. The idea was conceived by the then-owner of the Padres, Tom Werner, a television producer and mega-investor whose crown jewel show at the time was—you guessed it!—*Roseanne*. Werner had hoped that getting Barr to perform the National Anthem would be a great way to promote the show. Unfortunately, Barr caterwauled her way through a sixty-second rendition of the National Anthem, where she managed to be both off key and offensive. When the performance—which was met with loud boos—was over, Barr grabbed her crotch and spit on the field. She then hugged her then-husband, Tom Arnold, and got off the field.

33. It goes without saying that this would be medically impossible, but the humor in the sketch is also found in the absurdity.

34. Of all the Wayans family members, Marlon is the only one who has successfully ventured into more dramatic roles, to the point that he's now better known for them than for his comedic fare. Keenen tried his hand at the more dramatic fare with roles in films like *Most Wanted* and *The Glimmer Man*, but Marlon found more success—and critical acclaim—with roles in films like *Requiem for a Dream*, *On the Rocks*, and—as of 2021—the Aretha Franklin biopic, *Respect*.

35. Here, "other races" refers to other *non-white* races. There's no such thing as "being racist against white people"—or "reverse racism"—because white people, historically and especially in Western civilization, are the ones who hold the power *and* the money. ("Prejudice" is not the same as "racism"—white people can experience the former, but not the latter, in Western society.) As long as whiteness continues to be centered in American society—and other Eurocentric societies—white people will *never* experience the levels of systemic racism and discrimination that non-white races have experienced. "The Black man's joke hurt my feelings" is nowhere near in the same category as "The white man made laws that have stripped me of my voting rights and made it perfectly legal to own me as a slave," and any intimation that they're even in the same universe, let alone the same league, is deliberately disingenuous.

36. There's some comment and controversy regarding the term "Latino" (or, in its more preferred gender-inclusive version, "Latine"). The catch-all term is used to describe anyone who speaks Spanish—regardless of country of origin—and often interchangeably

with "Hispanic." But in reality, "Hispanic" refers to someone from Spain, whereas "La-tino" (and the feminine "Latina") refers to someone from a Spanish-speaking country that was once conquered by Spain (and, as such, has Spanish as its primary language). As of 2022, there has been some suggestion that "Latine" is preferred because of its all-encompassing gender inclusivity; however, "Latine," as of this writing, has not en-tered common parlance, either in the Spanish-speaking community or in the English-dominant community.

37. Oprah Winfrey, "What I Know for Sure about Making Peace with My Body," Oprah.com, August 1, 2002, https://www.oprah.com/omagazine/what-i-know-for-sure-weight.

38. In a 2002 essay penned for her own *O Magazine*, Oprah wrote that she eventu-ally messed up her metabolism so much from all the dieting that she suffered from heart palpitations.

39. In 1988, Oprah made headlines when she appeared on her show with a fashion-able outfit and a nearly seventy-pound weight loss. But she achieved the weight loss from a "liquid diet," and needless to say, she wasn't able to keep the weight off. Within two years, she'd gained it all back—and then some.

40. The PSAs would feature a hot skillet, then a voice-over that said, "this is drugs." Then, a raw egg would get cracked into the skillet, and as it fried, the voice-over would say "this is your brain on drugs. Any questions?"

41. Celia Viggo Wexler, "Coca-Cola's Tab Soda Has Been Discontinued: Its Retire-ment Should Have Come Decades Ago," NBC News, October 20, 2020, https://www.nbcnews.com/think/opinion/coca-cola-s-tab-soda-has-been-discontinued-its-retire ment-ncna1243950.

42. The rise of the "thin" ideal in the United States came with the rise of the femi-nist movement. In the 1950s, women were lauded for more "zaftig" looks—one need only look at the old Marilyn Monroe centerfolds to see that "the hourglass ideal" was very much "in." But by the 1960s, Dame Leslie Hornby Lawson, DBE—aka Twiggy—presented a new, and completely different ideal of "thin is in." A thin woman was seen as active, vital, and able to hold her own against men—whereas curvier women were seen as homely and matronly. In the twenty-first century, that seems to be changing, with many women—especially white women—getting plastic surgery to fill out their lips and hips in an effort to emulate Black and Latina women who naturally inherited these traits. But at this point in history, *In Living Color* also seemed to ascribe to the "thin is in" philosophy, which is why they took aim at Oprah's weight.

43. Natalie Finn, "Oprah Winfrey's 40-Year Weight Loss Struggle: Inside the Bil-lionaire Star's Ongoing Quest for Self-Acceptance," *E! Online*, August 3, 2017, https://www.eonline.com/news/871198/oprah-winfrey-s-40-year-weight-loss-struggle-inside-the-billionaire-star-s-ongoing-quest-for-self-acceptance.

44. Lily Rothman, "The 1991 Crown Heights Riots: Read *Time*'s Explanation of the History," *Time*, August 19, 2015, https://time.com/3989495/crown-heights-riots-time-magazine-history/.

45. July and August are, notoriously, the hottest months of the year in New York City. Even though the average real temperature is 83 degrees Fahrenheit, the humid-ity and the congestion can make it feel like more than 100 degrees Fahrenheit and

better—and, certainly, global warming has done Manhattan no favors in the heat index department.

46. "The Hasidim set up an apartheid situation in Crown Heights," said Dr. Vernal Cave, a Black dermatologist who lived in the Crown Heights area for more than thirty years, to *Time* magazine at the time (Rothman, "The 1991 Crown Heights Riots"). In response, the Hasidim claimed that they were being persecuted by the Black community in methods reminiscent of the Holocaust. Both sides seemed prone to hyperbole because neither side liked one another very much.

47. The exact speed at which Lifsh was driving was never fully determined, but it was certainly fast enough to knock down a whole stone pillar that held up a Brooklyn building—so it's safe to say he was going *pretty* fast.

48. The *New York Times* claimed that more than 250 Black teenagers were shouting "Jews! Jews! Jews!" as they began to turn their violence on the police. While this number seems a bit excessive, there's more than a bit of evidence to indicate that the private ambulance that came to ferry Lifsh away to the hospital didn't do anything to help the young Black children pinned under the stone pillar—and there was a belief among the Black men and women in the crowd that the children might have been saved had the Hatzolah ambulance been willing to help.

49. John T. Mcquiston, "Fatal Crash Starts Melee with Police in Brooklyn," *New York Times*, August 20, 1991, https://www.nytimes.com/1991/08/20/nyregion/fatal -crash-starts-melee-with-police-in-brooklyn-668791.html.

50. The 1994 *Law & Order* episode "Sanctuary" was a dramatization based on the Crown Heights riots.

51. Three hours after the riots began, a group of twenty Black teenagers surrounded— and killed—twenty-eight-year-old Yankel Rosenbaum, who was a foreign exchange student in New York studying for his doctorate. Before his death, Rosenbaum ultimately identified Lemrick Nelson Jr. as his attacker, but Nelson was acquitted of the crime at trial. "A pound of flesh," indeed.

52. This sketch would have benefited from a Hasidic writer—or, at the very least, a Jewish writer who was familiar with Hasidim—in the writer's room. And, to put a finer point on it, this example is a perfect illustration of why Black men and women call for Black writers in the writer's room for shows that have more than one Black actor on the set: because there's an authenticity that a Black writer will have about his or her own culture that a white writer—even if the white writer in question was raised exclusively around Black people—would not. If we can understand why it would be a bad idea for a predominantly Black writer's room to write a sketch about Hasidim—and where depictions border on parody—we can *certainly* understand why it would be a bad idea for a predominantly white writer's room to write a sketch about Black men and women. It's *not* that difficult, really.

53. It's hard to believe today, given his ties to—and subsequent defense of—Jeffrey Epstein, but there was a time that Alan Dershowitz was considered a great lawyer. He was a professor of law at Harvard University, was a special adviser on the O. J. Simpson case, and won thirteen of the fifteen murder and attempted murder cases he handled as a criminal appellate lawyer.

54. The choice to cast Grier as a Black activist was an interesting one, considering his history. Grier's father, William H. Grier, was a psychiatrist who wrote an influential book, *Black Rage*, that was one of the first to tackle the ravages of racism on the Black American psyche. Dr. Grier's observations about the psychological behaviors of victims of systemic racism—Black men who exhibit hostility against Black women, Black women who have low self-esteem thanks to Eurocentric beauty standards—are both prescient and valid today.

55. Damon and Keenen also play off one another very well when they perform together, but their fraternal relationship—and their birth order—gives their interactions a more deferential dynamic. As the older brother, Keenen often sets up the joke, and Damon delivers the punchline. But Damon and Grier's interactions are those of two equals, and their dynamic—as evidenced by this sketch and the "Men on Film" sketches, to name a few—is one of masters of their craft flexing their muscles for and at one another, which is why their chemistry is so top notch.

56. It goes without saying that none of the three descriptors are accurate—Farrakhan is problematic, to put it mildly, and Sharpton decidedly less so, but the only thing these two men threaten is the white patriarchal structure that keeps racism firmly entrenched in American society. In fact, racism is so entrenched in American society that when it's tackled head-on, some people think those who attack it are attacking America. And when you consider that fact—when you consider that all Sharpton et al. really want (however problematic their messaging) is to afford Black men and women the same rights afforded to their white counterparts—it makes some of the criticisms against men like them suspicious, to say the least.

57. While accepted by a certain subset today, Farrakhan was seen by most in the mainstream in the 1990s as a separatist and an outlier. And while Farrakhan's calls for Black equality and equity are nothing if not noble, these calls are often ignored or otherwise ridiculed because they're wrapped in a thick coat of anti-Semitism. Farrakhan also blames Jewish people for everything from the Transatlantic Slave Trade (when it was the Dutch who were the foremost enslavers and human traffickers) to plantation sharecropping (when, in reality, it was the white descendants of the predominantly Protestant Western European settlers who engaged in sharecropping the most). As a result, the Southern Poverty Law Center has classified Farrakhan as an extremist.

58. At this point in history, Sharpton was embroiled in the Tawana Brawley controversy. While the actual Brawley case is filled with twists and turns—and gets messier with each detail—for the purposes of this book, it's enough to know that Brawley was a fifteen-year-old girl who was found dumped among trash bags outside her home in Wappingers Falls, New York. Feces had been smeared on her, and "KKK" and the n-word were scrawled on her face. Later, she'd accused four white men—many of whom were in positions of power, including a New York prosecutor—of raping her, but no medical evidence substantiating the rapes was ever produced. Sharpton had thrown his support behind Brawley, even after a jury concluded that she'd fabricated the attack, and the story drew further racial lines in the sand between those who did, and didn't, believe her claims. Ultimately, the New York prosecutor sued Brawley, Sharpton, and Sharpton's advisers for defamation—and won. Today, shellshocked by the controversy, Brawley lives in Virginia Beach, Virginia, and works as a private nurse under a new name and identity.

59. There's a scene in the 1994 hit film *A Low Down Dirty Shame*—written by, and starring, Keenen—in which his character, Shame, provokes a group of white supremacists, then points them in the direction of the bad guy, Luis, by telling them "Luis said the white man can kiss his butt!" He then whispers to Luis, "tell them you're friends with Al Sharpton," before speeding off—with his fist in the air and screaming "Black power! Black power!"—and leaving the group of skinheads to do what they wish with Luis.

60. In June 2021, the Biden administration shifted the American focus away from foreign terrorist threats and toward domestic terror threats thanks to the rise in politically and racially motivated terrorism from the likes of the Ku Klux Klan, the Proud Boys, the Oathkeepers, and other white supremacist groups.

61. The pushback against a Black Bond in the twenty-first century, perhaps unsurprisingly, comes from more conservative types—and the late Rush Limbaugh was particularly vocal about this, claiming that some roles should be "whites only," and James Bond is one such role. Limbaugh also claimed that casting a Black actor—like Idris Elba, who has long been a rumored favorite as the first Black Bond—in the role of James Bond would be the equivalent of casting George Clooney as Barack Obama or Kelsey Grammer as Nelson Mandela, even though Obama and Mandela are real people, whereas Bond is a fictional character.

62. Christina Dugan Ramirez, "Connie Chung on the 'Embarrassing' Reason She Agreed to Marry Maury Povich after 2 Proposals," *People*, October 29, 2020, https://people.com/tv/why-connie-chung-agreed-to-marry-maury-povich-after-multiple -proposals/.

63. Fans of Povich's show will recall that Povich would often comfort devastated fathers—especially—by recounting how "he is not the birth father" of Matthew, yet the love Povich has for him remains the same.

64. Today, it's very common for women of all stripes to be open about their fertility struggles. But back in the 1990s, women journalists—especially those like Chung, who was only the second woman *in history* to coanchor a network newscast when she was added to the *CBS Evening News*—were expected to comport themselves with what was seen as "decorum" but what was, in actuality, quite stifling. While their male counterparts were free to strut their sexuality as they pleased, and wore their struggles like a badge of honor, women were required to exhibit a humanoid-like demeanor, devoid of personality outside of being a talking head, lest they be seen as salacious or trying to seduce their audience, their interview subject, or both. Even today, women journalists— especially those in the entertainment arm of the industry—are sometimes viewed by both their male *and* female audience as little more than well-connected groupies. As such, Chung frequently commented that discussions about her fertility struggles were "difficult" and "uncommon."

65. By twenty-first-century standards, "Me So Horny" is juvenile and asinine, and the song sounds like something written by a Midwestern teenager who has been raised on a steady diet of *Beavis and Butt-Head*. But by 1990s standards, "Me So Horny" was obscene—so much so that the group was successfully prosecuted on obscenity charges, and the album *As Nasty as They Wanna Be* was banned from being sold in Florida. (The ban was later overturned.) "Me So Horny" was also under fire for what was seen as racist depictions of Asians—but the blame for the line "me so horny/me love you long time"

falls squarely on the shoulders of Stanley Kubrick's *Full Metal Jacket*, from where the line was sampled.

66. The pregnancy ultimately didn't happen, and in 1995, Povich and Chung adopted Matthew. Povich also has two biological daughters from his first marriage.

67. A dragon lady stereotype is one that depicts Asian women as exotic temptresses and prostitutes who use their sexuality to gain whatever it is that they're after in that given transaction. Credit (or, more correctly, blame) for this stereotype can be traced all the way back to 1875, when the Page Act of 1875 limited the number of Chinese women who were allowed to emigrate into the United States. Those who were allowed to emigrate were often forced into prostitution—and this bled into the media, where Asian women were depicted as good enough for a romp in the sack but not good enough to become wives to American men (well, *white* American men, since this is *yet another* unfortunate side effect of white supremacy in the United States). "It's a sexual connotation that cannot be removed from race, and it's attributed to a particularly long history of the hypersexuality of Asian American women in our international consciousness, and in the fantasies that have been offered by the theater and film," said Celine Parreñas Shimizu, director of the School of Cinema at San Francisco State University (Celine Parreñas Shimizu, *The Hypersexuality of Race: Performing Asian/American Women on Screen and Scene* [Durham, NC: Duke University Press, 2007, 17]).

68. In 1997, Park took to "the internet"—as the news referred to it at the time—and released a three-page mission statement after he became the victim of a racist incident on the set of *Friends*. In what was probably one of the first incidences of a statement "going viral," Park detailed how the set of *Friends* was "lacking in generosity of spirit and basic human courtesy," and explained his embarrassment when he witnessed a *Friends* production assistant launch into a tirade about "I don't have time for this! Where's Hoshi, Toshi or whatever the [f-word] his name is. Get the Oriental guy!" He also rightly called the *Friends* set—which included the actors, it should be noted—as part of "white exclusionary culture" and called upon Hollywood to "wake up" and stop with their negative depictions of Asians and Asian Americans (Steve Park, "Steve Park's Mission Statement," Model Minority: A Guide to Asian American Empowerment, October 7, 1992, https://web.archive.org/web/20070928140952/http://modelminority.com/modules.php?name=News&file=article&sid=1). You might say Park was "woke" before "woke" was a thing. And even in the twenty-first century, Park's call to action to Hollywood, especially in how it treats Asian characters in popular media, is still relevant.

69. In 1989, Lyle and Erik Menendez shot their parents to death while they slept in their Beverly Hills, California, home. Their father, Jose, was an immigrant who had worked his way up in the world, eventually becoming an entertainment executive responsible for signing such bands as Duran Duran and the Eurythmics to their super-smash record deals. But according to Lyle and Erik, their parents were abusive—and they accused their father of being emotionally, physically, and sexually abusive, which was their motive behind his murder. They also claimed that they shot their mother "to put her out of her misery." Ultimately, the Menendez brothers were sentenced to life in prison without the possibility of parole—but there's little, if any, humor to be found in such a ghoulish crime. To this day, few comedians (with the brilliant exception of George Carlin, who used the Menendez brothers as an example of people *not* to emulate if one

wishes to go to heaven) tell jokes at the expense of the Menendez brothers, because some things are just too morbid to joke about on any level.

Chapter 5

1. Bobby Quinn, dir., *The Tonight Show Starring Johnny Carson,* season 30, episode 54, "Keenen Ivory Wayans / Jimmy Brogan / Siskel & Ebert," aired January 16, 1992, on NBC, https://www.imdb.com/title/tt2990102/?ref_=ttep_ep10.

2. Bernadette Giacomazzo, "*In Living Color*: The Show and the Modern-Day Super Bowl Halftime Show," Showbiz Cheat Sheet, February 5, 2022, https://www.cheatsheet.com/entertainment/in-living-color-birthed-modern-super-bowl-halftime-show.html/.

3. Thurman Thomas is a former running back who played with the Buffalo Bills for twelve seasons—after having been picked in the second round of the 1988 NFL draft—and spent his final season playing for the Miami Dolphins. He was inducted into the Pro Football Hall of Fame in 2007.

4. Iceman: "Sign it to Laquita! L-A-yo, you figure it out!"

5. This sketch, and the "Homeboyz Shopping Network," were actually pretaped to give the censors enough time to "dead" any potentially offensive remarks. All the other sketches were performed live, which was a risky proposition but one that ultimately paid off. According to Keenen, the executives recognized the possibility for controversy if things did, indeed, get a little too crazy in the live sketches.

6. He asked every single actor if they were "enjoying the nachos—enjoying the guacamole," and they all, inevitably, were.

7. Though best known as the bass player for the band Filter—whose hit songs included "Take a Picture" and "Hey Man Nice Shot"—Buckman was also an established actor who had roles in *Days of Our Lives, Frasier,* and *Beverly Hills 90210.*

8. This generated raucous laughter from the audience.

9. Antoine: "It's like playing cowboys and Indians!" The Redskins won, 37 to 24.

10. "Fish" is a term in queer slang that has several meanings, and the meaning depends on the context of the conversation. "Fish"—as Blaine/Damon is using it here—is a derogatory slang term for a biological female, and its insinuation is that her genitals smell bad (and, more specifically, of fish). But "fishy" can also be used as a compliment, especially when said about a drag queen who "serves realness" (that is, can pass for being a biological female) in her look. "Serving fish" (and, more derogatorily, "serving cunt") is when a drag queen is going for a "girly" look and successfully pulls it off.

11. Antoine referred to them as "scallops on the sidelines," and Blaine held his nose.

12. The setup of the Richard Gere joke began with a Joe Namath reference. In 1973, Namath wore a pair of nylon stockings in a commercial for Beautymist, which was considered controversial for its time for what are, perhaps, obvious reasons (the commercial was meant to show that Beautymist nylons were more durable than its counterparts; however, many took it to mean that Namath was a cross-dresser, and the 1970s was neither the time nor the place for such things). Blaine thought it was wonderful that "Broadway Joe"—as he was known at the height of his career, before he began hawking

Medicare supplemental insurance—was being "who he was," implying that he was an out and proud gay man. This prompted Antoine to remark that Namath was a married man, to which Blaine replied, "well, so is Richard Gere"—as Gere was in a highly publicized marriage, at the time, to supermodel Cindy Crawford—"and you should have seen the gerbil in the wedding dress." The "gerbil" reference stems from an old urban legend about Gere getting a gerbil stuck so far up his rectum during an alleged gay sexual encounter that he had to go to the hospital to get it removed. Aside from the fact that "gerbiling" is not a real sexual practice by either gay or straight people—no cases of "gerbiling" exist in any medical journals, past or present—the origin of the story can be traced back to 1984, when it started out as just "an anonymous gay man," but became "Richard Gere" somewhere along the line. And though it's not clear how Gere got lobbed with the accusation, many pop culture commentators believe it was because Gere played a gay Holocaust victim in the stage play *Bent*. Others believe it was Sylvester Stallone (whose beef with Gere is long-standing and well documented since Stallone had Gere fired from *The Lords of Flatbush*) who started the rumor (a claim Stallone vehemently denies—in fact, Stallone claims it was *Gere himself* who started the rumor that Stallone started the rumor. Confused yet?).

13. "Keenen Ivory Wayans," Television Academy, accessed August 30, 2021, https://www.emmys.com/bios/keenen-ivory-wayans.

14. Though the term has now entered common parlance, "reading" was once an exclusively queer slang term that means exposing someone's flaws wittily, but mercilessly. This is not to be confused with "shade," which is a more sarcastic and caustic way of pointing out someone's flaws. If "intent follows the bullet," as the old law adage goes, "reading" is friendly, funny, and honest, while "shade" is mean, funny, and honest.

15. "Opening the library" is a term used in queer slang that invites drag queens to "read" one another. When "the library is closed," it means the time for "reading" is over. This call-and-response is used extensively on *RuPaul's Drag Race*, where host RuPaul—who knew the "ball" circuit inside and out—often invites the queens to read other queens by saying that the library is open "because reading is *what?* Fundamental!"

16. This is the formal scientific name of the asteroid that landed in what is now the Gulf of Mexico 66 million years ago, which singlehandedly wiped out the dinosaur population. And that description of *In Living Color*—as the asteroid that wiped out the network dinosaurs—is accurate on far too many levels.

17. Ericka N. Goodman-Hughey and Charlotte Gibson, "Super Bowl Halftime Show Never the Same after Jennifer Lopez and *In Living Color*," ESPN, January 30, 2020, https://www.espn.com/espn/story/_/id/28592073/super-bowl-half-show-never-same-jennifer-lopez-living-color.

18. "Keenen Ivory Wayans."

Chapter 6

1. Damon Wayans was no longer a cast member when this sketch aired, so he was billed as a "special guest star."

2. As with "Men on Cooking," Damon Wayans was no longer a cast member when "Men on Fitness" aired, so he was billed as a "special guest star."

3. *Fresh Air*, "David Alan Grier's 'Sporting Life' on Broadway," NPR, May 22, 2012, https://www.npr.org/2012/05/22/152848779/david-alan-griers-sporting-life-on-broadway.

4. Greg Braxton, "Hip-Hop TV's Leading Edge: Along with Its Emmy Awards and Enviable Ratings, *In Living Color* Has Attracted Criticism That the Show Deals in Negative Stereotypes," *Los Angeles Times*, November 4, 1990.

5. Braxton, "Hip-Hop TV's Leading Edge."

6. No modern evidence exists of any active campaigning against *In Living Color*—or "Men on Film"—by GLAAD. It is highly likely that the show did receive some pushback from various activist groups—Keenen, himself, admitted as much—but there doesn't seem to be a concerted effort against "Men on Film" and/or *In Living Color*.

7. Riggs was best known as a documentary filmmaker whose works included *Tongues United* and *Black Is . . . Black Ain't*. He died in 1994 at the age of thirty-seven due to complications from AIDS.

8. Gay men often use descriptors to identify other men within the gay community, and the descriptors are used to classify both the man's body type and his personality. Bulls, bears, otters, pups, and daddies are just a few of the seemingly endless descriptors used by gay men, and this is just one of many clues that give insight as to how diverse the gay community is. And these descriptors don't even consider men who are bisexual, or men who are more fluid with their sexuality. So, Riggs's assertion that gay men—especially gay Black men—aren't effeminate by default is the correct one, and this is especially more noticeable in the twenty-first century, given what we know about the broad spectrum of human sexuality today.

9. Carleton Atwater, "Looking Back at *In Living Color*," *Vulture*, January 27, 2011, https://www.vulture.com/2011/01/looking-back-at-in-living-color.html.

10. John J. O'Connor, "Review/Television; Bringing a Black Sensibility to Comedy in a Series," *New York Times*, May 29, 1990.

11. "*In Living Color* 25 Year Reunion," YouTube, 2019, https://www.youtube.com/watch?v=QQSM7ltyFfY.

12. "*In Living Color* 25 Year Reunion."

13. "*In Living Color* 25 Year Reunion."

14. This is a message that Keenen has conveyed, and has been consistent with, for more than thirty years—which proves that Keenen isn't engaging in "spin" about the sketch or the show or begging off his responsibility with the passing of time. When the cast of *In Living Color* appeared on *The Phil Donahue Show* in 1990, Donahue questioned him about the pushback the show was reportedly getting about the "Men on Film" series from GLAAD, and Keenen's response was "all the sketches on the show have to be looked at within the context of the show. And it's not as though we isolate any particular group. We make fun of everybody," he said. "The sketch is not a bashing sketch. We don't do jokes about any issues related to gay people. It's really a play on the extremes of the stereotype" ("*Donahue in LA*: The Cast of *In Living Color*," YouTube, posted August 2, 2020, https://www.youtube.com/watch?v=2ulrnAxm0KI).

15. "*In Living Color* 25 Year Reunion."

16. Kiko Martinez, "Ahead of San Antonio Gigs, Andrew Dice Clay Says He's 'Grand-fathered in' When It Comes to Cancel Culture," *San Antonio Current*, August 10, 2021, https://www.sacurrent.com/sanantonio/ahead-of-san-antonio-gigs-andrew-dice-clay-says-hes-grandfathered-in-when-it-comes-to-cancel-culture/Content?oid=26882964.

17. Candi Nichols Carter, prod., *The View*, season 20, episode 124, "Damon Wayans / Hot Topics," segment "Damon Wayans Talks *In Living Color*," aired March 15, 2017, on ABC, https://www.facebook.com/watch/?v=10154296387031524.

Chapter 7

1. Alan Carter, "Leaving *In Living Color*," *Entertainment Weekly*, January 15, 1993.

2. Carter, "Leaving *In Living Color*."

3. The modern colloquial parlance is "feeling yourself," which, in this context, implies that the person thinks more of himself or herself than is warranted or merited—or in such a way that it causes harm to others around him or her.

4. Tyler Malone, "The Uncanny Valleys of Martin Scorsese's *The Irishman*: Features: Roger Ebert," RogerEbert.com, December 17, 2019, https://www.rogerebert.com/features/the-uncanny-valleys-of-martin-scorseses-the-irishman.

5. Auteur theory is a film theory that suggests the director is the "author" of the film. First popularized by French director François Truffaut in his 1959 film *The 400 Blows*—which launched the French New Wave movement in cinema—auteur theory suggests that a film reflects a director's artistic vision, and that he or she is solely responsible for the creative output of the film.

6. Jamie Foxx was also absent from the special, but that's because he was in New Orleans filming *Django Unchained*, a film by Quentin Tarantino, which was released in 2012.

7. DJ Envy, Angela Yee, and Charlamagne tha God, hosts, *The Breakfast Club*, episode "Damon Wayans Interview at *The Breakfast Club* Power 105.1," YouTube, September 4, 2015, https://www.youtube.com/watch?v=n52uSXCKdLs.

8. Dominic Patten and Nellie Andreeva, "Damon Wayans' Mysterious Absence from *In Living Color*'s TV Land Awards Tribute," *Deadline*, April 29, 2012, https://deadline.com/2012/04/damon-wayans-mysterious-absence-from-in-living-colors-tv-land-awards-tribute-263704/.

9. Joe Flint, "*I Love Lucy* Still a Cash Cow for CBS," *Los Angeles Times*, September 20, 2012, https://www.latimes.com/entertainment/envelope/la-xpm-2012-sep-20-la-et-ct-cbslucy-20120920-story.html.

10. Before his exodus from the network, Les Moonves infamously bragged that *I Love Lucy* generated more than $20 million a year for the network thanks to its syndication.

11. Flint, "*I Love Lucy* Still a Cash Cow for CBS."

12. While today's shows are often recommended to have eighty-eight episodes for syndication thanks to the presence of streaming networks, the "magic number" was one hundred episodes back then.

13. Carter, "Leaving *In Living Color*."

14. Carter, "Leaving *In Living Color*."

15. Once again, the question begs itself: who financially benefits from Keenen and Damon being at odds with one another—the Wayans family, or the Fox network? Actions speak louder than words, and the fact that Damon and Marlon chose to follow their brother out the door than remain on the show that made them famous speaks volumes as to where their priorities—and loyalties—lie, and it was to one another, first and foremost. Even if they fought—and all brothers and sisters do, and sometimes more brutally than either side would like to admit—a family sticks together when the times get rough.

16. Mara Reinstein, "'We Were Warped Out of Our Minds': *In Living Color* Stars Recall Fox Censors, Spike Lee's Disdain in Dishy Oral History," *Hollywood Reporter*, July 10, 2019, https://www.hollywoodreporter.com/movies/movie-features/living-color-oral -history-fox-censors-spike-lees-disdain-1219192/.

17. Greg Braxton, "Fox's *In Living Color*: Life after Wayans' World," *Los Angeles Times*, March 26, 1993.

18. In 2019, Carrey tried to downplay these comments to the *Hollywood Reporter* and said that he stayed on with the show even after Keenen was gone because "things were happening for me. I spent nights in my office with Steve Oedekerk writing the *Ace Ventura: Pet Detective* script" (Reinstein, "'We Were Warped Out of Our Minds'"). Carrey also took umbrage with Grier cracking jokes at *Ace Ventura*'s expense, even though the comedy on *Ace Ventura* is juvenile at best, and tired at worst. Carrey also conveniently forgot to mention that were it not for *In Living Color*, his career wouldn't be where it is today—and were it not for Damon Wayans, Keenen's brother, he never would have gotten on the show to begin with.

19. It's entirely possible that Carrey was being darkly humorous, as is typical of his reputation. Even if that were the case, however, the statement is in *extremely* poor taste, especially given that Keenen, Damon, and Kim were all being very vocal with their claims of racism against the new "management." And when weighed against his subsequent comments in 2019, the entire situation is—to put it mildly—suspicious.

20. The only time Carrey publicly showed a modicum of deference to the Wayans family was when the "original five"—Keenen, Damon, Kim, Shawn, and Marlon—appeared on *Oprah* in 2004, and Carrey recorded a "shout-out" where he thanked Keenen for the opportunity to appear on *In Living Color*, and thanked Damon for being a friend. It's the least he should have done.

21. Braxton, "Fox's *In Living Color*."

22. Can you imagine this happening in the age of social media? At the first sign of a white man trying to wrest control of a property created and singularly envisioned by a Black man, social media would be ablaze with hashtags—#InLivingKeenen maybe, or #IvoryWayisTheOnlyWay—calls to the advertisers, and backlash unlike anything they'd seen before. Fox's stocks would have taken a tumble, advertisers would have pulled out of the show, think-pieces would have hit both the niche and mainstream outlets—with one side calling for Keenen to retain control of his creation, and the other side (most likely penned by Ben Shapiro) claiming that Keenen not turning over his show to the hands of the white men is "racist" and somehow contributing to the decline of Western civilization as we know it, alongside "WAP" by Cardi B and Megan Thee Stallion. And,

ultimately, Keenen would have retained control of his show and gotten a standing ova-
tion at the Primetime Emmy Awards.

23. Carter, "Leaving *In Living Color*."
24. Braxton, "Fox's *In Living Color*."
25. Braxton, "Fox's *In Living Color*."

Chapter 8

1. Mara Reinstein, "'We Were Warped Out of Our Minds': *In Living Color* Stars
Recall Fox Censors, Spike Lee's Disdain in Dishy Oral History," *Hollywood Reporter*, July
10, 2019, https://www.hollywoodreporter.com/movies/movie-features/living-color-oral
-history-fox-censors-spike-lees-disdain-1219192/.

2. Ta-Nehisi Coates, "It Was No Compliment to Call Bill Clinton 'the First Black
President,'" *Atlantic*, August 27, 2015, https://www.theatlantic.com/notes/2015/08
/toni-morrison-wasnt-giving-bill-clinton-a-compliment/402517/.

3. Coates, "It Was No Compliment to Call Bill Clinton 'the First Black President.'"

4. A Sapphire caricature is part of a larger "angry Black woman" trope found in popular culture that traces back to the days of the Transatlantic Slave Trade. The "Sapphire"
is a woman who is loud and brash and henpecks her mate—always a Black man—for
everything from not having a job to dating a non-Black woman. While the Sapphire caricature can be found in modern Black comedy, most recently in the works of Tyler Perry
and his *Madea* series—and it can arguably be seen as a way for Black men and women
to reclaim tropes that were used to displace them in greater society for so long—it also
has a lasting negative effect in modern American culture as well. Many Black women—
especially in professional/corporate settings—report feeling unsafe and unable to express
themselves effectively out of fear of being perceived as a Sapphire caricature. (The sole exception is Black women who are in a "majority-minority" office—that is, an office that's
predominantly run, and staffed, by Black men and women.) That's changing, albeit very
slowly, but gender studies professor Deborah Gray White says that the ravages of slavery
continue to pervade the Black American psyche, and seeing themselves as Sapphire caricatures on television and in film does the psyche no favors. "Slave women understood the
value of silence and secrecy . . . like all who are dependent upon the caprices of a master,
they hide their real sentiments and turn toward him with a changeless smile or enigmatic
passivity," she writes, while drawing a straight line between the attitudes of slaves that
were victims of the Transatlantic Slave Trade and today's modern Black women who feel
uncomfortable speaking up in the workplace out of fear of being viewed as a stereotype
(Deborah Gray White, *Ar'n't I a Woman? Female Slaves in the Plantation South* [London:
Norton, 1999, 89]).

5. The same year that the "Ugly Wanda Gives Birth" sketch was released, Fox began
airing *Living Single*, a show that featured *In Living Color* alum Kim Coles alongside
Queen Latifah, Erika Alexander, and *The Facts of Life* alum turned reality superstar Kim
Fields. All four of the women were young, beautiful, and professional—nowhere near the
Sapphire stereotype embodied by Ugly Wanda. Then again, the women on *Living Single*

were the singular vision of a Black woman, Yvette Lee Bowser—and this is again worth noting, because the contrast between how Black women characters are depicted when they're written by Black men and women, and how Black women characters are depicted when they're written by *white* men and women, is rather striking—especially in this case.

6. At one point, Keenen hid the master *In Living Color* tapes above the ceiling panels in his office to prevent the new executives from getting their hands on them. It didn't work, but no one can accuse him of not trying his best.

7. Luaine Lee, "Wayans Feel [*sic*] Vindicated as *Living Color* Fades," *Baltimore Sun*, August 23, 1994, https://www.baltimoresun.com/news/bs-xpm-1994-08-23-1994 235015-story.html.

8. In this same interview, Damon said, "once they disrespected my brother, then the right thing to do was to go" (Lee, "Wayans Feel [*sic*] Vindicated as *Living Color* Fades"). Once again, the question must be asked: who benefits, financially, from Keenen and Damon being at odds with one another, and where would people get the idea that Keenen and Damon—who were the older version of Shawn and Marlon—would be at loggerheads when Damon's own actions—and words—suggest otherwise? And even if you ignore everything else, consider this: Damon's daughter, Cara Mia, gave birth to a son in September 2021, and she named him "Damon Ivory" (Cara Mia Wayans [@caramiawayans], "The best month of my life thus far with our little love, Damon Ivory," Instagram photo, October 27, 2021, https://www.instagram.com/p/CVjrv portQo/). That doesn't sound like someone who has watched her father and her uncle tear at each other's throats all the time.

9. In 2017, Disney announced that they were acquiring FX and FXX as part of a larger deal that had a price tag of $52.4 billion. The deal was ultimately completed in 2019. With this deal, FX and FXX—among other Fox-owned properties—became Disney properties, and *In Living Color* became distributed through Disney-ABC Domestic Television. If you want to look at it another way: the cast of *In Living Color* became Disney princes and princesses.

10. In September 2015, the body of Cathriona White was found in her apartment. White overdosed on prescription medication, which Carrey allegedly provided to her. White's estranged husband, Mark Burton, and her mother Brigid Sweetman commissioned Michael Avenatti—yes, *that* Michael Avenatti—to file a wrongful death lawsuit against Carrey for White's death. The lawsuit was dismissed in 2018.

11. In 2008, Carrey and his then-girlfriend Jenny McCarthy led a charge against vaccines based on the since-disproven theory postulated by quack doctor Andrew Wakefield that substances in vaccines are linked to autism. McCarthy's son, Evan—a product of her first marriage—was diagnosed with autism, and McCarthy believed—and continues to believe—that his diagnosis was connected to his vaccine schedule, despite countless independent and mainstream studies that prove otherwise. In 2015, Carrey called then California governor Jerry Brown a "corporate fascist" for passing a law that removed the religious exemption from vaccine requirements to enter the state's primary and secondary schools. In response, Carrey received critical blowback from the scientific community, and Jeffrey Kluger of *Time* magazine wrote an op-ed blasting Carrey for being "all about rage, all about echo-chamber misinformation" (Jeffrey Kluger, "Vaccines: 'Jim Carrey, Please Shut Up,'" *Time*, July 2, 2015, https://time.com/3944067/jim-carrey-vaccines/).

12. In 2017, a note written by White in 2013 revealed that Carrey allegedly transmitted several STIs to her (while refusing to disclose that he had them) and introduced her to a life of hard drugs and prostitution.

13. During his 2015 interview with *The Breakfast Club*, Damon recounted that Keenen regretted not signing the top-tier *In Living Color* talent to his own roster, since he had such a—wait for it—keen eye for identifying the best of them. "Too late now, though," Damon snarked. "Would-a, could-a, should-a" (DJ Envy, Angela Yee, and Charlamagne tha God, hosts, *The Breakfast Club*, episode "Damon Wayans Interview at *The Breakfast Club* Power 105.1," YouTube, September 4, 2015, https://www.youtube.com/watch?v=n52uSXCKdLs).

14. Charles infamously said, "The kid's got it!" when asked about Foxx's performance.

15. That same year, he was also nominated for a Best Supporting Actor Oscar for his role in *Collateral*, but he lost to Morgan Freeman in *Million Dollar Baby*. But Foxx is only the third actor in history—after Barry Fitzgerald and Al Pacino—to be nominated for two Oscars in the same year but in two different categories.

Chapter 9

1. The title of this penultimate chapter is both a reference and a tribute to the classic Public Enemy track "Black Steel in the Hour of Chaos"—from the album *It Takes a Nation of Millions to Hold Us Back*—which is told through the eyes of a militant conscientious objector of the American government who gets locked up . . . and who overcomes untold amounts of systemic racism and stress from the prison industrial complex to ultimately break free, and takes his brothers-at-arms with him.

2. Alicia Bell, "The Case for Media Ownership Reparations (Guest Column)," *Hollywood Reporter*, October 11, 2021, https://www.hollywoodreporter.com/business/business-news/media-ownership-reparations-guest-column-1235027772/.

3. Michael Chui, Brian Gregg, Sajal Kohli, and Shelley Stewart, "A $300 Billion Opportunity: Serving the Emerging Black American Consumer," McKinsey, December 13, 2021, https://www.mckinsey.com/featured-insights/diversity-and-inclusion/a-300-billion-dollar-opportunity-serving-the-emerging-black-american-consumer.

4. "Why Inclusive TV Matters to the Black Community—and the Media Business," Nielsen, November 2, 2021, https://www.nielsen.com/us/en/insights/article/2021/why-inclusive-tv-matters-to-the-black-community-and-the-media-business/.

Conclusion

1. Greg Braxton, "Hip-Hop TV's Leading Edge: Along with Its Emmy Awards and Enviable Ratings, *In Living Color* Has Attracted Criticism That the Show Deals in Negative Stereotypes," *Los Angeles Times*, November 4, 1990.

Appendix

1. As hard as it is to believe today, there was a time when Kirstie Alley was an in-demand actress, and television shows clamored to say that she was even in the same building as many of their cast and crew.

2. Unlike the other musical guests, who would perform their song at the close of the show, Heavy D and the Boyz performed their musical number to open the show—which made sense, considering they were performing the theme song.

3. Although he shot to mainstream superstardom thanks to his "Club Quarantine" performances on Instagram during the COVID-19 pandemic, Derrick "D-Nice" Jones got his start with Boogie Down Productions (with his bandmates KRS-One and DJ Scott La Rock) in the 1980s. He also—unfortunately—discovered Kid Rock in 1988 and got him his first record deal. File this performance under *yet another* way *In Living Color* was ahead of its time in recognizing hot talent.

4. Credited as the first female rapper signed to Def Jam Records, Nichelle Strong—aka "Nikki D"—currently works in the fashion industry for the parent company that manufactures the "Phat" series of clothing (Baby Phat, Phat Farm, etc.).

5. Credited as the first rapper signed to Motown Records, Rich Nice went on to become a Columbia University fellow and a producer for SiriusXM's *Sway in the Morning*.

6. At the time that Leaders of the New School first performed on *In Living Color*, they hadn't released an album yet. But they quickly became an audience favorite, and it wasn't long before they were invited back to perform several times. The breakout star of Leaders of the New School was none other than Busta Rhymes.

7. Discovered by Michael Bivens of Bel Biv Devoe and New Edition, Another Bad Creation was a group of preteen and teen hip-hop and New Jack Swing stars who were the youngest performers on *In Living Color*.

8. "The Bridge Is Over" is considered a classic diss track, which Boogie Down Productions—at that time—wrote as a direct salvo against the Juice Crew, Marley Marl, and other rappers from Queens, New York. "The Bridge" in the song refers to the Queensbridge projects in Long Island City, New York, where many of the rappers in the Juice Crew were from.

9. Ice Cube, who was known for his work with N.W.A. and as a solo act at the time, introduced the group to the stage.

10. This was Keenen Ivory Wayans's last episode as a cast member.

11. Tupac Shakur was originally supposed to perform on this episode, but he was arrested outside the *In Living Color* production offices after getting into a fight. Heavy D filled in at the last minute.

12. This was the very last episode of *In Living Color*.

Bibliography

Abbott, Jim. "After *In Living Color*, Coles Gets on with Her Life." *Orlando Sentinel*, June 7, 1991.

Adams, Thelma. "Casting-Couch Tactics Plagued Hollywood Long before Harvey Weinstein." *Variety*, October 17, 2017. https://variety.com/2017/film/features/casting-couch-hollywood-sexual-harassment-harvey-weinstein-1202589895/.

Andrew, Scottie. "What These Trans Comedians Have to Say about Dave Chappelle's Jokes at Their Expense." CNN, October 24, 2021. https://www.cnn.com/2021/10/24/entertainment/trans-comics-dave-chappelle-netflix-cec/index.html.

Andrews, Travis M. "Comedians Have Long Used Rape as a Punchline: The Me Too Era Is Changing That." *Washington Post*, November 9, 2018. https://www.washingtonpost.com/lifestyle/style/comedians-have-long-used-rape-as-a-punchline-the-me-too-era-is-changing-that/2018/11/08/54ffc888-dd5b-11e8-b3f0-62607289efee_story.html.

Anjarwalla, Tas. "Inventor of Cell Phone: We Knew Someday Everybody Would Have One." CNN, July 9, 2010. http://www.cnn.com/2010/TECH/mobile/07/09/cooper.cell.phone.inventor/index.html.

Arkin, Daniel. "Toni Morrison Defended, Championed and Chastised Presidents." NBCNews.com, August 7, 2019. https://www.nbcnews.com/pop-culture/books/toni-morrison-defended-championed-chastised-presidents-n1039591.

Associated Press. "Mirage Hotel Volcano, Icon on Vegas Strip, to Be Demolished." KSTU, January 25, 2022. https://www.fox13now.com/news/national-news/mirage-hotel-volcano-icon-on-vegas-strip-to-be-demolished.

———. "Satellite Dishes Survive Great Scramble of 1980s." *Deseret News*, January 14, 1990. https://www.deseret.com/1990/1/14/18841125/satellite-dishes-survive-great-scramble-of-1980s.

Astin, John, dir. *CHiPs*. Season 6, episode 1, "Meet the New Guy." Aired October 10, 1982, on NBC. https://www.imdb.com/title/tt0534486/.

Atwater, Carleton. "Looking Back at *In Living Color*." *Vulture*, January 27, 2011. https://www.vulture.com/2011/01/looking-back-at-in-living-color.html.

Baldwin, James. *Everybody's Protest Novel.* Indianapolis, IN: College Division, Bobbs-Merrill, 1949.

Bandini. "The Cast of *In Living Color* Reunites to Discuss Changing TV 25 Years Ago (Video)." Ambrosia for Heads, April 30, 2019. https://ambrosiaforheads.com/2019/04/in-living-color-cast-reuninion-video-interview/.

Bareket, Orly, Rotem Kahalon, Nurit Shnabel, and Peter Glick. "The Madonna-Whore Dichotomy: Men Who Perceive Women's Nurturance and Sexuality as Mutually Exclusive Endorse Patriarchy and Show Lower Relationship Satisfaction." *Sex Roles* 79, no. 9–10 (2018): 519–32. https://doi.org/10.1007/s11199-018-0895-7.

Barron, T. "Condom Ads Debut on U.S. Network Television." *Family Planning World* 2, no. 1 (1992): 6, 18.

Bart, Peter. "Advertising: Color TV Set Output Spurred." *New York Times,* July 31, 1961.

Bascome, Erik. "10 of the Strangest Laws in New York State." silive, May 29, 2017. https://www.silive.com/news/2017/05/strangest_laws_in_new_york_sta.html.

Bates, Karen Grigsby. "Comer Cottrell, Creator of the People's Jheri Curl, Dies at 82." NPR, October 11, 2014. https://www.npr.org/sections/codeswitch/2014/10/11/354931324/comer-cottrell-creator-of-the-peoples-jheri-curl-dies-at-82.

Bátiz-Lazo, Bernardo. "A Brief History of the ATM." *Atlantic,* March 26, 2015. https://www.theatlantic.com/technology/archive/2015/03/a-brief-history-of-the-atm/388547/.

Baysinger, Tim. "*Designated Survivor* Revived at Netflix for a Third Season." TheWrap, September 5, 2018. https://www.thewrap.com/designated-survivor-revived-at-netflix-for-a-third-season/.

Bell, Alicia. "The Case for Media Ownership Reparations (Guest Column)." *Hollywood Reporter,* October 11, 2021. https://www.hollywoodreporter.com/business/business-news/media-ownership-reparations-guest-column-1235027772/.

Berlin, Erika. "What Dress Size Was Marilyn Monroe, Actually?" Mental Floss, July 30, 2015. https://www.mentalfloss.com/article/66536/what-dress-size-was-marilyn-monroe-actually.

Blake, Wayne M., and Carol A. Darling. "The Dilemmas of the African American Male." *Journal of Black Studies* 24, no. 4 (June 1994): 402–15. https://doi.org/10.1177/002193479402400403.

Bloom, Nicholas Dagen, and Matthew Gordon Lasner. *Affordable Housing in New York: The People, Places, and Policies That Transformed a City.* Princeton, NJ: Princeton University Press, 2016.

Bowley, Graham, and Julia Jacobs. "Bill Cosby Freed as Court Overturns His Sex Assault Conviction." *New York Times,* June 30, 2021. https://www.nytimes.com/2021/06/30/arts/television/bill-cosby-release-conviction.html.

Boyd, James. "Nixon's Southern Strategy." *New York Times,* May 17, 1970. https://www.nytimes.com/1970/05/17/archives/nixons-southern-strategy-its-all-in-the-charts.html.

Boyle, Louise. "Daniel Tosh Tells Female Heckler That It Would Be 'Funny If a Bunch of Guys Just Raped Her.'" *Daily Mail Online,* July 12, 2012. https://www.dailymail

.co.uk/news/article-2172277/Daniel-Tosh-tells-female-heckler-funny-bunch-guys -just-raped-her.html.

Brady, Jonann, and Stephanie Dahle. "Celeb Couple to Lead 'Green Vaccine' Rally." *ABC News*, June 4, 2008. https://abcnews.go.com/GMA/OnCall/story?id=4987758.

Braxton, Greg. "Fox's *In Living Color*: Life after Wayans' World." *Los Angeles Times*, March 26, 1993.

———. "Hip-Hop TV's Leading Edge: Along with Its Emmy Awards and Enviable Ratings, *In Living Color* Has Attracted Criticism That the Show Deals in Negative Stereotypes." *Los Angeles Times*, November 4, 1990.

Buck, Stephanie. "Condom Ads Were Banned in Mainstream Media, until Too Many People Were Dying of AIDS." Medium, January 27, 2017. https://timeline.com/aids -advertising-1980s-2b32b73beb7d.

Byman, Daniel L. "Assessing the Right-Wing Terror Threat in the United States a Year after the January 6 Insurrection." Brookings, February 1, 2022. https://www.brook ings.edu/blog/order-from-chaos/2022/01/05/assessing-the-right-wing-terror-threat -in-the-united-states-a-year-after-the-january-6-insurrection/.

Campbell, Richard, Christopher Martin, Bettina Fabos, and Ron Becker. *Media and Culture: An Introduction to Mass Communication*. New York,: Bedford/St. Martin's, 2021.

Carmody, John. "Arsenio Hall Bails Out as Ratings Plunge." *Washington Post*, April 19, 1994.

Carter, Alan. "Leaving *In Living Color*." *Entertainment Weekly*, January 15, 1993.

Carter, Candi Nichols, prod. *The View*. Season 20, episode 124, "Damon Wayans / Hot Topics." Segment "Damon Wayans Talks *In Living Color*." Aired March 15, 2017, on ABC. https://www.facebook.com/watch/?v=10154296387031524.

Chavez, Danette. "David Alan Grier on *The Carmichael Show*, the Prescience of *Blankman*, and Repeatedly Turning down *In Living Color*." *A.V. Club*, August 31, 2018. https://www.avclub.com/david-alan-grier-on-the-carmichael-show-the-pre science-1828686418.

Chiles, Nick. "8 Black Panther Party Programs That Were More Empowering than Federal Government Programs." *Atlanta Black Star*, February 16, 2019. https:// atlantablackstar.com/2015/03/26/8-black-panther-party-programs-that-were -more-empowering-than-federal-government-programs/.

Chui, Michael, Brian Gregg, Sajal Kohli, and Shelley Stewart. "A $300 Billion Op-portunity: Serving the Emerging Black American Consumer." McKinsey, December 13, 2021. https://www.mckinsey.com/featured-insights/diversity-and-inclusion/a-300 -billion-dollar-opportunity-serving-the-emerging-black-american-consumer.

Coates, Ta-Nehisi. "It Was No Compliment to Call Bill Clinton 'the First Black Presi-dent.'" *Atlantic*, August 27, 2015. https://www.theatlantic.com/notes/2015/08/toni -morrison-wasnt-giving-bill-clinton-a-compliment/402517/.

"'Comedy Is Tragedy plus Time.'" Quote Investigator, February 17, 2020. https://quote investigator.com/2013/06/25/comedy-plus/.

Comen, Evan. "Check Out How Much a Computer Cost the Year You Were Born." *USA Today*, October 3, 2018. https://www.usatoday.com/story/tech/2018/06/22 /cost-of-a-computer-the-year-you-were-born/36156373/.

Cormier, Roger. "22 Things You Might Not Know about *In Living Color*." Mental Floss, April 15, 2015. https://www.mentalfloss.com/article/62630/22-things-you-might-not-know-about-living-color.

Cosby, Bill. *Childhood*. New York: Berkley, 1992.

"Damon Wayans." IMDb, accessed December 16, 2021. https://www.imdb.com/name/nm0001834/.

"Damon Wayans on the Inspiration behind Homey D. Clown, 'Men on . . .' and More." *UPROXX*, April 15, 2015. https://uproxx.com/hitfix/in-living-color-damon-wayans-on-the-inspiration-behind-homey-d-clown-men-on-and-more/.

Davidson, Tommy, Tom Teicholz, and Stedman Graham. *Living in Color: What's Funny about Me*. New York: Kensington, 2021.

Davies, Dave. "'The Uncensored Story' of the Smothers Brothers." NPR, October 15, 2010. https://www.npr.org/transcripts/130569467.

DeVega, Chauncey. "How *The Cosby Show* Duped America: The Sitcom That Enabled Our Ugliest Reagan-Era Fantasies." Salon, July 13, 2015. https://www.salon.com/2015/07/12/how_the_cosby_show_duped_america_the_sitcom_that_enabled_our_ugliest_reagan_era_fantasies/.

Dibdin, Emma. "*In Living Color* Creator, Cast Reflect on Show's Impact: 'America Needed Something New.'" *Hollywood Reporter*, April 27, 2019. https://www.hollywoodreporter.com/tv/tv-news/living-color-creators-reflect-shows-impact-25th-anniversary-1205371/.

DiPrinzio, Harry. "At NYCHA's Fulton Houses, a Bitter Divide over the Future of the Development." City Limits, August 27, 2019. https://citylimits.org/2019/08/21/at-nychas-fulton-houses-a-bitter-divide-over-the-future-of-the-development/.

DJ Envy, Angela Yee, and Charlamagne tha God, hosts. *The Breakfast Club*. Episode "Damon Wayans Interview at *The Breakfast Club* Power 105.1." YouTube, September 4, 2015. https://www.youtube.com/watch?v=n52uSXCKdLs.

"*Donahue in LA:* The Cast of *In Living Color*." YouTube, posted August 2, 2020. https://www.youtube.com/watch?v=2ulrnAxm0KI.

Drew, Mike. "Upstart Fox Has Pounced, and the Networks Are Getting Jumpy." *Milwaukee Journal*, April 19, 1990.

Ebert, Roger. "*I'm Gonna Git You Sucka* Movie Review." RogerEbert.com, December 14, 1988. https://www.rogerebert.com/reviews/im-gonna-git-you-sucka-1988.

"18 U.S. Code § 2721—Prohibition on Release and Use of Certain Personal Information from State Motor Vehicle Records." Legal Information Institute. https://www.law.cornell.edu/uscode/text/18/2721.

Englebrecht, Leandra. "Lenny Kravitz Reveals Bill Cosby Fired Lisa Bonet from TV Show over Pregnancy News." Channel24, October 9, 2020. https://www.news24.com/channel/TV/News/lenny-kravitz-reveals-bill-cosby-fired-lisa-bonet-from-tv-show-over-pregnancy-news-20201009-2.

Evans, Erin E. "Nafessa Williams: Breaking Barriers as TV's First Black Lesbian Superhero." NBCNews.com, February 1, 2019. https://www.nbcnews.com/news/nbcblk/nafessa-williams-breaking-barriers-tv-s-first-black-lesbian-superhero-n962796.

Evans, Kelley D. "Now We Can Find *Hidden Figures* in the Classroom." Andscape, April 21, 2017. https://theundefeated.com/features/now-we-can-find-hidden-figures-in-the-classroom/.

Evans, Shalwah. "United States House of Representatives Passes the CROWN Act." *Essence*, September 23, 2020. https://www.essence.com/beauty/house-of-representatives-passes-crown-act/.

Farrakhan, Louis, and Henry Louis Gates. "Farrakhan Speaks." *Transition*, no. 70 (1996): 140. https://doi.org/10.2307/2935354.

Farrow, Rachel. "Here's How Much Jennifer Aniston and Other Actors Get Paid for Their Reruns." Yahoo!, May 25, 2021. https://www.yahoo.com/now/much-jennifer-aniston-other-actors-220000357.html.

Field, Miranda. "Empowering Students in the Trauma-Informed Classroom through Expressive Arts Therapy." *in education* 22, no. 2 (2016): 55–71. https://doi.org/10.37119/ojs2016.v22i2.305.

Fink, Jameson. "Enjoy a 200-Dollar Bottle of Ripple." Grape Collective, April 7, 2021. https://grapecollective.com/articles/enjoy-a-200-dollar-bottle-of-ripple.

Finn, Natalie. "Oprah Winfrey's 40-Year Weight Loss Struggle: Inside the Billionaire Star's Ongoing Quest for Self-Acceptance." *E! Online*, August 3, 2017. https://www.eonline.com/news/871198/oprah-winfrey-s-40-year-weight-loss-struggle-inside-the-billionaire-star-s-ongoing-quest-for-self-acceptance.

Flanders, Annie, ed. *"In Living Color."* *Details*, 1989.

Flint, Joe. "*I Love Lucy* Still a Cash Cow for CBS." *Los Angeles Times*, September 20, 2012. https://www.latimes.com/entertainment/envelope/la-xpm-2012-sep-20-la-et-ct-cbslucy-20120920-story.html.

"47 U.S. Code § 223—Obscene or Harassing Telephone Calls in the District of Columbia or in Interstate or Foreign Communications." Legal Information Institute. https://www.law.cornell.edu/uscode/text/47/223.

Fresh Air. "David Alan Grier's 'Sporting Life' on Broadway." NPR, May 22, 2012. https://www.npr.org/2012/05/22/152848779/david-alan-griers-sporting-life-on-broadway.

George, Nelson. "How Rosie Perez Got Her Start on *Soul Train*." *Esquire*, March 24, 2014. https://www.esquire.com/entertainment/tv/a27953/rosie-perez-soul-train/.

Giacomazzo, Bernadette. "How Byron Allen Became One of the Wealthiest Black Men in Entertainment Today." AfroTech, August 24, 2021. https://afrotech.com/byron-allen-net-worth-companies-bio-wife.

———. "How the Wayans Family Went from *In Living Color* to a $300m Empire." AfroTech, October 15, 2021. https://afrotech.com/wayans-family-net-worth-entertainment.

———. *"In Living Color*: The Show and the Modern-Day Super Bowl Halftime Show." Showbiz Cheat Sheet, February 5, 2022. https://www.cheatsheet.com/entertainment/in-living-color-birthed-modern-super-bowl-halftime-show.html/.

———. "Inside the Controversial Life and Career of Stepin Fetchit, the First Black Movie Star." All That's Interesting, August 9, 2021. https://allthatsinteresting.com/stepin-fetchit.

Gooden, Tai. "The Lasting Impact of *In Living Color*'s Fly Girls." Nerdist, April 9, 2021. https://nerdist.com/article/fly-girls-in-living-color-impact-hip-hop-dance-fashion/.

Goodman-Hughey, Ericka N., and Charlotte Gibson. "Super Bowl Halftime Show Never the Same after Jennifer Lopez and *In Living Color*." ESPN, January 30, 2020. https://www.espn.com/espn/story/_/id/28592073/super-bowl-half-show-never-same -jennifer-lopez-living-color.

Graves, Lucia. "Hannibal Buress: How a Comedian Reignited the Bill Cosby Allegations." *Guardian*, April 26, 2018. https://www.theguardian.com/world/2018/apr/26 /hannibal-buress-how-a-comedian-reignited-the-bill-cosby-allegations.

Gray, Jonathan W. "'Why Couldn't You Let Me Die?' Cyborg, Social Death, and Narratives of Black Disability." In *Disability in Comic Books and Graphic Narratives*, edited by Chris Foss, Jonathan W. Gray, and Zach Whalen, 125–39. London: Palgrave Macmillan, 2016. https://doi.org/10.1057/9781137501110_9.

Greenberg, Jan Crawford. "Clarence Thomas: A Silent Justice Speaks Out." ABC News, September 30, 2007. https://abcnews.go.com/TheLaw/story?id=3665221&page=1.

Greenfield Sanders, dir. *The Black List: Volume One*. New York: HBO, August 2008.

Grimes, William. "William H. Grier, Psychiatrist Who Delved into 'Black Rage' in 1960s, Dies at 89." *New York Times*, September 12, 2015. https://www.nytimes.com /2015/09/13/books/william-h-grier-psychiatrist-who-delved-into-black-rage -in-1960s-dies-at-89.html.

Grove, Rashad. "5 Times Eddie Murphy and Arsenio Proved to Be Bros for Life." BET, April 1, 2021. https://www.bet.com/article/zecb9y/5-times-eddie-and-arsenio -celebrated-their-bromance.

Grover, Ronald. "Chernin Buys Anime Site Crunchyroll to Expand Online Video Assets." Reuters, December 2, 2013. https://www.reuters.com/article/us-chernin -crunchyroll-idUSBRE9B10X320131202.

"H. Ross Perot, Sr." *Forbes*, September 13, 2021. https://www.forbes.com/profile/h-ross -perot-sr/?sh=4dcda957470f.

Harmetz, Aljean. "Why My Sons Watch *The Waltons*." *New York Times*, February 25, 1973. https://www.nytimes.com/1973/02/25/archives/why-my-sons-watch-the -waltons.html.

Harrington, Amy, and Keenen Ivory Desuma Wayans. "Keenen Ivory Wayans: Archive of American Television Interview Part 1 of 3." YouTube, November 5, 2013. https:// youtu.be/auR49MoW6yY.

Harrington, Richard. "The Music Industry's Court Hits." *Washington Post*, May 30, 1990.

Hayford, Vanessa. "The Humble History of Soul Food." Black Foodie, June 3, 2021. https://www.blackfoodie.co/the-humble-history-of-soul-food/.

Hdogar. "Dreadlocks Are Much More than Just a Fashion Statement." History of Yesterday, November 11, 2021. https://historyofyesterday.com/dreadlocks-are-much-more -than-just-a-fashion-statement-b365f21e258a.

Headgeek. "Stallone Answers December 9th & 10th Questions in a Double Round." Ain't It Cool News, December 29, 2012. http://legacy.aintitcool.com/node/30932.

"History of the Improv." Improv, accessed December 9, 2021. https://improv.com /history/.

Hood, Micaela. "The New Damon Wayans." *South Florida Sun-Sentinel*, November 10, 2013. https://www.sun-sentinel.com/entertainment/events/sf-go-damon-wayans -improv-111013-20131107-story.html.

Horovitz, Bruce. "Trojan Gets a Condom Ad on Network TV." *Los Angeles Times*, November 19, 1991.

Howard, Jessica. "It Still Stings: The Uncomfortable Legacy of *Girls*." *Paste Magazine*, December 2, 2020. https://www.pastemagazine.com/tv/hbo/girls-tv-show-legacy/.

Hutchinson, Sean. "8 Suave Facts about Billy Dee Williams." Mental Floss, April 6, 2017. https://www.mentalfloss.com/article/93906/8-suave-facts-about-billy-dee -williams.

"*I'm Gonna Git You Sucka*." Box Office Mojo, accessed November 23, 2021. https:// www.boxofficemojo.com/release/rl122979841/weekend/.

"*In Living Color*: Back in Step with the Fly Girls." YouTube, 2004. https://www.you tube.com/watch?v=eMbgcdem8XU.

"*In Living Color* 25 Year Reunion." YouTube, 2019. https://www.youtube.com /watch?v=QQSM7ltyFfY.

Jacobs, Julia. "Remembering an Era before *Roe*, When New York Had the 'Most Liberal' Abortion Law." *New York Times*, July 19, 2018. https://www.nytimes.com /2018/07/19/us/politics/new-york-abortion-roe-wade-nyt.html.

Jacobs, Paul. "Addresses at DMV Remain Accessible : Privacy: New Rules Were Written to Keep Information Confidential. Critics Say There Are Too Many Loopholes." *Los Angeles Times*, August 19, 1991. https://www.latimes.com/archives/la-xpm-1991-08 -19-mn-608-story.html.

James, Kendra. "Why *In Living Color* Is Still Relevant Today." Shondaland, January 9, 2018. https://www.shondaland.com/live/a14532256/why-in-living-color-is-still -relevant-today/.

Jancelewicz, Chris. "Jim Carrey Lawsuit: Unearthed Note from Ex-Girlfriend Makes Shocking Claims." Global News, October 3, 2017. https://globalnews.ca/news /3780493/jim-carrey-lawsuit-cathriona-white-note/.

Johnson, Robert Edward, ed. "Pick Duke's Granddaughter as June Taylor Dancer." *Jet*, September 26, 1963.

Johnston, David. "Survey Shows Number of Rapes Far Higher than Official Figures." *New York Times*, April 24, 1992, sec. A.

Jones, Jeffrey M. "LGBT Identification Rises to 5.6% in Latest U.S. Estimate." Gallup, November 20, 2021. https://news.gallup.com/poll/329708/lgbt-identification-rises -latest-estimate.aspx.

"Keenen Ivory Wayans." Television Academy, accessed August 30, 2021. https://www .emmys.com/bios/keenen-ivory-wayans.

Keltner, Dacher, and George A. Bonanno. "A Study of Laughter and Dissociation: Distinct Correlates of Laughter and Smiling during Bereavement." *Journal of Personality and Social Psychology* 73, no. 4 (1997): 687–702. https://doi.org/10.1037/0022 -3514.73.4.687.

Kempley, Rita. "*The January Man*." *Washington Post*, January 13, 1989.

Kilgore, Alexcia M., Rachel Kraus, and Linh Nguyen Littleford. "'But I'm Not Allowed to Be Mad': How Black Women Cope with Gendered Racial Microaggressions through Writing." *Translational Issues in Psychological Science* 6, no. 4 (2020): 372–82. https://doi.org/10.1037/tps0000259.

Kluger, Jeffrey. "Vaccines: 'Jim Carrey, Please Shut Up.'" *Time*, July 2, 2015. https://time.com/3944067/jim-carrey-vaccines/.

Koblin, John. "After Racist Tweet, Roseanne Barr's Show Is Canceled by ABC." *New York Times*, May 29, 2018. https://www.nytimes.com/2018/05/29/business/media/roseanne-barr-offensive-tweets.html.

Kohut, Andrew. "From the Archives: 50 Years Ago, Mixed Views about Civil Rights but Support for Selma Demonstrators." Pew Research Center, July 28, 2020. https://www.pewresearch.org/fact-tank/2020/01/16/50-years-ago-mixed-views-about-civil-rights-but-support-for-selma-demonstrators/.

Kornacki, Steve. "1984: Jesse Jackson's Run for the White House and the Rise of the Black Voter." NBC News, July 29, 2019. https://www.nbcnews.com/politics/elections/1984-jesse-jackson-s-run-white-house-rise-black-voter-n1029596.

Kurtzleben, Danielle. "Understanding the Clintons' Popularity with Black Voters." NPR, March 1, 2016. https://www.npr.org/2016/03/01/468185698/understanding-the-clintons-popularity-with-black-voters.

LaFraniere, Sharon. "Barry Arrested on Cocaine Charges in Undercover FBI, Police Operation." *Washington Post*, January 19, 1990.

Lara, Dulcinea, Dana Greene, and Cynthia Bejarano. "A Critical Analysis of Immigrant Advocacy Tropes: How Popular Discourse Weakens Solidarity and Prevents Broad, Sustainable Justice." *Social Justice* 36, no. 2 (2009): 21–37.

LaSalle, Mick. "Taking on Hollywood's Asian Take / Actor Steve Park Posts Critique after *Friends* Epithet." *SFGate*, May 27, 1997.

Lee, Luaine. "Wayans Feel [sic] Vindicated as *Living Color* Fades." *Baltimore Sun*, August 23, 1994. https://www.baltimoresun.com/news/bs-xpm-1994-08-23-1994235015-story.html.

———. "Wayans Started Making People Laugh at Early Age." *Baltimore Sun*, April 3, 1995. https://www.baltimoresun.com/news/bs-xpm-1995-04-03-1995093127-story.html.

Levin, Marc, dir. *Prisoners of the War on Drugs*. DVD. New York: HBO, 1996.

Lewis, John. "Robert Johnson Sells His Souls to the Devil." *Guardian*, June 15, 2011. https://www.theguardian.com/music/2011/jun/16/robert-johnson-sells-soul-devil.

"LL COOL J." Billboard, accessed November 18, 2021. https://www.billboard.com/artist/ll-cool-j/chart-history/.

Longsdorf, Amy. "Jamie Foxx Hits All the Right Notes as He 'Becomes' Ray Charles." *Potsdam Mercury*, October 25, 2004.

Machkovech, Sam. "The Best Game-Breaking Speedruns of Summer Games Done Quick 2020." Ars Technica, August 24, 2020. https://arstechnica.com/gaming/2020/08/the-best-game-breaking-speedruns-of-summer-games-done-quick-2020/.

Malone, Tyler. "The Uncanny Valleys of Martin Scorsese's *The Irishman*: Features: Roger Ebert." RogerEbert.com, December 17, 2019. https://www.rogerebert.com/features/the-uncanny-valleys-of-martin-scorseses-the-irishman.

Marable, William Manning. "Rediscovering Malcolm's Life: A Historian's Adventure in Living History." In *The Portable Malcolm X Reader*, edited by Garrett Felber, 580–83. New York: Penguin, 2013.

Marie, Erika. "Tommy Davidson Left *In Living Color* for Rehab, Says He Would Be Dead If He Hadn't." HotNewHipHop, January 30, 2020. https://www.hotnew hiphop.com/tommy-davidson-left-in-living-color-for-rehab-says-he-would-be-dead -if-he-hadnt-news.102336.html.

Maron, Marc, host. "Jim Carrey." Episode 1140 of *WTF with Marc Maron* (podcast), July 16, 2020. http://www.wtfpod.com/podcast/episode-1140-jim-carrey.

Martin, Murilee. "Once Status Symbols, These 1990s Factory Car Phones Will Face the Crusher." *Autoweek*, September 6, 2020. https://www.autoweek.com/car-life /a1821071/once-status-symbols-these-1990s-factory-car-phones-will-face-crusher/.

Martinez, Kiko. "Ahead of San Antonio Gigs, Andrew Dice Clay Says He's 'Grand-fathered in' When It Comes to Cancel Culture." *San Antonio Current*, August 10, 2021. https://www.sacurrent.com/sanantonio/ahead-of-san-antonio-gigs-andrew-dice -clay-says-hes-grandfathered-in-when-it-comes-to-cancel-culture/Content?oid =26882964.

Maslin, Janet. "Review/Film; *Sucka*, a Sendup." *New York Times*, January 13, 1989.

McKerrow, Steve. "Even on Radio, *Star Wars* Has the Force." *Baltimore Sun*, July 9, 1993. https://www.baltimoresun.com/news/bs-xpm-1993-07-09-1993190241-story .html.

Mcquiston, John T. "Fatal Crash Starts Melee with Police in Brooklyn." *New York Times*, August 20, 1991. https://www.nytimes.com/1991/08/20/nyregion/fatal-crash -starts-melee-with-police-in-brooklyn-668791.html.

Mejia, Zameena. "How Inventing Liquid Paper Got a Secretary Fired and Then Turned Her into an Exec Worth $25 Million." CNBC, July 23, 2018. https://www.cnbc .com/2018/07/19/inventing-liquid-paper-got-a-secretary-fired-and-then-made-her -rich.html.

Michel, Alexandra. "The Science of Humor Is No Laughing Matter." Association for Psychological Science, March 31, 2017. https://www.psychologicalscience.org /observer/the-science-of-humor-is-no-laughing-matter.

Miller, Adrian. "From Pig's Feet to Corn Bread, a History of Soul Food in the White House." *Washington Post*, June 12, 2017. https://www.washingtonpost.com /lifestyle/food/from-pigs-feet-to-corn-bread-a-history-of-soul-food-in-the-white -house/2017/06/12/49b966f2-4c69-11e7-a186-60c031eab644_story.html.

Miller, Kelsey. "*Friends* Is 25 Years Old: It's Still Extremely Popular—and Polariz-ing." Vox, September 20, 2019. https://www.vox.com/culture/2019/9/20/20875107 /friends-25th-anniversary-polarizing-legacy-homophobia.

Murphy, Keith. "The Undisputed Ranking of Every Black *Saturday Night Live* Cast Member." Level, May 18, 2020. https://level.medium.com/the-undisputed-ranking -of-every-black-saturday-night-live-cast-member-c1d0efbeb7ca.

"Muscular Dystrophy Association Announces Relaunch of Iconic Telethon Hosted by Actor and Comedian Kevin Hart." Muscular Dystrophy Association, September 9, 2020. https://www.mda.org/press-releases/the-mda-kevin-hart-kids-telethon-2020.

Myers, Dvora. "Diary of a Fly Girl: Rosie Perez Tells Her Story." *Elle*, March 25, 2014.

National Museum of African-American History & Culture, ed. "The Foundations of Black Power." National Museum of African American History and Culture, July 5, 2019. https://nmaahc.si.edu/explore/stories/foundations-black-power.

Neddenien, Erika. "We Tracked down the Kid Vice President Dan Quayle Made Misspell 'Potato.'" BuzzFeed News, September 12, 2019. https://www.buzzfeednews.com/article/buzzfeednews/dan-quayle-potato-spelling.

Netter, Sarah, Russell Goldman, and Sabina Ghebremedhin. "Michael Jackson's Friend Not Convinced Pepsi Accident Caused Lifelong Addiction." ABC News, July 15, 2009. https://abcnews.go.com/Business/MichaelJackson/story?id=8096762&page=1.

Newkirk, Vann R. "How the Myth of Reverse Racism Drives the Affirmative-Action Debate." Atlantic, June 15, 2021. https://www.theatlantic.com/education/archive/2017/08/myth-of-reverse-racism/535689/.

NYPR Archive Collections. "Statement on Harlem Riot: WNYC." WNYC, July 22, 1964. https://www.wnyc.org/story/statement-on-harlem-riot/.

O'Connor, John J. "Review/Television; Bringing a Black Sensibility to Comedy in a Series." New York Times, May 29, 1990.

———. "TV: Pryor's Art Is Strong Stuff, 'Soap' Weak." New York Times, September 13, 1977.

Oldenburg, Ann. "MDA Ends Jerry Lewis Labor Day Telethon." USA Today, May 1, 2015. https://www.usatoday.com/story/life/people/2015/05/01/muscular-dystrophy-association-ends-labor-day-television-telethon/26709717/.

Oppenheim, Maya. "People Are Furious with Chrissy Teigen because She Doesn't Find the Term 'Oriental' Offensive." Independent, September 15, 2016. https://www.independent.co.uk/news/people/chrissy-teigen-oriental-offensive-twitter-outrage-a7309531.html.

Ovide, Shira, and Peter Sanders. "Peter Chernin to Leave Post as President of News Corp." Wall Street Journal, February 25, 2009. https://www.wsj.com/articles/SB123542374683052407.

Park, Steve. "Steve Park's Mission Statement." ModelMinority: A Guide to Asian American Empowerment, October 7, 1992. https://web.archive.org/web/20070928140952/http://modelminority.com/modules.php?name=News&file=article&sid=1.

Patten, Dominic, and Nellie Andreeva. "Damon Wayans' Mysterious Absence from In Living Color's TV Land Awards Tribute." Deadline, April 29, 2012. https://deadline.com/2012/04/damon-wayans-mysterious-absence-from-in-living-colors-tv-land-awards-tribute-263704/.

Pew Research Center, Journalism and Media Staff. "The American Newsroom." Pew Research Center's Journalism Project, Pew Research Center, May 30, 2020. https://www.pewresearch.org/journalism/2006/10/05/the-american-newsroom/.

Pham, Elyse. "Here's How Pop Culture Has Perpetuated Harmful Stereotypes of Asian Women." TODAY.com, April 1, 2021. https://www.today.com/popculture/here-s-how-pop-culture-has-perpetuated-harmful-stereotypes-asian-t213676.

Pinak, Patrick. "Joe Namath's Controversial Pantyhose Commercial Was ahead of Its Time." FanBuzz, November 4, 2021. https://fanbuzz.com/nfl/joe-namath-commercial/.

Pitt, Sofia. "Credit Scores Put Black Americans at a Disadvantage: Here's How." Grow from Acorns + CNBC, June 18, 2020. https://grow.acorns.com/how-credit-scoring -contributes-to-racial-wealth-gap/.

Porter, Lauren. "Billy Dee Williams Is a Colt 45 Spokesperson Again." *Essence*, March 29, 2016. https://www.essence.com/news/billy-dee-williams-colt-45-spokesperson -once-again/.

Pryor, Richard. *Dinah!* Season 1, episode 144. Aired May 23, 1975, in syndication.

Psychology Today Staff. "Humor | Psychology Today." *Psychology Today*, accessed November 6, 2021. https://www.psychologytoday.com/us/basics/humor.

Quinn, Bobby, dir. *The Tonight Show Starring Johnny Carson.* Season 16, episode "Bruce Dern / Robert Klein / Susan Sullivan / Dr. Carl Sagan." Aired March 2, 1978, on NBC. https://www.imdb.com/title/tt5444166/.

———. *The Tonight Show Starring Johnny Carson.* Season 30, episode 54, "Keenen Ivory Wayans / Jimmy Brogan / Siskel & Ebert." Aired January 16, 1992, on NBC. https:// www.imdb.com/title/tt2990102/?ref_=ttep_ep10.

Quintanilla, Michael. "*In Living Color* Fly Girls Start a Fashion Buzz." *Baltimore Sun*, August 7, 1991.

Ramirez, Christina Dugan. "Connie Chung on the 'Embarrassing' Reason She Agreed to Marry Maury Povich after 2 Proposals." *People*, October 29, 2020. https://people .com/tv/why-connie-chung-agreed-to-marry-maury-povich-after-multiple-proposals/.

Ramm, Benjamin. "What the Myth of Faust Can Teach Us." BBC, September 26, 2017. https://www.bbc.com/culture/article/20170907-what-the-myth-of-faust-can -teach-us.

Reinstein, Mara. "'We Were Warped Out of Our Minds': *In Living Color* Stars Recall Fox Censors, Spike Lee's Disdain in Dishy Oral History." *Hollywood Reporter*, July 10, 2019. https://www.hollywoodreporter.com/movies/movie-features/living-color-oral -history-fox-censors-spike-lees-disdain-1219192/.

"Repeal of 'Don't Ask, Don't Tell.'" Human Rights Campaign, accessed December 5, 2021. https://www.hrc.org/our-work/stories/repeal-of-dont-ask-dont-tell.

Rizzo, Monica. "*Dancing with the Stars*' Carrie Ann Inaba." *People*, October 16, 2006.

Robinson, Bryan. "Convicted Killer of Ennis Cosby Confesses." ABC News, February 9, 2001. https://abcnews.go.com/US/story?id=94100.

Roemer, Christian. "When Did the VCR Become Popular?" Legacybox, November 19, 2020. https://legacybox.com/blogs/analog/when-did-vcr-become-popular.

Rose, Mickey, writer. *The Tonight Show Starring Johnny Carson.* Season 21, episode "Sean Connery / Keenen Ivory Wayans / Tania Maria." Aired October 5, 1983, on NBC. https://www.imdb.com/title/tt5340482/?ref_=ttep_ep139.

Rosenfeld, Megan. "A Pregnant Pause for Chung?" *Washington Post*, July 31, 1990.

Rosenthal, Gay, writer. *Behind the Music.* Season 1, episode 1, "Milli Vanilli."Aired August 17, 1997, on VH1. https://www.imdb.com/title/tt0394380/fullcredits/?ref _=tt_cl_sm.

Rossitto, Rayna. "Why I've Decided to Stop Watching Reruns of *Friends*: For Good." POP-SUGAR Entertainment, June 13, 2019. https://www.popsugar.com/entertainment /Why-Friends-TV-Series-Problematic-46071047?stream_view=1#photo-46101377.

Rothman, Lily. "The 1991 Crown Heights Riots: Read *Time*'s Explanation of the History." *Time*, August 19, 2015. https://time.com/3989495/crown-heights-riots-time-magazine-history/.

Rotondi, Jessica Pearce. "Before the Chinese Exclusion Act, This Anti-immigrant Law Targeted Asian Women." History.com, March 19, 2021. https://www.history.com/news/chinese-immigration-page-act-women.

Russell, Calum. "The Controversy Surrounding *Driving Miss Daisy*." *Far Out Magazine*, December 13, 2021. https://faroutmagazine.co.uk/driving-miss-daisy-controversy/.

Sanders, Jeff. "Padres History (July 25): Barr-Strangled Banner Creates Controversy." *San Diego Union-Tribune*, July 25, 2020. https://www.sandiegouniontribune.com/sports/padres/story/2020-07-25/padres-history-july-25-roseanne-sing-national-anthem.

Santhanam, Laura. "How Has Public Opinion about Abortion Changed since *Roe v. Wade*?" PBS, July 20, 2018. https://www.pbs.org/newshour/health/how-has-public-opinion-about-abortion-changed-since-roe-v-wade.

Schrader, Stuart. "How Global Counterinsurgency Transformed American Policing." *Badges without Borders* 56 (January 15, 2019): 79–112. https://doi.org/10.2307/j.ctvp2n2kv.7.

Schwindt, Oriana. "Super Bowl LI Pulls in 111.3 Million Viewers on Fox, Shy of 2015 Ratings Record." *Variety*, February 6, 2017. https://variety.com/2017/tv/news/super-bowl-li-ratings-patriots-falcons-24-1201978629/.

"The 77th Academy Awards: 2005." Oscars.org, accessed December 2, 2021. https://www.oscars.org/oscars/ceremonies/2005.

Shimizu, Celine Parreñas. *The Hypersexuality of Race: Performing Asian/American Women on Screen and Scene*. Durham, NC: Duke University Press, 2007.

Simpson, Heather. "Famed Cold Duck Wine Unearthed in Blenheim Drinks Cabinet." Stuff, December 24, 2015. https://www.stuff.co.nz/life-style/food-wine/75436070/famed-cold-duck-wine-unearthed-in-blenheim-drinks-cabinet.

"Southern-Fried Genius." TV Tropes, accessed November 25, 2021. https://tvtropes.org/pmwiki/pmwiki.php/Main/SouthernFriedGenius.

Steinberg, Brian. "NBC Seeks Record $6 Million for Super Bowl Commercials (Exclusive)." *Variety*, June 16, 2021. https://variety.com/2021/tv/news/super-bowl-commercials-price-record-1234998593/.

Stern, Marlow. "Spike Lee Blasts *Selma* Oscar Snubs: 'You Know What? F*ck 'Em.'" *Daily Beast*, July 12, 2017. https://www.thedailybeast.com/spike-lee-blasts-selma-oscar-snubs-you-know-what-fck-em.

Stowe, Harriet Beecher. *Uncle Tom's Cabin*. Geneva, Switzerland: Edito-Service, 1985.

Sukii, King. "*In Living Color*: Remember That Time Tupac and Jamie Foxx Weren't Seeing Eye to Eye?" Global Grind, March 22, 2018. https://globalgrind.com/4259055/tupac-in-living-color-throwback-clip/.

Sullivan, Andrew. "The Golden Age of TV Drama." The Dish, November 29, 2012. http://dish.andrewsullivan.com/2012/11/28/how-television-drama-came-of-age/.

Summers, Chelsea. "The Tongue-Twisting History of the Many Euphemisms for Eating Ass." Vice, June 10, 2015. https://www.vice.com/en/article/3bjqx3/tongue-twisting-history-of-the-many-euphemisms-for-eating-ass.

Tapley, Kristopher. "25 Years Later: How *In Living Color* Broke Sketch Comedy's Race Barrier." *UPROXX*, April 15, 2015. https://uproxx.com/hitfix/how-in-living-color -broke-sketch-comedys-race-barrier/.

Tate, Crystal. "Jamie Foxx and Keenan [*sic*] Ivory Wayans' Daughters Hit the Runway at New York Fashion Week." *Essence*, September 13, 2017. https://www.essence.com /fashion/fashion-week/jamie-foxx-keenan-ivory-wayans-daughter-nyfw/.

"Top Fire Causes." National Fire Protection Association, accessed December 7, 2021. https://www.nfpa.org/Public-Education/Fire-causes-and-risks/Top-fire-causes.

Tsuchiyama, Jayne. "The Term 'Oriental' Is Outdated, but Is It Racist?" *Los Angeles Times*, June 1, 2016. https://www.latimes.com/opinion/op-ed/la-oe-tsuchiyama -oriental-insult-20160601-snap-story.html.

uDiscover Team. "Let's Talk about the Female Rappers Who Shaped Hip-Hop: Udiscover." uDiscover Music, September 24, 2021. https://www.udiscovermusic.com /stories/the-female-rappers-who-shaped-hip-hop/.

VanHooker, Brian. "A Highly Questionable Cultural History of Richard Gere's Ass Gerbil." *MEL Magazine*, September 29, 2021. https://melmagazine.com/en-us/story /richard-gere-gerbil-incident-story-fact-check.

Voland, John. "Turner Defends Move to Colorize Films." *Los Angeles Times*, October 23, 1986.

Wallenstein, Andrew. "What Disney Bought: A Billion-Dollar Breakdown of Assets." *Variety*, December 14, 2017. https://variety.com/2017/biz/news/what-disney-bought -fox-merger-1202641234/.

Walters, Suzanna Danuta. *All the Rage: The Story of Gay Visibility in America*. Chicago: University of Chicago Press, 2001.

Wayans, Cara Mia (@caramiawayans). "The best month of my life thus far with our little love, Damon Ivory." Instagram photo, October 27, 2021. https://www.instagram .com/p/CVjrvportQo/.

Wenzel, John. "Wayans Brothers to Reunite for 2014 Comedy-Sketch Tour." The Know, October 4, 2013. https://theknow-old.denverpost.com/2013/09/17/wayans -brothers-news-comedy-sketch-stand-up-tour-2014/77468/.

Wexler, Celia Viggo. "Coca-Cola's Tab Soda Has Been Discontinued: Its Retirement Should Have Come Decades Ago." NBC News, October 20, 2020. https://www.nbc news.com/think/opinion/coca-cola-s-tab-soda-has-been-discontinued-its-retirement -ncna1243950.

"What Is Auteur Theory and Why Is It Important?" Indie Film Hustle, May 20, 2022. https://indiefilmhustle.com/auteur-theroy/.

White, Deborah Gray. *Ar'n't I a Woman? Female Slaves in the Plantation South*. London: Norton, 1999.

"Why Inclusive TV Matters to the Black Community—and the Media Business." Nielsen, November 2, 2021. https://www.nielsen.com/us/en/insights/article/2021 /why-inclusive-tv-matters-to-the-black-community-and-the-media-business/.

Williams, Stereo. "The Story behind Salt-N-Pepa and Hip-Hop's Grammy Boycott." Rock the Bells, accessed December 19, 2021. https://rockthebells.com/articles/salt-n -pepa-hip-hop-respect-and-the-grammy-boycott/.

Willis, Kelcie. "*In Living Color*' Star Kim Wayans Urges Voting in Benita Butrell Video." *Atlanta Journal-Constitution*, October 25, 2020. https://www.ajc.com/news/nation-world/in-living-color-star-kim-wayans-urges-voting-in-benita-butrell-video/HJWDGA2DX5FZLAL3LJBART5FPY/.

Winfrey, Oprah. "What I Know for Sure about Making Peace with My Body." Oprah.com, August 1, 2002. https://www.oprah.com/omagazine/what-i-know-for-sure-weight.

Winter, Christine. "Credit Cards Charge into the 90s." *Orlando Sentinel*, December 27, 1989.

Yang, George, and Tracey Ann Ryser. "Whiting Up and Blacking Out: White Privilege, Race, and White Chicks." *African American Review* 42, no. 3/4 (2008): 731–46.

Zurcher, Anthony. "Rush Limbaugh and His 'Black Bond' Outrage." BBC News, December 29, 2014. https://www.bbc.com/news/blogs-echochambers-30594460.

Index

About the Author

Bernadette Giacomazzo is an editor, journalist, author, photographer, and publicist with more than twenty years of experience in the entertainment arm of the industry. Her work has been featured in *People, Teen Vogue, Us Weekly*, the *Los Angeles Times*, the *New York Post*, and more. She is also CEO and founder of G-Force Marketing & Publicity, which has been featured in the *Hollywood Reporter*, and she has secured film, television, and radio placements for blue-chip clientele throughout the world. In addition to her contributions to the *Cultural History* series, Giacomazzo is the author of the critically acclaimed fiction series *The Uprising Series* and works in various roles behind the scenes in Hollywood. A native of Queens, New York, she lives in Atlantic Beach, New York, and works in Las Vegas and Los Angeles. Visit her online at www .bernadettegiacomazzo.com.

CPSIA information can be obtained
at www.ICGtesting.com
Printed in the USA
BVHW041133111122
650638BV00001B/1

9 781538 166574